LIFE IS A YO-YO

By the same author:

On and Off the Flight Deck: Reflections of a naval pilot in World War II
published by Pen & Sword Aviation

To: Geoffrey,
I hope you enjoy the read!

Hank Adlam
MAR. 2010

LIFE IS A YO-YO

AN AUTOBIOGRAPHY

HANK ADLAM

BOOK 2: MIDDLE, BEGINNING AND NEAR THE END

ARROWSMITH

First published in Great Britain in 2009 by
Arrowsmith
34 Hill Grove
Bristol BS9 4RQ

Copyright©Henry Amyas Adlam 2009

ISBN 978-0-9562919-0-5

The right of Henry Amyas Adlam to be identified as Author
of this work has been asserted by him in accordance with the
Copyright, Designs and Patents Act 1988.

A CIP catalogue record for this book is
available from the British Library.

All rights reserved. No part of this book may be reproduced or transmitted in
any form or by any means, electronic or mechanical including photocopying,
recording or by any information storage or retrieval system, without
permission from the Publisher in writing.

Jacket design by Mousemat Design Ltd
Illustrations scanned by 4Word, Bristol
Typeset in 10 on 12 point Palatino by
Victoria Arrowsmith-Brown, Bristol

Produced by Macmillan Production Asia

Dedication

If she had not coaxed me into writing my memoirs, it would never have occurred to me, at the then age of eighty-four, to do so and I would have missed the fine and closer relationship such writing has given us. Without her constant encouragement this book would never have been written, and therefore it is dedicated to Aza, my daughter.

Contents

	List of illustrations	viii
	Preface	ix
Chapter 1	Decommissioning	1
Chapter 2	At Home with the Leamans	21
Chapter 3	166 Gulson Road	35
Chapter 4	Recalled to the Royal Navy	39
Chapter 5	In the Beginning	52
Chapter 6	My Father's Will	93
Chapter 7	Civilian Life	99
Chapter 8	A Desk Job with Shorts and a New Home	109
Chapter 9	Painting and Promotion	119
Chapter 10	At Home	132
Chapter 11	Back to the Mainland	150
Chapter 12	Rolls-Royce	159
Chapter 13	Clifton College and Preparatory School	166
Chapter 14	At Clifton: Years 1971 – 74	187
Chapter 15	The Norman Years, 1973 – 78	198
Chapter 16	Clifton College, June 1978 – 82	208
Chapter 17	Clifton College, the Final Year, 1982	222
Chapter 18	Early Retirement	228
Chapter 19	Pensionable Retirement	242

Chapter 20	A Private Family Matter	261
Chapter 21	The Residential Home	265
Chapter 22	The Last Lap	281
	Index	289

Photographs illustrating the chapters follow page 150

Preface

When at the age of eighty-four I started to write these memoirs I intended to begin at the beginning, naturally enough, and thus, starting myself off as a ten-year old schoolboy, to continue the story right through to the present day. But, on reaching the wartime period of my life, the memories of my five years in a fighter squadron of the Fleet Air Arm began to flow out of my mind in such a deluge of personal experiences that they formed a complete and separate book of their own which I call Book 1, and which has been published under the title of *On and Off the Flight Deck: Reflections of a naval pilot in World War II*.

This means that the format of this autobiography is changed and needs some explanation. In this, Book 2, I leap into the story from where I left it in Book 1, in 1948 and shortly after my marriage. The period of the 1930s before the war covering my boyhood and earlier years is described at Chapter Five, In the Beginning.

I resume the natural chronology of my yo-yo life in Chapter Six.

CHAPTER ONE

Decommissioning

After our marriage at Yeovilton church on July 17th, 1948, my wife, Heather, and I were looking for a cottage to rent in the fishing village of Coverack in Cornwall. My new appointment was as an Instrument Flight Instructor and Examiner at the Royal Naval Air Station, Culdrose, a few miles away from the village. Without any success in our search so far, we had ended up in the local pub, the Paris, where we had talked to fishermen and others over our pints. We told them that we hoped to find somewhere to live in Coverack and the landlord, overhearing our conversation, mentioned that he knew of a converted cottage nearby at a very reasonable rent. When he told us the rent, Heather and I downed our pints and wasted no time in going to see it.

Painted white, with bright yellow wooden clapboard and a dark slate roof, the Watch House stood alone, with the rocks and sea immediately below it. Entry was either through the big front door from a path running alongside the house to the upper cliffs, or straight into the kitchen at the lower level where there was also a bedroom and the bathroom. The main bedroom upstairs was next to the sitting-room. Heather was enchanted with it and so indeed was I, but it did cross my mind briefly to wonder why, at such a low rent, it should be empty.

But I couldn't fault it as a place to live happily for what might possibly be the final nine months of my service in the Royal Navy.

The short service commission of four years, which I had taken in 1945 immediately after the war, had another nine months to go and I had not as yet formally applied for a permanent commission, which I must do before the last three months of the four years. I didn't feel in any hurry about it; I felt certain that the Navy would want me on a permanent basis. After all, although I hadn't served with any distinction, I had as good a war record as most other aircrew having flown from aircraft carriers as a fighter pilot for nearly five wartime years. Subsequently, I had completed two years as the senior Flying

Instructor at Yeovilton from where the Captain had given me a super report, as evidenced by the 'flimsy' copy of it in my possession. And thirdly, nonsense though I regarded it to be, I guessed that there was an advantage in having been to school at Harrow because the Royal Navy, even now after the war, was still the type of service to regard such an irrelevant factor as important.

Nevertheless, neither one of us was entirely certain about staying on in the Navy. Heather didn't ever fuss me about it, but I knew that she hated and feared my flying job and longed for me to have normal work without the inevitable risks associated with service flying, even in peacetime. For my part, while I wasn't particularly keen to fly, I treated it as my function in life since, as I had concluded three years earlier, flying was all I knew and a career as an experienced naval aviator had seemed to offer good opportunities for senior rank. However, I was no longer so sure about this. It was noticeable already that appointments as commanding officers of squadrons, for example, were tending to go to Lt/Commanders who were ex-Dartmouth and regular officers of the Royal Navy. The reality was that they had less flying experience, although more seniority as officers, than ex-wartime RNVR pilots like me. Meantime we had several months ahead, living in this perfect little house, during which we could consider our future Moreover, Heather was pregnant and the house would be an ideal home as a start for the baby.

As it turned out, neither the Watch House nor my appointment as an Instrument Flight instructor at Culdrose, were quite as ideal as they had at first seemed. First as regards the house, we were very happy there except for some small but disturbing incidents, which we were sure had occurred from time to time. Please don't laugh, but each of us separately had the impression that articles, such as plates on the old Welsh dresser, had moved slightly of their own volition. Eventually we told each other of our suspicions and I became convinced that there had in fact been such movements. Moreover, sometimes at night, I thought I heard the wooden rings, which held up a heavy green baize curtain over the big front door, clack noisily, as they did whenever the door was being opened. Those who have read the wartime experiences in my autobiography *On and Off the Flight Deck* will know that I suffer from a nervous disposition and therefore these apparent strange happenings worried me. But Heather, although not an unimaginative person, took these weird occurrences in her stride, and would refuse to let them interfere with her enjoyment of the house and its lovely surroundings.

In the pub one evening we told the locals, mostly fishermen, of our suspicions. 'Most likely young George up to his tricks again,' said Archie Rowe, coxswain of the Coverack lifeboat. A gale of laughter swept the bar and I demanded to know, rather edgily, 'Who's George?' Silence descended. Then old Major Perkins, the local squire, spoke up. 'Well, here's the story – make what you will of it. A passenger ship, the *Paris*, was wrecked years ago on the nearby Manacle rocks. Many drowned, a newly married couple amongst them, but only the wife's body was found.' He paused and looked at us significantly. 'The story goes that the young husband, as a ghost, forever searches for her, particularly where the recovered bodies were placed. They laid them out in the Watch House.' I laughed uneasily and said, 'I don't believe it.' Jackie Ringo, another fisherman, shrugged. 'Then why do so many holiday tenants leave early and why do you think your rent is so low?' he demanded. 'And haven't you noticed that no one passes your front door after dark? They use the much longer way round the village.'

My throat went dry and I could find nothing to say to that. Then after a moment's silence, Heather spoke angrily. 'I don't know why you people are so keen to frighten us with your damned ghost story, but you are wasting your time. We don't care if a few ornaments get shoved around or whatever else your ghostly George does, because Hank and I intend to stay in the Watch House and to enjoy living there. It's a lovely cottage and we aren't going anywhere else, so stop trying to put the frights on us, because we are not interested.' Toni, an Italian one-time opera singer and now one of the local fishermen, apologised. 'We are really sorry, we had no intention of frightening you away, it's just a story we like to tell to newcomers.' There was a murmur of approval round the bar for his genuine apology.

We made many friends in Coverack during the succeeding months. Friends not only among the local people including Toni and his wife Maggie, who incidentally had won the George Cross for her bravery during the London blitz, but with several young married couples who, like ourselves, worked at the Naval Air Station and were living in Coverack. It was a lovely late summer and autumn that year and it was such a pleasure living with Heather in that house that I overcame my fears about George and the creepy atmosphere which I still felt existed there. Maybe it was all in my mind anyway. One of the simple pleasures, if I may describe it as such, was using the outside loo. Although it worked in a modern way, it was built as a little hut added on to the far end of the house and, with the door left open, one could look out over the sea crashing against the rocks immediately below and to the fishing boats in the near distance. I have a joyful memory of watching and hearing Toni, on a calm day out at sea among the other fishing boats, singing at the top of his fine voice as he pulled up the lobster pots. Fishermen often mended their pots and their nets sitting outside a large shed located near the back of the house and, during the day while I was away flying, Heather enjoyed their company chatting over mugs of tea, which she would make for them. In return, sometimes we would find a couple of live lobsters clanking about in a bucket, left as a gift outside our kitchen door.

For a special occasion I arranged to take the lifeboat coxswain, Archie Rowe, to the Air Station with me for a flight in a Harvard. It was beautiful weather on a Saturday morning and, having somehow crammed this huge barrel of a man into the rear cockpit, I took off and flew out over the sea to the fleet of small boats fishing in sight of the harbour at Coverack. I swooped around low over the fishing fleet so that Archie could wave at his friends down below and then, after climbing up to a safe height over them, flew some gentle aerobatics before heading back to the aerodrome. By the time we had landed and driven back to Coverack, all the fishermen and locals were awaiting Archie's return and had congregated in the Paris pub where they presented him with a huge pair of cardboard wings to hang round his massive neck and shoulders. There had to be a party in the pub after that with pints of beer flowing to celebrate Archie's wings.

After we had been settled into the house and village for some time, we received a letter from my Mother suggesting a visit to us for a few days. Of course we telephoned back to say how delighted we would be to have her and her companion, Maddie, and a date was fixed a week ahead. In fact, neither Heather nor I looked forward to the visit with pleasure. We had visited Mother for four days at her house in Taplow at the end of our honeymoon, some months earlier, and the visit had been a disaster. The truth is that she had always been a possessive sort of mother to me and, regardless of whichever girl I had married, I think that Mother would have resented her. On that first visit, therefore, she had been critical of almost everything Heather said, did or wore and in fact she developed, even during that brief visit, into a domineering mother-in-law of pantomime proportions. My dear Mother, whom I revered as such, could sometimes be horrid and when she was, she was very, very horrid. But she had more than met her match with Heather who, confident of our love, kept her temper and quietly rejected most of the criticisms without letting them become a cause for argument. I was justifiably proud of her for how, under pressure, she had remained gentle with my Mother and handled a difficult situation calmly and, yes, with dignity too. Nevertheless, I prayed that the forthcoming visit was not intended by Mother to be round two of the match, but rather I hoped she would see it as an opportunity to make friends with Heather.

Mother and Maddie were due to arrive by train at Penzance on the following Saturday where we would fetch them in an old saloon car which I had borrowed from a naval friend. For the purpose, I had arranged to swop my sporty little MG with him for the few days of Mother's visit since she would never have been able to fit into the MG. Mother was normally a jolly personality and loved meeting people, so we had arranged a big party in the Watch House for that evening and had invited a mixture of local villagers and naval friends. The main room upstairs was L-shaped and large enough for about eighteen of our friends and, as was the style in those days, we had laid on plenty of gin and tonics or whisky and sodas and Heather, with the help of two other friendly naval wives, had prepared lots of the sort of food easy to gobble down at the same time as drinking and talking. The party had been going very well indeed and everybody, including Mother in particular, had appeared happy and enjoying themselves. At least, that was until I happened to see her at the other end of the room, sitting on a chair and looking up, ashen faced, at Major Perkins while the damned old fool was holding forth, telling her all about our ghostly George. I had expressly briefed all our friends beforehand not on any account to mention George to my Mother (from whom I had no doubt inherited my own nervous disposition) and now there was old Perkins in full verbal spate and obviously giving her a terrible fright. I rushed over to them, gave old Perkins a kick on his shin and hissed in his ear, 'Don't talk about George.' He caught on to the realisation of her fear, and to give her some reassurance said, 'Oh no, me dear lady, not up here; he don't operate up here – downstairs is where George usually appears.' That did it. Earlier that day we had shown Mother and Maddie the spare room downstairs … where they were to sleep! Mother's face became even more ashen and she fell totally silent. The party broke up soon after that.

The next morning, I prepared a nice pot of tea on a tray for Mother and Maddie, knocked on their bedroom door and entered on hearing a quavering 'Come in.' They were sitting bolt upright in their beds, both of them looking desperately haggard and white and obviously so very relieved to see me. They looked as though neither had slept a wink all night. Mother immediately launched into a prepared story about how she had completely forgotten about a doggie customer she was due to see (she bred and sold bull terriers) and therefore they must return home without delay. So I drove them to the station and off they went, both looking immensely glad to be leaving, but Mother protesting, genuinely I think, how sorry she was at having to spoil the visit.

As it was, I felt relieved that she was departing, albeit so soon, without any awkward fusses and indeed during that very short period her manner to Heather had been pleasant enough. Good old George, I thought, as it was he who was responsible for the curtailed visit. I had been able to obtain a couple of days leave for their visit and now Heather and I could spend the two days just relaxing quietly together at home and going for walks along the cliff tops. It was an opportunity too to think about my job and my future in the Navy.

My new job as an Instrument Flight Instructor had turned out to be not quite as simple, safe and easy as I had imagined it would be. Hitherto in bad weather, pilots in the Fleet Air Arm, and particularly fighter pilots without an observer to provide precise navigation, had tended to fly around and sometimes over the top of clouds but mostly under them. However, flying through thick cloud was frequently unavoidable and coming down through such cloud was always dangerous unless the pilot by some means had a firm fix on his position or, alternatively, if he was letting down through cloud over the sea, since there would be no fear of hitting mountains or hills. But aviation now had entered a new era. It had become normal now for aircraft to take off straight into cloud and to be controlled by surveillance radar through thick cloud all the way to their destination, without ever seeing the ground. On approaching the aerodrome in cloud, the Controller on the ground using GCA (Ground Control Approach) radar would give detailed instructions to the incoming pilot who, flying on instruments with absolute precision in response to the instructions, would be able to let down to within two hundred feet over the aerodrome runway for a landing.

In consequence, our Instrument Flight Squadron had been formed to convert pilots to this modern and more complex form of bad weather flying, which was new to many otherwise experienced naval pilots and, in doing so, to raise their standard of instrument flying. At the end of the course, we would give them a formal instrument flight rating without which any flight, particularly in bad weather, could be restricted by the Air Traffic Controllers. By the time I arrived, the squadron had been undertaking this task for about two years and already many naval pilots had passed through the course. But the job of instructing this type of flying, although tedious and boring most of the time, was more onerous than I had expected, particularly because the only landing approach aid available, on our own aerodrome at Culdrose, was the imprecise Navy Y.G. beacon. This merely transmitted six letters of the alphabet in Morse code along six sectors of a circle. In wartime, this had given the pilot the general direction back to his Aircraft Carrier but, as an aerodrome and runway approach aid in the very bad weather which often prevailed at Culdrose, it was ludicrously inadequate.

To train our pupils, we could use the modern GCA landing aid available at a RAF aerodrome some thirty miles away but we had to rely upon the YG beacon, using it as an approach aid, to return and land at Culdrose. In bad weather and a low cloud base, the procedure was to let down over the sea, even down to a little over two hundred feet, tune the YG to identify the direction sector for the aerodrome and approach the land to fly over and just clear of the cliff tops. Select wheels and flaps down at that stage to slow-fly along a tract of well-known and recognisable flat countryside, then, sweating profusely usually, to plonk the Oxford down on the first bit of runway which came into view. Needless to say, I never allowed the pupil, whoever he was, to bring the aircraft in to land under those conditions. Flying with such limited equipment in such conditions was all too often absurdly dangerous but, as instrument flight instructors, we were expected to cope with the situation.

During that winter in the Watch House, which faced out to the Atlantic and its associated bad weather, my first action every morning was to go to the bedroom window, still in my pyjamas, to see what the weather was like. I was not even aware that I was doing it, or realise that this nervous habit was causing Heather to worry about me. And so, those two days when Mother had left us rather abruptly, provided the opportunity for reflection about my potential career in the Royal Navy. Heather and I took account of two factors; firstly that regular RN officers tended to be getting the plum jobs as squadron commanders, despite their relative inexperience. Secondly that my current job, whether it was a typical example or not, could at times be damn near as bloody dangerous as wartime flying had been. On the other hand, it could be foreseen even then that jet aircraft and improvements on Aircraft Carriers to accommodate them, would make flying in the Fleet Air Arm so very much safer in the future.

We didn't make a definite decision at that time, but it had begun to occur to me that this type of work was not worth the risk if, in competition with regular RN officers, it might not provide the opportunity for reaching the higher ranks. Moreover, it seemed irresponsible to take the inevitable risks associated with service flying, now that I was starting a family. Heather, I realised, had reached these conclusions long ago but had forborne to worry me with her thoughts and fears. Anyway, there was time yet before we needed to make a final decision and so we let it lie in our minds for a while. In the meantime, we resolved to start saving money in readiness for leaving the Navy, in case that is what we would eventually decide to do. From now on, for instance, there would be no more expensive parties.

The aircraft used by the squadron for instrument flight instruction consisted of a couple of Harvard trainers, but the main complement was six rather elderly Airspeed Oxfords. These were twin-engined aircraft of wooden construction large enough to take four passengers and originally used, I suppose, as communication aircraft between naval air stations. In fact, they were remarkably suitable for their purpose now as instrument flight trainers because, although wooden, they were robust and their two radial engines gave a good single-engine performance, if one should fail. I had flown an Oxford before at Yeovilton, quite casually on a flight to Lee-on-Solent just to see what it was like to fly a twin, and had found it to be a simple and pleasant thing to fly. Now though, with responsibility to my pupils, I would have to take flying it more seriously and learn its performance and capabilities. The pupil sat in the seat alongside me on my right hand side in the cockpit of the Oxford and, if the weather was cloudless, there was a gadget for him to wear which prevented him from seeing out and limited his view to the instrument panel only. But, during winter on the Cornish coast, the weather was usually cloudy and on many days very bad indeed. Thus the aerodrome would have been ideal for an Instrument Flight course, if only radar approach and landing aids had been available.

There were six instructors in the squadron, including the CO, all of whom had completed the course at the Central Flying School with the RAF at Little Rissington, as I had done. Most of them had been in this instrument flight squadron since qualifying as instructors. I gathered that, other than my particular friend Nigel Gardner, not many of them had experience of wartime flying from Carriers but, none the less, they were experienced as instructors. They were a good bunch of colleagues who had accepted in a relaxed manner the difficulties of trying to do their job without adequate aerodrome facilities. The pick of the bunch as an instructor was Duncan Lang who, with abundant self-confidence, was the only one who seemed to revel in the bad weather conditions under which frequently we all had to fly. The CO, a Lt/Commander who had done well indeed to be promoted as a seaman from the lower deck, rarely ever flew. He was engrossed in paperwork of some sort most of the time and would emerge from his office from time to time to check that we were working in accordance with the flying programme he had scheduled. He had become a martinet type of RN officer, totally out of character for a pilot in the Fleet Air Arm, who was obsessed to ensure that the petty regulations of the Admiralty were observed. Having to serve under him was an irritation but, since he never flew in bad weather, he lost our respect and was generally ignored.

The birth of our first child was getting near and was expected sometime near Christmas; rather too soon I suppose to be proper since our marriage had only been in July, but neither Heather nor I were fussed about that sort of thing and we were both looking forward to becoming parents. We had been persuaded by Doreen, who had been a close friend of ours at Yeovilton, to make arrangements for Heather to have the baby at Westminster hospital in London where Doreen's husband, Charles, was a senior Consultant. Mother had an empty flat in London awaiting a new tenant and our plan was to stay there for my Christmas leave. Heather would travel up to London ahead of me by train, stopping off at Salisbury to visit her parents, and I would follow in our small MG sports car three days later when my leave was due.

And so, when Heather had left for London, I found myself in the situation of having to stay in the Watch House by myself and I did not relish the prospect with thoughts of George the ghost still in my mind. It was a dark early evening as I drove back to Coverack from the aerodrome and, after a day of flying in highly unpleasant weather, I felt tired but looked forward to a couple of large whiskies and to cooking myself a supper of bacon and eggs before an early bed. I parked the car close to the house and, with a torch, started to walk in the dark along the footpath to the lower kitchen door of the house. The main door at the higher level was always kept locked from the inside with a huge old key. A heavy green curtain hung on wooden rails, which would clack noisily whenever the door was opened.

But this approach and entrance was rarely used.

I entered by the kitchen door and switched on the light and there on the floor were the smashed remains of one of the old plates, which we had placed for decoration, along the ledge of the old Welsh dresser. It was difficult to imagine how it could have fallen down. I felt an immediate chill but made myself look everywhere in the house to see if anyone was about – but there was no one. I picked up the pieces of plate to put them in the bin and, shades of my wartime days, looked immediately for the whisky bottle to pour myself some courage. I tried to act normally and so, humming cheerily to myself, I cooked the bacon and eggs, ate them and armed with another strong glass of whisky went up the wooden stairway to the sitting-room and to our bedroom upstairs. After drinking the whisky, I went straight to bed.

Something woke me. It was pitch black and I imagined that I heard movements downstairs. Surely, that was the sound of footsteps climbing the wooden stairs from the kitchen and now, was there someone in the sitting-room next door? 'Get up, get up,' I told myself. 'Open the bedroom door and confront them.' Then I heard it; it seemed to be the noise of someone quietly sobbing. I felt my scalp prickle and I shivered. I simply hadn't the guts to get up and open that door; I just couldn't do it. A moment later I heard what sounded like the key turning in the lock of the front door, the clacking of the curtain-rails as the door was opened and shut. Then utter quiet.

I did not move until daylight. When I looked in the sitting-room nothing had been moved, nothing touched and the green curtain was in position and the heavy door still locked. I wanted to get away from this nightmare of a house, so I quickly washed up the supper dishes, packed my clothes for London and left. There were still three days before I was due to leave to join Heather in London, but no way would I remain in that house any longer by myself. I arranged for an officer's cabin to be available for me at the Air Station for the period. And I took the opportunity to volunteer as the duty officer for those three nights to build up a reserve, which would enable me to avoid future duties at night. I vowed never to leave Heather and our child, once they came back from hospital, alone in that house.

However, once in London together, Heather and I had precious little time to enjoy the few pleasures we had planned for Christmas, such as a theatre visit and maybe an inexpensive lunch or two, because in the event the birth was rather sudden! On Christmas Eve, a week or so before ETA (the expected time of arrival to use flying jargon), Heather called anxiously out to me, 'It's time to go, and hurry!' I telephoned for an ambulance, which thankfully arrived quickly to rush Heather to Westminster Hospital where, shortly afterwards, our first child, a boy, was born.

Despite being Christmas, I was unable to visit Heather to talk to her and to see our son, except at the customary specified time during each day. Thus it was not until nearly mid-day on Christmas day itself that I could make my first visit to see them. The baby was a fine, healthy-looking infant with a surprisingly dark complexion and dark hair on his head. I was a bit surprised by this as I had always imagined our children would have Heather's blonde hair and colouring, but it simply didn't matter to me. I had a son and, although I wasn't very good at cuddling him at the time, I felt sombre and warm with the feeling of being his Father.

Just as well too that I had belatedly felt the importance of the occasion because, feeling lonely and bereft of Heather's companionship on the previous evening, I had not behaved well. I had spent several hours in an unknown pub, somewhere in the west-end of London, talking to other lonely single people and had become, unusually for me, quite drunk before finding a taxi to return me to the flat. All I had brought for Heather therefore, in appreciation for presenting me with a son, was a thundering hangover and a very small bunch of tatty flowers with six sad-looking soft oranges. These were all I could find available at the last minute from the hospital shop downstairs. But Heather took them with a smile, almost as if they had been the traditional gold and myrrh, and told me that all had gone well with the birth and now we really must decide upon names for our son. For weeks past, we had been mulling over two names, if the child were to be a boy, of either Jasper or Jeremy but with little argument now, we settled on Jeremy, which Heather had favoured.

The ward Sister informed me that Heather and the baby ought not to be released from hospital until another five days at least, which was a miserable prospect for me since I was very lonely living on my own in mother's little flat and knowing nobody in London at that time. It wasn't like my old wartime days in London of cavorting around the Cavendish Hotel where Rosa Lewis used to hold court, and when I had plenty of money to burn. I assumed that Heather would be happy having Jeremy to care for and the company of the other patients.

Despite my selfish attitude, I had been strongly affected by the first sight of my family and it brought me round to consider once more whether or not to apply for the permanent commission. The more I thought about leaving the Navy the more I favoured it and, of course, I knew that this was what Heather really wanted. I had in mind our earlier discussion about saving and building up a pot of cash in readiness for leaving the Navy, should we decide definitely to do so. These few days while Heather and the baby were in hospital and while I was stuck in London with nothing to do, seemed to be the ideal opportunity for selling the MG car, or maybe to exchange it. This would enable us to stash some money away because, as a result of the profligate manner in which I had always lived during and since the war, I had absolutely nothing in the bank or invested for our future.

I visited a number of garages in London to see what sort of price I could get for the MG and was alarmed to find how little I was offered. She was a 1936 model and was therefore, I had to realise, about thirteen years old with an apparent value now in the region of £80. New cars were by this time in full production and so my beloved little MG was not only old but had lost her scarcity value. Moreover, none of the main garages in the city had decent old bangers to offer me in part exchange. I drove out to Colnbrook, on the Bath road out of London, where I remembered a garage which I knew dealt in car exchanges. So stupid was my next action that I hate writing about it and so, to cut the story as short as I can, I sold the MG in exchange for an even older Renault saloon car, plus a sum of £50. The old Renault was jet black all over, high off the ground, a long sharp nose and a luggage boot like a huge female bottom at the back, reminding me of a Madame of a French brothel. Let me explain that on our way back from the south of France, at the end of our honeymoon, we had arrived in Dieppe very late at night (dirt in the petrol tank had delayed us) and, desperate to find accommodation, the only room I could find for us had been in a brothel, where in desperation I had negotiated with the Madame for a room. So I knew what a Madame looked like.

Anyway, for some unjustifiable reason, I liked the look of the old car. I undertook to accept the deal but only if the Renault were to start up immediately when I pressed the starter button, which I very much doubted it would do. But it did and the horrible old car thus became mine. At least, I had cash of £50 to put into our bank account and, knowing my spendthrift ways, I did so without delay before I could begin to lose it.

It was on the day before Heather was due to leave that I drove the Renault to the hospital and parked it in the area at the back of the building below a window in Heather's ward. The old car had performed quite well in the meantime but I had the worried feeling now, too late of course, that Heather would be truly upset at losing the MG and I knew that I should have consulted her first and that it was unfair of me to have acted so impetuously. Right now, however, I had to put a brave face on what I had done and hope that I could make it appear as a totally justifiable and sensible move.

And so I bounded into the Ward, all bogus and cheerful-like, to find Heather up and dressed, nursing the baby and obviously happy at the thought of leaving the hospital the next day to return home to Coverack. I started by reminding her how badly we needed some money in the bank and that the sporty MG, with its rather tatty hood, was too draughty and cold and obviously unsuitable now that we had a child. I explained that I had exchanged it for a comfortable saloon car which would be much more appropriate for our needs, now that we had started a family. And to top it all, I told her, we have some money in the bank, but I didn't tell her at first how little it was. It must have sounded as a good and sensible argument, I thought, but Heather was watching my face cautiously and obviously knew me too well, so she said simply, 'Let me see it.' I took her over to the window and we gazed down upon that battered old Renault, looking what it truly was; an ugly old car and no disguising the fact.

I couldn't bear to see the hurt and disappointment in her eyes that I could have done such a thing without discussing it with her first. However, all Heather said was, 'It is a hell of a long way to Cornwall and I just hope that dreadful-looking old heap will get us and our son there safely.' She suggested that we should stop on the way at my Mother's, in Taplow, to see how it performed. 'While we are there for a day, we can buy the things we need for the baby including extra shawls and a hot water bottle to keep him warm for the journey. Get cracking,' she said laughing at me by now, 'and organise that old dragon of a Mother of yours to put us up.'

Mother looked upon our visit benignly and was obviously glad of the opportunity to help us and to see the baby. 'Lucille', as we had decided to call our Renault, had taken us through London and to Taplow safely and with reasonable comfort, although rather slowly and ponderously. It was no good trying to push her along fast; she would have none of it and so the journey to the far end of Cornwall was obviously going to be a very long one indeed, probably taking ten or twelve hours (no motorways in those days) and we would have to stop somewhere half-way. The baby was left with Mother and Maddie while we spent the whole morning in the town of Maidenhead buying a carry-cot and stocking up with baby food, extra shawls, a hot-water bottle and a flask for hot water, in preparation for the journey. It was a cold mid-January in 1949, the heating in Lucille was non-existent, her serviceability was suspect, we had a journey of some three hundred and fifty miles to go and we had to care for a two-week old baby on the very long journey. A modern-day young married woman, sensible, responsible and cautious as she would have been brought up to be, would probably have wet herself at the thought of such a journey, in those circumstances, and would never have even considered undertaking it. But Heather seemed to have enough confidence in herself and in me to cope with difficulties. For my part, at least, I had taken the sensible precaution of buying a new battery for Lucille.

The next morning, we set off very early in the dark and Lucille ground to her first halt five hours later somewhere between Bath and Bristol. Luckily, after many years of owning old cars since a teenager, I had built up a comprehensive tool-kit and a sound knowledge of what made elderly car-engines tend to stop. So armed with this trusty tool-kit containing plenty of pliable wire and pliers, a large roll of black tape and two tins of Radweld, I reckoned I could cope with most stoppages. And so, after taping up the spark condenser whose electric leakage I had diagnosed and found, we were off again. There was no more trouble and we arrived in the dark at Taunton where I found a nice little family hotel, more of a guest-house really, where we warmed ourselves at an open fire, had a good meal and so to bed. Jeremy had been no trouble all day, just vaguely gurgling in his cot and, as for some reason Heather's own milk supply was inadequate, he was being bottle-fed which was easier under the circumstances.

The next day was a disaster as, for a start, Lucille chose the middle of Bodmin Moor in the pouring rain to express her disgust loudly at the excessive demands on her by dropping the rear end of her exhaust pipe so that it clattered along the road behind us making a fearful din. I fixed it back on to its bracket using the wire and pliers. Then she wouldn't restart until I found and repaired a leak in a petrol pipe connection to her carburettor. I was very wet, cold and miserable until, two miles further on, we sighted that famous pub halfway across the moor. After two large hot whiskies and a bowl of hot soup each, with a change of nappies and warm milk for Jeremy, we were off again with our hot-water bottles recharged ready again for the cold journey. Heather, however, seemed to be quite enjoying the challenge of it all when, as a young mother with a new baby, she should have been complaining about the thoroughly uncomfortable predicament into which her husband had led her. While at the pub, I had telephoned Nigel and Margery Gardner, our naval chums in Coverack, and had asked them to light the fires in the Watch House and get the house warm for our arrival, which I hoped would be late that evening. But Lucille hadn't finished yet. Her little flat-four engine started clanking and rattling and, when I stopped, she emitted clouds of steam from her radiator. Never mind letting the radiator cool first, as I should have done, I poured the Radweld straight in and set off again determined to have no more nonsense from Lucille.

Whatever fears of George I had experienced as I left the Watch House three weeks earlier, were forgotten as Lucille at last clanked and steamed her way along the back lane towards the house. And what a relief and joy it was at the end of that journey to see the house looking so welcoming with all the lights on, ready for our return. Inside, we were greeted by the warmth from the fires, which our friends had lit, and the smell of a hot stew cooking on the hob. Such is friendship and, oh yes, there was a half-bottle of whisky on the table waiting for us. Heather bathed and fed Jeremy before putting him to bed in the carry-cot while I sank back into an armchair with a large whisky. I rang Nigel to thank them and to ask if they would like to join us and, thank heavens, he said certainly not and we were to enjoy a quiet evening. He would give me a lift to the aerodrome in the morning.

The months which followed were very happy. The village of Coverack provided a close community of friends among whom was one of my pupils, Herbert Ellis and his wife Margaret. Herbert was that rarest of all creatures in the Royal Navy, a flying doctor, and indeed I do believe that he was the only one the Navy had ever produced. When he first came to me as my pupil on the instrument flight, for completion of his flying course, I assumed that the Admiralty had at long last recognised the need for aviation doctors, who would specialise in the care of aircrew and would understand their fears and problems. Dear me no, that would have been the very last role suitable for Herbie because he was not only an unusually good aviator but, as I had found in bad weather, the man simply did not know the meaning of the word fear.

On completion of his course with me, he went straight to Farnborough, the aerodrome where government test flying took place and where he flew every one of the new jet fighter aircraft. More particularly, he flew so as to subject his body to the most appalling strains and stresses to discover the safety limits in the air for future aircrews, for which he properly earned an AFC. But, bless his heart, if for example I had come to him for help in the days of my wartime 'twitch', I think he would have been genuinely puzzled to understand what I was talking about. Anyway, we became chums and, at the christening ceremony in the local Coverack church, Herbie became Jeremy's Godfather. And typical of most godparents, contributed a silver napkin ring and promptly forgot Jeremy's existence.

Close to us lived a naval engineering officer, Doidge, with his wife and three-year old daughter. It is important that I mention this family on two counts; firstly because Doidge was an excellent artist and, although I didn't actually start to paint until much later, he initiated my interest in painting. But secondly and much more importantly, he and his wife were at the forefront of what in the 1950s was the new ideology on the upbringing of children. This dictated that children must be allowed 'to do their own thing' without repression or order imposed by parents to enable the child, as the parents quaintly expected, to develop naturally into a lovely and charming adult. It was a method of bringing up children, never saying 'no' to them, which took strong root in the UK, inevitably growing even stronger as each weak generation followed the previous one, and thus undoubtedly became one of the causes of our current yobbo culture, in which there are people who have little respect for others in the community around them.

Our concern, whenever that family visited us, was that their little girl would inevitably rush into every room to seize whatever ornament or object she could reach on a table, or wherever, and either break it or demand to keep it. Meantime, her dotty parents would follow behind the child, never once saying 'no' to it, and cajoling the little creature to give up whatever it had grabbed. The point was reached where one of the parents would arrive in advance of the child to suggest that we move any ornaments first. It became impossible to disguise our dislike of the child, which of course it instinctively recognised, and so responded by being even more unpleasant and difficult.

Our experience of that awful child, without doubt a nice-enough little girl had she been sensibly brought up, did a great service to Heather and me and our family. For we solemnly vowed together that we would bring up Jeremy, and any other children we had, with kindness and love but always with normal discipline. Not to be over-strict but enough so that there would be order in their lives, and for them to understand that there were standards to be respected. We were determined that we would never have reason to see loathing of our children in the eyes of those adults who might meet them during their formative years.

I don't remember precisely how it happened but I think that it was about this time that Heather became 'Saccie,' a nickname which stayed with her all her life and one which her family and the many, many friends she made in her life used affectionately always. I think that we were probably having a row, a very rare occurrence between us because she absolutely loathed any such thing, but which I might perhaps enjoy for the pleasure of the cuddle and make up afterwards. In any case, I don't remember our rows ever lasting more than twenty minutes or so. It was part of Heather's nature, and my good fortune, that she was incapable of indulging in that well-known and female weapon, so dreaded by all men; a long period of tight-lipped, grim silence. Instead, I think she must have referred to herself as being regarded by me as 'my old bag,' which turned into, 'my old sack,' and eventually became affectionately, 'Saccie.' Thus, much in the same way that I had become 'Hank' instead of Henry (as the result of a chance encounter with an American soldier), so Heather became 'Saccie' from a chance remark made during a bit of a row. So there you are, and though in my mind and privately my lovely wife is always Heather, from now on I usually refer to her as Saccie, but always with affection.

The end of my short service commission was drawing near when I was called for an interview with the Captain of the Naval Air Station, who wanted to know whether I had made up my mind to apply for a permanent commission and he implied that he would certainly support my application. However, Saccie and I had already discussed our future at length and we had made the firm decision for me to bale out of the Royal Navy. It was not an easy decision because, in reality, neither of us had a clue about civilian life and we recognised the decision to be a gamble. Had I only known then how much of a gamble and how bloody difficult life was going to be, I would probably have gone running back to the Navy. I had been such an utter clot for failing to make up my mind much earlier, when I would could have at least studied some profession, under a correspondence course, before leaving. I didn't know it then but, in three months' time, I would have to learn in a very hard school indeed how to grow up in Civvie Street.

Only then, after our decision had been made and in the short time left to me in the Navy, did I begin to think vaguely about getting a job. The financial support offered by the Attlee government to ex-service men immediately after the war, to attend university and polytechnics, was no longer available. And now, four years later because of the short service commission which I had so rashly chosen, I had missed that opportunity. But in my mind was the idea that companies, of whatever sort, would offer training to a young ex-service officer and I intended to buckle down to seeking such training and a job just as soon as I was a civilian. In the meantime, there was my work as a flying instructor to be done and it occupied most of my mind each day.

Lucille was an absolute pain and constantly unserviceable, so that I had to rely on others to give me a lift to the aerodrome and back. At one stage, coming down the steep hill into Coverack, her transmission shaft came completely adrift and fell with a great clatter onto the road. The small local garage coped with the situation, but it was Lucille's most expensive failure so far. Later, the rear starboard wheel took to coming off and running on gaily ahead of the car. The only way that I could afford at first to deal with that particular problem was to drill right through the hub of the wheel, through the half-shaft, and knock a large thick nail through them both. I found that each nail would last for about eight miles, when I would replace it before the wheel came off. Saccie, being mindful of the care of our son, had lost all confidence in Lucille and understandably would only travel very short journeys in her.

After a while, I took Lucille to a garage and had her wheel welded on; too bad if I had a puncture as I wouldn't have been able to take the wheel off.

George, our ghost, we felt was still around and we were aware that he would quietly move the occasional plate slightly when we weren't looking, and he seemed prone to do so particularly after Jeremy had been in the room. We never left Jeremy by himself in any room; he was always with us except, during the day, when Saccie would put him outside in his pram where she could watch him. It was such a lovely place for him to be, gurgling happily away within sound of the sea beating against the rocks below, and with seagulls wheeling about above his head for him to watch.

I had not told Saccie about my awful experience with George on that night when she had gone to London and I had been on my own in the Watch House. As a result of it I was convinced that George set out, with malicious intent, to frighten inhabitants of the house, particularly when they were left on their own in the house. But I had made such arrangements as were possible at the Air Station to avoid any night duties, so that I would be there with Saccie and Jeremy in the house every night until we left Coverack. I didn't see myself as some Galahad capable of seeing George off the premises, I was much too frightened of him for that, but I reckoned that, in the company of Saccie and with my son to protect, I wouldn't be quite such a wimp as I had been the last time.

Then one evening, when we had only two weeks remaining before we were due to leave Coverack and the Navy, I was summoned to take part in a search for an aircraft which had ditched some thirty miles off the Lizard, at the far end of the Cornish coast.

It was an emergency and, of course, with my experience it was essential that I took my part in it. I would have to leave Saccie alone with Jeremy, probably for the whole night, though I hated the thought of doing so. On the other hand, this was not the time to warn her about George and the possibility of his more frightening form of visitation. Perhaps he might not come near her although, on the other hand, he had seemed to be particularly attracted by the presence of our baby son. I left the house in a worried state of mind, but I had to go.

At the aerodrome, I went through the briefing with a part of my mind on my family but made myself concentrate because the weather at first light, when we were due over the search area, was expected to remain very bad, and there was a crew of three men out there somewhere in the sea, whom we must try to find. One of the other instructors was with me in the cockpit but, in that weather and with a night take-off, I preferred to do the flying and for him to do most of the looking. We were allocated an area over the sea for our search but, when we arrived there, the visibility was so very poor that it limited the size of our square search to the point where there was little likelihood of seeing anybody down there in the rough sea. After only an hour, all aircraft on the search were recalled because of the weather. The three aircrew who had ditched were never found.

At the end of the de-briefing, I drove home as fast as Lucille could go, with my heart racing in fear for Saccie and Jeremy. On arrival, I ran along the path and crashed open the kitchen door and there was Heather … feeding Jeremy. She smiled but couldn't disguise the strain and fear she had been through alone in that house with him. She told me that, after going to bed with Jeremy in the cot next to her, she had been awakened and terrified by precisely the same pattern of events which I had suffered. I felt sick and angry at the thought of this damnable 'thing,' this ghost, whatever it was, causing us such fear. And I felt completely helpless.

We talked about it and I thought that we should move straight away to a hotel for the two weeks remaining of my time in the Navy. But Saccie said firmly, 'No, we can't afford that sort of thing any more. We shall be fine,' she said, 'provided that we are all three together after dusk and not one of us is ever alone.' And so we stayed. (Who was it who said that a man was always the boss in a family?)

But Heather was right, or so it seemed, until our last night in the Watch House. We had packed everything up in readiness for our journey to Salisbury, where we were going to stay with Heather's parents for a short while until I found a job. We went to bed as normal with Jeremy in the cot next to us and we both awoke at the same time. Something was downstairs. We held each other tight as we heard it start up the wooden stairs, as before, and come into the sitting-room next to us. When it started its sobbing noises, I suddenly felt absolute fury at this ghastly thing, which so threatened and frightened us. I forced myself out of bed, followed closely by Saccie. At the door, I hesitated … then, as the sobbing continued, I flung open the door shouting 'Get out, get out of here you wretched, miserable, vile thing. Get out!'

Suddenly I realised that I was shouting at a total silence. There was nothing there. I crossed to the switch and flooded an empty room with light.

In the morning we packed Lucille and took a final look at the Watch House, lovely in its solitary seaside setting … it was such a happy-looking house in the sunshine and made it difficult to believe in the misery which lurked within. Many months later we learned by chance from a book we found in a library, written by Harry Price, the famous author and ghost-hunter, that he featured the Watch House as one of the most haunted houses in England. If only we had known it earlier, we would never have rented it. It was subsequently exorcised so that George left it in peace, and many young families over the past fifty years have spent happy holidays there.

Well, all that and the Navy were behind us now and, had we but known it, there was a lot worse than a haunted house to worry us in the life ahead.

CHAPTER TWO

At Home with the Leamans

My situation, on leaving the Navy in May 1949 at age twenty-seven, was that I had a sum of £65 in the bank, no income whatsoever, no job or any prospect of one, no qualifications or training for any work or profession and no home for my wife and child. Oh, and no car as sorrowfully, I had taken Lucille into a knackers' yard and received a mere fiver for what was left of her. I was damn lucky that Alice, mother of Heather, bottled up her strong dislike of me and joined her husband, Stuart, in offering us a temporary home with them. Alice considered me to be an absolute bounder and, under those circumstances to which I had reduced her daughter, who could say she was wrong.

Heather's parents had a nice four-bedroom house and large garden in a pleasant suburb on the outskirts of Salisbury. By that time her father, Stuart, had been the City Treasurer of Salisbury for many years and it wasn't until weeks later that I came to realise what a hugely important appointment and position he held in the City. He was in control of the massive budget, which he himself set each year for the running of the City, and in effect therefore he was a minor god to whom, as I found later, the Mayor, members of the Council, the city Clerk and his staff all deferred. To have control of the money-bags in any organisation is to command respect and, at the council offices where Stuart held sway, there was absolutely no lack of that, despite his quiet and always pleasant manner. I should add that he was also the Grand Master of the Masons in that area of the UK, whatever that might mean, as I never found out. Stuart was a good-looking man who had been athletic in his youth and a good pianist. He appeared to me as rather an unimaginative type of man, a bit of a plodder perhaps, but one who had achieved his position by determination and hard work. I liked him a lot as he was a modest and kindly person, as well as being a strong enough character to achieve most of his objectives in life.

If I have painted this picture of a powerful, quietly commanding man, at his place of business at the council offices, then it will be difficult to believe what a subdued man he was in his home. ... He was like a mouse.

Alice, in the domain of her house, ruled like Queen Victoria and her every word was law.

She had been the second eldest of a family of seven sisters and a brother. Their mother had died very young, so that Alice and her elder sister had perforce to take responsibility for the care and upbringing of the other six younger siblings. This background may explain the autocratic manner in which she conducted her own household after she had married Stuart who, significantly, had wooed her with his typical determination for over three years before she had eventually accepted him. Moreover, after the loss of her second child at its birth, she had become an apparent invalid for whom Stuart, in his devotion to her, would sacrifice all his spare time. For example, he would have enjoyed his two hobbies of stamp collecting and photography, had he not been expected to keep Alice company almost every evening, listening to the radio. Alice needed his company because she was shy to an extraordinary degree and even dreaded rare visits of friends to her house. Thus, but for the companionship of her husband, her life would have been a lonely one. In particular, she declined to join her husband at many of the formal occasions and dinners to which, because of his position at the Council and as the Grand Master, they were frequently invited. Consequently Heather, when she became a teenager, often had acted as escort to her father. They must have made quite a pair on such occasions, the handsome father, a power in the community, with his escort of a beautiful honey-blonde young daughter.

And so, after spending most of our adult life in the Navy with the vigorous and lively lifestyle peculiar to it, Saccie and I had now found ourselves in an altogether different environment to which we would have to adapt. And it wasn't going to be easy. The pattern of life with the Leamans was such that, as her priority, Alice kept the house absolutely spotlessly clean and tidy with the help of a daily maid. Her kitchen, where she produced plain but delicious mid-day meals, was sacrosanct and no one, not even her daughter, was allowed in there when she was cooking. Stuart came home each day for lunch, which Alice served at precisely 1 p.m., for Stuart to get back to his work at 2 p.m. We had high tea at 6 p.m., which consisted of bread and butter with something or other, followed by listening to the radio until bedtime at about 9.45 p.m. About twice a month we went to the pictures.

This regime was dreary beyond words for Saccie and me, but it acted as a spur to our desperate intention, firstly for me to find a job and, secondly and in the meantime, to save as much money as we could towards our own home. Our bank balance at that time, what with one thing and another, was £67 as I remember. Hence, in the evenings with Jeremy in his cot asleep, Saccie was stuck listening to the radio with her mother, which gave Stuart the rare opportunity to play with his stamps and to print photographs in his study. Most of my mornings and evenings were spent in the dining-room with the newspapers around me, writing letter after letter applying for jobs or for some sort of work. After a while and in the end, any work would have done so long as I could get it, and I didn't care where I would have to go or to live, and neither did Saccie, if only I could get a job.

In great desperation, because I hated the thought of grovelling to the company which, if Father hadn't sold it, rightfully should have been mine, I bottled up my pride and travelled to Bristol to see if there might be any possibility of work or training with my family firm of George Adlam & Sons. But there was only one man remaining from the time when my Father had been the owner and chairman of this very successful company of brewers' engineers. He was Mr. Farquhar, the chief draughtsman, who was now elderly and about to retire, but he remembered me and my brief apprenticeship in 1940, before I had joined the Navy. When he realised that I wanted to come back and work for the company, he was sympathetic, but told me that there was little chance of the current Chairman, the major shareholder, wanting anyone from the Adlam family anywhere near the place. That foolish and incompetent man of business, at a time when the brewing industry was beginning to boom as never before, was busy dismantling the brewing machinery in the factory and sacking the skilled brewing workforce, to replace all that expertise with his absurd scheme to develop and manufacture a silent road drill. The road drill was already a failure and the company, the family firm over which my Father should have retained control, was failing with it, and fast.

Farquhar told me that the very name of Adlam was anathema to this Chairman, he was so sick of being reminded how hugely successful the company had been in all the years since 1820 when it had been developed and managed by my family. Father had a lot to answer for in selling the company at a time when I was still a boy and too young to show ability or promise. According to my Mother, he had an obsessive hatred and fear both of socialism and the trade union movement, which were becoming so much stronger in the 1930s and these fears, plus the gain of even more wealth from the sale of our family business, were presumably his main reasons for selling my inheritance. It was not possible for me to visualize then in 1951, as a destitute young man unable even to provide a home for my wife and children, that sometime in the future I would become a company director and a skilled negotiator with the trade unions. Therefore, although I would never have been an engineer, as was my Father, I would have been eminently capable of directing and leading the family business during the boom years of the fifties through to the eighties. Well, it was not to be and no good to bewail it.

I returned sadly to Salisbury and, in my continuing search for work or training, I ran out of those companies prepared to train young men because they all apparently had an age maximum of twenty-five for that purpose. None of the companies or anyone else seemed remotely interested in my service background or of employing a man of my age who had absolutely no previous training. Two evenings a week, therefore, I attended night-school in Salisbury where I had enrolled to learn basic book-keeping and accountancy. But these lessons weren't enough and moreover the teaching from an inexperienced young accounting clerk was amateur and inadequate. One evening each week, Saccie and I just had to bale out to a pub where, slowly drinking a pint of beer each, we could talk privately together about our problems and how to cope with them. Alice, whose life had been so sheltered, was appalled that we should go out to a pub instead of quietly enjoying the benefit of her home.

Saccie, thank heavens, had Jeremy to look after and to keep herself focused and reasonably happy would take him in the pram for long walks in the local area which she knew well from her childhood. Alice, fortunately, enjoyed and was very good at caring for infants of Jeremy's age and so therefore, after we had been there a while, Saccie persuaded Stuart to find a clerking job for her in the Council offices for two hours a day, during the mornings, which he was able to do for her easily enough. We banked all her earnings each week.

At last came a reply from one of the many firms to whom I had written and, although it was as a salesman, the last thing I wanted, I responded immediately. The office in Bristol, when I arrived there for interview, consisted of a barely-furnished room with lots of big cardboard boxes lying about. There was a desk in the middle at which sat a dark rather saturnine-looking gentleman wearing thick glasses. However, he was a pleasant-enough chap who explained that he and his brother held distribution contracts with producers of office equipment such as paper, carbons, stationery and all that kind of thing for sale in the Bristol, Wiltshire and Somerset area. But he became really excited about his sales distributorship of a machine called the Copycat, which he showed me. It was a photographic machine, rather like a huge flat camera, designed to copy letters, book pages or large drawings and maps. He reckoned that he was on to an absolute winner and he even managed to enthuse me about the thing, as he described how it worked.

I had dressed up in my only suit for the interview and he evidently liked the impression I gave with my comparatively plummy accent, and so I got the job. The brother was the main salesman for their firm and, to start with, I accompanied him as he called upon his list of potential customers for the Copycat. These were generally the offices of Solicitors, Accountants and local Councils plus anyone else who conceivably might have need for such a machine. I marvelled at his manner of brushing aside the rude attitude we so frequently met from junior clerks and typists when we went into the offices, and in response to them, his firm demand that he speak with a partner or the chief clerk. I admired too his smooth sales patter and explanation of how the Copycat worked and what it could do. Even when we failed to sell a Copycat, he would usually obtain an order for stationery. My job was to carry the heavy machine in its case and, of course, to learn how to sell it.

The time came inevitably when I would have to go out into the streets of Salisbury on my own in an endeavour to sell a Copycat machine to some office or other. The first attempt was the pattern of nearly all the others, as I sat in a café opposite a firm of solicitors, trying to gird up my courage to cross the street and enter their offices. What I really needed, instead of a cup of coffee, was a large but unaffordable glass of whisky. Eventually, putting a brave face on it, I would enter the office of the solicitors to be greeted, probably by some teenage boy with brylcreamed hair, who would assess immediately by my manner and the case I was carrying that I was a salesman. 'I wish to speak with Mr. So and So,' I would say to the boy having noted earlier the name of a partner. 'What time is your appointment with him?' would ask the boy, going through the pretence that he believed me to be a client. 'I don't have an appointment but I wish to discuss with a partner or with your chief clerk a matter of equipment.' 'Oh well, if you want to flog us some stuff, I can tell you that we order direct from suppliers and we don't deal with salesmen, so you'd better 'op it, Mister.' Would be a typical response from the grinning boy. And I had lost so much confidence and pride in myself that I could do no more than leave. I was only earning thirty shillings a week as wages, the real earnings should have been as commission on the sales, which I seemed incapable of achieving.

For two weeks, I kept forcing myself into various offices with the same result. The truth was that I was a hopelessly bad salesman and knew it. The ridiculous situation was that, despite my background as an officer and carrier pilot who had taken part in a long war at the sharp end, I was quite unable in these new circumstances to cope with being rebuffed and shown the door by oily-haired young clerks. It never occurred to me that I might gain some advantage by mentioning my wartime background. That would be something I, or any man of similar war experience, simply could not do and which I never ever did during all the years ahead. With regard to the Copycat machine, only once did I reach someone in authority to whom I could deliver my sales pitch on it, but even then I failed to impress him. I had lost confidence and felt myself to be a failure as a man and without hope for the future. I could have collapsed entirely but for Saccie who never once lost faith in me and my ability to succeed eventually.

One evening, Stuart found an opportunity while Alice was preparing the high tea, to question me about my job and to ask the reason for the misery I appeared to be suffering. Two days later, I received a letter to invite me to the offices of the City Council with a request that I demonstrate the Copycat machine to members of senior staff. They were genuinely interested once I had shown them the machine and this gave me the confidence to demonstrate it reasonably well. After I had finished and answered questions adequately, the Council bought two machines; a large one for their map room and a smaller one for office use. I telegraphed the good news of the sales to my boss in Bristol, who sent me a cheque for £7 as my commission, together with his congratulations.

If he thought that he had found himself a super salesman, then he would have been disappointed by my subsequent letter in which I gave him my notice. I reckoned that the sale of the two machines (thanks to Stuart) had paid off what I owed him for giving me a job. But I had decided that any job, anything at all, would be preferable to the degradation of having to submit myself, as a salesman, to those sniggering rebuffs from the young clerks and office typists who confronted me.

Instead, I enrolled with a small firm of contract office cleaners in Salisbury, who allocated me to the offices of one of the main banks, where I would start work at 6.30 a.m. every morning for two hours to clean the lavatories and hallways of the building each day. The work was well paid at 24 shillings per week and enabled me to plough through the newspapers and write job-hunting letters during the rest of the day. As a job, it was one hundred times preferable to being a door-to-door salesman, which I had learned to regard as the nadir of all forms of work. Whereas, unexpectedly in fact, I found some pleasure in keeping those lavatories as immaculate as I could make them. Perhaps I was affected by my memory of how nauseating the lavatories had been at the naval barracks, years ago when I was a sailor.

Nearly all the money Saccie and I earned with our part-time jobs was put into our bank account as we were obsessed with the desire to save enough money to live in our own home. Particularly now was a home so vital because Heather was pregnant again. The pregnancy must have been conceived before we left Coverack, because we dared not make any noises in our bedroom next to Alice, who would flush in embarrassment if Saccie and I so much as held hands in the house. Alice would even turn off the radio if an intimate play was on, which led Saccie and me to wonder, having a bit of a giggle together, how Saccie had ever come into being in the first place? A strange factor of our continued living with her parents was that Alice, who had found it impossibly difficult to disguise her dislike of me when I was a naval officer, became friendly and nice to me the lower I sank. Now, instead of being ashamed of a son-in-law who was no more than a lavatory cleaner, she appeared to warm to me. Her warmth reached the point at which, on Saturday mornings sometimes, Stuart would drive all four of us to a pub where Alice would have a small glass of Guinness. Alice's problem, as I had recognised early on, was her extreme shyness, which made her so prickly and difficult a person for a stranger to befriend.

But Alice was immensely proud of Stuart and his achievement as City Treasurer. The only sibling who could match their social position was her immediately younger sister, Rowena, who was an entirely different character; a vivacious woman with dark flashing good looks and an obvious and rather loud enjoyment of the money earned by her husband, who was manager of an oil-rig in Persia. On rare visits from this sister and her husband, I found it interesting and rather fun to listen and watch these two wives fighting for one-upmanship over the other. Alice might come out fighting with an account of how Stuart had presided over an important city dinner, to which Rowena would riposte with dining at the Captain's table on the ship from Persia, and so it would go on. Meanwhile the two husbands, great friends, would be chatting amicably in the background. However, Alice was never going to match Rowena's comparatively exotic lifestyle abroad, and eventually, flushed and bridling with anger, little Alice would fall silent. I wanted to help her and commented how, from my experience, the pleasure of travel could so soon pall whereas nothing could compare with living at home in England with the children. This was a double-edged thrust from me because it would remind Rowena that, while she was abroad, she had been glad that her young son, John, had lived with the Leamans and indeed, while Alice had been like a mother to him, Saccie had been like an elder sister to the boy.

At long last, I received a response to one of my many letters seeking work or training. It was from the Rootes Group of car manufacturers in Coventry; a very big company which made the well-known Humber and Hillman cars. They had advertised for young men suitable to be trained as managers and, unusually, they had not specified a maximum age limitation, which had given me some hope. In consequence, I did not state my age of twenty-seven in the CV which I sent them, and implied in it that I was younger. Their letter invited me to attend for interview at their main offices in Coventry in eight days' time. I arrived at the due time to be greeted by a pleasant man aged about fifty who introduced himself as the Trainee Manager. There were several other young men also waiting to be interviewed and I noted that they all appeared to be younger than me.

The interview itself took place in an annex to the boardroom and, when I went in, I was asked to sit in a chair facing, on the other side of a table, a group of four important-looking men of middle age, including the Trainee Manager. To begin with I seemed to be doing quite well in describing my interests which, of course, included cars, and I made much of my time as an apprentice in an engineering company without mentioning my family connection with it, also I mentioned that I was attending night-school to learn accountancy. I kept off the subject of wartime experience because I had learned, as all ex-servicemen who fought at the sharp end do, that those who had not taken part would rather not hear about war. Despite my caution, the subject of my flying experience was inevitably raised since, after all, I had done little else, and I let slip that I had flown Hurricanes. This was seized upon by the chairman who, aware that the Hurricane was a fighter aircraft of the earlier period of the war, queried my age. The upshot was that I had to admit that I was nearly twenty-eight and I was told, as pleasantly as possible by the interview committee, that they were only recruiting young men in their early twenties. I found myself shamefacedly almost pleading for an opportunity to train with their company, or even for any job they could offer me … but it was a case of sorry but goodbye, and I was to wait outside to receive my travel expenses from the Manager.

I was sitting outside the interview room alone, the other young applicants, mostly local men, having gone, and I was in despair at having to return to Saccie without a job, when the Trainee Manager came out to give me my expenses back to Salisbury. He was sympathetic and kind, realising from the interview how desperate I was for any job, and he told me that he was in charge of a secondary entry into the company management structure via the shop floor. He had the authority to select young men for training as managers, if they were sufficiently outstanding, from anywhere in the company. But, he added, that in his ten years as Trainee Manager only two had so far been good enough to come up for such selection from the shop floor. He explained that he could arrange for me to have work in the factory as a semi-skilled machine operator, which would provide me with a good wage, and then it would be up to me to make my mark in some way and perhaps find promotion. I jumped at the chance he was giving me. Accordingly, he wrote a brief note and suggested that I hand it into the office of the Personnel department early on the following morning when I would have to queue with other men looking for work with the company.

The note he had given me was effective and it was arranged that I would report for work in one of the machine shops on the following Monday morning at 7.30 a.m. It was then Tuesday and this would give me five days to find digs in Coventry, return to Salisbury, collect a case of clothes, say goodbye to Saccie and then to take the train back to Coventry on the Sunday afternoon. The Personnel office had provided me with a short list of 'digs' in the area near to the factory and I was lucky enough to find a vacancy in a house run by a youngish widow whose husband, a sergeant pilot in the RAF, had been killed in the war. She had two rooms which she let out as digs to working men, two men to a room, at twenty-five shillings a week each, to include a cooked breakfast, except on Sundays. Having secured the room with a week's rent in advance, I hotfooted it back to Salisbury, anxious to tell Saccie my news and to discuss it with her and worried because I thought she was bound to be disappointed that I had been unable to get a job as a trainee.

As soon as we could on my first evening back in Salisbury, Saccie and I were off to the local pub to talk privately together about the job in Coventry and the possibilities it presented. My view was that I would never be able to obtain any management job anywhere, because of my total lack of training, so I might as well start at the ground floor and, with the help of learning at night-school, grind myself upwards and gradually to a responsible position. The work which had been offered to me in the machine shop was pretty lowly but the wages, as in all the car factories in the UK at that time, were very high and I would be able to earn nearly £5 per week. Saccie agreed entirely with my attitude to the situation but fiercely told me that our first absolute priority was to find a home. Therefore, when I got back to Coventry, I must forget about night-school and, with a decent wage now, spend every spare moment looking for accommodation to rent. 'It doesn't matter,' she said, 'how grotty a place you find because, whatever it is like, I will make a home of it.'

So I returned to Coventry, heartened by her resolve, and ready to start work in the factory.

Next morning, after I had clocked in at one of the huge machine shops, I reported to the foreman who, threading his way through lines of lathes and other variety of machines, led me to a comparatively small vertical drilling machine. Here, over the clattering cacophony of noise from all the other machines, he explained how to work the drill and showed me the large stack of metal cylinders, about four inches in diameter and eight inches long, into each of which two holes had to be drilled. There was nothing particularly difficult about the task and so, by the time I had done four cylinders, I was able to launch myself at the job and worked with increasing speed at it. Eventually, towards the end of the morning, feeling rather pleased with myself, I eased down reckoning it must be about time for the mid-day break for lunch. For the first time, I took a glance around at all the other operators around me and gave them a tentative smile, rather hoping for an encouraging smile back since I had started quite well, I thought. Instead, I received a whole lot of boot-faced looks. It occurred to me that perhaps they were impatient while waiting for their lunch-break and I looked at my watch, which seemed to have stopped. But it hadn't stopped; the actual time as I came to realise was only 9.15 a.m., and I had been working for just over one hour! I had yet to learn that, in repetitive work such as this, time stood still. It was the most horrifying factor of such work and somehow my mind would have to learn to deal with it.

And so I pressed on, even faster, with the totally mistaken notion that the more cylinders I completed, the faster would pass the time. And moreover, I hoped obviously that the foreman would appreciate the effort I was making. Gormless twit that I was. Hours and hours later, as it seemed, there was a choking noise behind me and a voice saying, 'Stop, stop, you bleeder, what the hell do you think you are fucking doing, you bloody bleeder.' I turned round and there was this small, bald man, sporting a Hitleresque moustache and wearing a brown overall coat (a recognisable badge of his office, I was to learn) and nearly jumping up and down and spitting his filthy words out with rage. 'What is your problem?' I enquired. 'It has taken hours of negotiation with the management and the time and motion boys, you bleeding fool,' he spluttered, 'to agree a rate and time for each of these cylinders which, in turn, fits in with all the other jobs. And here you are, you steaming little twerp, pissing them out at three times the normal rate and ruining the money I had negotiated.' I asked him who and what he was. 'I am the union convenor for this machine shop and I run it,' he shouted in answer, 'and if you so much as piss out one cylinder too many from now on, I will 'ave you out of this factory on your arse before you can bloody well blink.' Around me the other operators were nodding approvingly.

Well, I tried. Oh, how hard I tried to comply with the agreed slow rate of work because I so badly needed the job. The hours and interminably long days passed doing what all operators on repetitive work learn to do, i.e., wander off to the loo, get some water, fill the tea can, have a chat, (but I had no mates to chat with), borrow a fag, ask for a match, then return to the drilling machine to clean it and sweep the floor around it and always to go off for the permitted washing of hands well before each official break. During my enforced wanderings, I noticed a works suggestion box fixed to a wall. It gave me the idea to spend my time trying to think of sensible suggestions and, to this end, I resolved to watch and observe all the work and the shop arrangements around me and I would contrive to put in at least one suggestion every week. All very well, since I hadn't a clue about car or any other production, but I kept my mind busy trying to think of anything at all worth putting into the suggestion box. I almost blush now to remember some of the naïve suggestions I must have put into that box during that time.

Despite my best efforts, my output of drilled cylinders was still too many and, true to his word, the union convenor had me out of there, just like that. The man seemed to be all-powerful. My guardian angel, in the form of the Trainee Manager, must have found a place for me in the engine assembly shop, as this was where I was moved on my third week.

I was given very fiddly work on the production line of inserting small guides with their valves into the Humber engine. It was a type of work requiring dexterity and concentration, but not necessarily any engineering knowledge, and I quite liked it as time passed once again like real time. I continued with my input of suggestions, which began to include my ideas of improved layout of the engine assembly shop. They were absolute nonsense, of course, but couldn't do any harm, so I thought.

All this time, I had been searching for a flat or even a house to rent for Saccie and Jeremy and very soon now there would be a second child as well. But Coventry at that time was a booming city and nowhere could I find a place for us to live. Not only was everywhere expensive and beyond my means but no accommodation whatsoever seemed available. I had given up on night-school to give myself more time to search for a flat, but also because the poor quality of teaching made it such a waste of time. Instead, I intended to use some of our precious capital to pay for a correspondence course. But not yet, however, because it would be difficult to learn while sharing a room with the young man at the digs who at times, being a skilled car worker with so much money to spend, was often quite loud and boozy.

I telephoned Saccie at agreed times twice each week as I needed the encouragement of her voice. Also I took the train to Salisbury once a month and reckoned the cost for the Saturday night and Sunday morning spent there was well worth every shilling. Christmas came, with Alice and Stuart going to some trouble to make it a happy occasion for all of us, with good food and even a bottle of wine. My Mother was cross that I had not visited her and found it difficult to understand my problems or even to believe the type of jobs I was doing. I understood her disappointment with me but could do nothing about it, but also, listening between the sentences of her telephone conversation, I sensed that she was beginning to find her dog business too much for her and too tiring at her age. It was sad to hear her so low but again there was nothing I could do about it. In fact, I couldn't bring myself to tell Mother that I had been working as a lavatory cleaner, as that really would have been the last straw.

Saccie was expected to have our second child towards the end of March that year, 1950, and still I had not been able to find a home for us in Coventry. We discussed my idea of breaking back into the more moneyed and influential society, more typical of our previous lifestyle, by my joining the Coventry Cricket and Squash Club, rather a posh outfit in the middle of the city and reasonably near my digs. I thought that maybe I might meet someone at the club, with influence enough to help me find somewhere to live or perhaps even with their own property to let. I would have to keep quiet about my lowly factory work, of course. Subscription to the club would mean using some of our meagre capital and I would have to pay for expensive drinks in the bar, that sort of thing, but Saccie didn't hesitate and urged me to have a go at it, regardless of the cost.

I joined the club easily enough and very shortly afterwards was invited to play in the first team. Squash, after all, was the one game which I had been able to play frequently, particularly at Yeovilton and Culdrose, and I had even been a good enough player to sneak in at number five for the Navy team twice against county sides. Among the spectators at all my home and some of my away matches for the club was a rather large young woman, Anne, who very evidently as it transpired fancied me in my white vest and brief shorts. Inadvertently, I really had struck gold because, later when we became friends, Anne told me that her mother owned a number of properties in the working class area of Coventry. I had concealed from other members of the club that I was an unskilled labourer at a factory, but I had told Anne of my circumstances and of my desperation to find a home for my wife and family. So I didn't cheat; but this knowledge seemed not to make any difference to her relationship with me.

Came the time when Anne, quite flushed and excited about her news, said that her mother had a small terrace house now available and that she could secure it for me immediately, if I wanted it? Did I want it, indeed! I could kiss her there and then and did so, even though we were walking! The house was number 166 Gulson Road and I could have it at the same longstanding rent of 15s. 6d. per week. It was then Thursday and Anne suggested that I view the house on the coming Saturday morning and, if I liked it, I could sign the rental agreement for it that morning. I told her that I didn't even care about seeing it first, as I wanted it whatever it looked like or its condition. 'If that's the case,' said Anne, 'let's celebrate on Friday evening and, as mother will be away for the weekend, I will cook a super dinner for the two of us at our house and, in the meantime, I shall collect the keys of the house and have them ready to give you.'

Well, it was obvious what would be required of me and, although it was not exactly a case of Barkis is willin', I was to my shame prepared to do whatever might be required to win such a desperately needed prize as the house in Gulson Road. In the event, the evening went well until, after a very good dinner, we inevitably had to romp together on the large settee. It was no good; despite having Saccie and the prospect of a home for us paramount in my mind, or perhaps because of that, I failed miserably as a lover for Anne. During similar affairs in the past, before I was married, I had so often been a lousy lover but now, confronted with Anne's large bottom and weighty thighs, I was even worse and quite useless. After a while, we gave up and I apologised miserably to Anne for my failure, while fearing that she might with justification withhold from me the promised keys of the house in Gulson Road. I don't think it occurred to her to do such a thing. She was genuinely fond of me and was crying as she gave me the keys when we kissed goodbye.

CHAPTER THREE

166 Gulson Road

Gulson Road connected two main roads in Coventry and consisted of a long row of about two hundred and eighty small terrace houses on one side of it. Number 166 was on a corner of an entry road but otherwise it was exactly the same as all the others. It had the small inevitable front room, which traditionally should be furnished but unused, a large living-room cum kitchen with a coal fired black range and oven and a long table for general use and meals. There was an outside flush lavatory and a scullery wash basin behind the kitchen. Upstairs were two bedrooms with one double bed in the front room. It was unfurnished, of course, except for the bed upstairs and kitchen table.

After my excited telephone call to Heather to tell her the wonderful news that we had our own house at last, she wasted no time in organising her father to drive her and Jeremy up to Coventry and he, dear man, willingly took a day off from work. But he did so only on condition that Saccie returned to Salisbury to have our second child, which was due in six weeks' time. He was insistent that she have the baby in the hospital there where he had booked a room and where he thought she would receive the best care. So my little family arrived at Gulson Road in Stuart's car, which was filled to the roof with luggage, bedding, crockery, cutlery, cooking pots, a kettle, the carry-cot and the old Tan-Sad pram tied on at the back. Typical of the selfish young, we couldn't wait to bundle poor Stuart back home in his car so that, alone together, we could really look round our house and savour the pleasure of having it. It seemed a potential palace to us and we each put behind us the misery of our separation during the past months.

Heather was determined that, during the few weeks ahead before having to return to Salisbury, she would transform the rather dirty and shabby little house into a comfortable home to be proud of. She started immediately the next day to clean the whole house from top to bottom, including the wooden floors, which she scrubbed. Then she set about repainting all the walls of each room. In the evenings and on Saturdays we took turns, one to stay at home looking after Jeremy, the other using the pram to hunt for wooden orange boxes and any old bits of furniture we could find and afford. In particular we found and had delivered two old and comfortable armchairs to put on either side of the kitchen range. With the orange boxes we had accumulated, Saccie made dressing tables and side tables, which she covered with cheerful materials. She made curtains for all the windows. She found cheap, colourful rugs to cover the newly scrubbed wooden floors. Also Saccie had brought with her our family photographs and the few ornaments we possessed to place around the rooms. As time moved towards the end of March, when the baby was due, I tried to make her slow down but she would crack on so, absolutely intent on having the house ready for when she came back with the new baby and Jeremy. In effect, with her hard work, her flair and her love, Saccie created a home for us.

On March 31st, Aza, our daughter was born at the hospital in Salisbury. I had asked for and received a week off work (unpaid) and was able to accompany Saccie when Stuart drove us to the hospital. This time, I remembered the next day to bring a decent bunch of flowers and a present when I visited Saccie after the birth of Aza, who turned out to be the most constantly cheerful infant, rarely wailing or crying. We had decided upon the unusual name of Aza, because we reckoned it couldn't be shortened but, more significantly, because of a great-aunt of Saccie's with that name.

And so back to our own home in Gulson Road where Saccie and I and the children were quietly content and happy. Our social life consisted of one pint of beer each on Saturday lunchtimes at the local pub, which was filled with young families who, unlike us, all appeared to be rich from the high wages paid to skilled workers on car production. Our battered little second-hand Tan-Sad pram looked incongruous alongside their large and ornate prams. We branched out and bought a linoleum covering for the bare boards of the kitchen floor and, although it was paper thin as we later discovered, we were still rather proud of it. Our major project, however, was to install a bath with a gas-fired hot water geyser in the scullery at the back of the kitchen. It was the first-ever such bath in Gulson Road and so we had a boozy party to celebrate, with beer provided mostly by the many friends Saccie had made amongst our neighbours. They all thought highly of her as she had 'no side' as they called it, and they had seen how hard she had worked to make our home. I too had made some friends by this time among my work-mates at the factory. It was an hilarious party started off by the explosion when I tentatively but ceremoniously lit the geyser. We were certainly not saving any money this way and we were very short of cash at the end of each week, but it was a cheerful and happy time.

Needless to say, I had ceased to attend or play at the squash club once we had secured the house; we could never have afforded to develop friendships with people from that sort of social life. I did at one time foolishly suggest to Saccie that it might be nice to invite Anne to see the house, bearing in mind that she had secured it for us, only to receive from Saccie a rare glint of anger in her eyes for my having suggested it. Of course, I had not spoken of my romp with Anne to obtain the house, but Saccie was no fool and had evidently guessed at the means I had used to get it.

Not long after my family had arrived and settled into the house, I was summoned to an interview with Mr Geoffrey Rootes, a director of the company and son of the Chairman. With him were his senior managers including my guardian angel, the Trainee Manager. At my meeting with them they decided, largely on the basis of that spate of mostly daft suggestions which I had put into the Works Box over the past months, that despite my age I was suitable for management training. Apparently, one or two of the suggestions had been quite sensible. The money was much the same, but oh what a wonderful boost it was to be specially selected for their management course.

My life at work was going to be very different and it seemed that at last I might be on my way up. I started to work and learn in various offices and departments at the factory, wearing normal clothes instead of oily overalls. I also had to visit the company offices in London, which normally would have involved staying in digs there for a month or more. Instead I bought a huge, very old and tatty 600cc Sunbeam motor-bike to blast my way there and back to Saccie and home as often as possible. Never having ridden a motor-bike before (I had always used four wheels), I was terrified of the thing with its awesome power and speed. I would have been happier and have felt much safer in one of the fighter aircraft of my earlier, wartime days.

At last there was a stable pattern to our lives and a possibility of a good career in the car industry for me while, as a family, Saccie and the children were settling down happily.

Then came a bombshell through the post in the form of a letter from the Admiralty appointing me, because of the new war in Korea, to a squadron at Lee-on-Solent and I was to report there in one week's time! I had dismissed entirely from my mind that the Royal Navy had the right to recall me at any time and it was just as though I had never left it.

My first action was to ask for an interview with Mr Geoffrey Rootes, who said he would do his best to offer me a job when I came out, but he could not guarantee it. I was more than fed up with the Royal Navy and its peremptory instructions and telephoned the appointments officer at the Admiralty to tell him that it would take me two weeks to make all my arrangements.

This summons from the Admiralty absolutely devastated both Saccie and me. We had made the adjustment to a new life-style, we had accepted that it was going to be hard going for both of us before a reasonable status and salary could be attained but, in the meantime, we had managed to slot ourselves into the car industry and among its people. We were happy in our achievement so far. In particular, we had come to love and to be proud of our little house in Gulson Road and of what Saccie had made of it. The thought of having to leave all this for the sake of another bloody war sickened us and, this time, against a people we had hardly even heard of before. What sort of job, I wondered, could be so important that I needed to be recalled? Presumably, it could only be that, once I was back in flying practice, I would be sent out to a Squadron in Korea where they were still using Corsairs, as well as the new Sea Furies. It was no good moaning; we would have to just get on with it, which would involve having to say goodbye to our home in Gulson Road, as there was no possibility of ever returning to it.

Two weeks later, we moved into a rented bungalow on the front at Lee-on-Solent which was comfortable enough and well furnished, compared to our little terrace house in Coventry.

CHAPTER FOUR

Recalled to the Royal Navy

The squadron to which I was appointed at Lee-on-Solent was a flight training unit and had a variety of service aircraft, such as Sea Furies and Seafires but mostly Fireflies, all with a second rear cockpit for an instructor. I found myself to be one of a team of experienced instructors, whose purpose was the training and retraining, as necessary, of pilots who for one reason or another had become out of flying practice. These trainees might be officers who had been in office jobs for some time or, perhaps, even ex 'Wings' from Carriers who needed to be reminded of their earlier flying ability. Whenever the weather was very good, there would be a gaggle of those officers who worked in the Admiral's offices at the main building of the Air Station, who would come down to the aerodrome to put in their flying hours as, otherwise, they might lose their flying pay. In addition there was a course each month of junior officers from Dartmouth, who were to be given an introduction to aviation to see if they might be interested enough to volunteer for the Fleet Air Arm. And finally, there was at the time a course of Indian Naval officers who, having been given basic flying training in India, now required to be converted onto service aircraft.

In other words, to put it bluntly, I had been pulled out of my burgeoning career in the car industry to retrain various odds and sods of the Navy how to fly. When this situation became apparent to me, I was angry and wrote a formal letter to their Lordships of the Admiralty, 'Sir, I have the honour to request your consideration, etc. ....,' type of letter in which I requested that I either be appointed to an operational squadron in one of the Carriers out in Korea, or be released to return to my job in Civvie Street since, in any case, there appeared to be little demand for my instructing skills here. It was a gamble because I was not at all keen on the former option but I was prepared to do it if absolutely necessary since, at least, it would make my recall seem to be for a more worthwhile purpose. I was as careful and polite in the wording of my letter as possible fearing to appear too critical of Admiralty for recalling me for such a paltry purpose as this wretched little training squadron, or for the unnecessary ruination of my civilian career. I had to be very cautious because these people at the Admiralty had me by the short and curlies; they could hold me for years in the Navy, if they wanted to, and they could send me to any ghastly job they liked. There was nothing I would be able to do about either. In the meantime while awaiting their reply, as there really was very little flying to be done and none of it that I could see of any significance, I applied to Commander Air for leave on the grounds that I needed to put my civilian affairs in order. And I was given a week's leave.

This leave was an opportunity at last to see my Mother and Maddie after many months and to find out why, once again, Mother had moved and this time to a house in the country near Shaftesbury. Since we were once again 'in the money' I had bought a moderately priced and sensible little saloon car (boring) and travelled down with Saccie and the two children to Shaftesbury. I was looking forward very much to seeing my Mother and Maddie after such a long time and hoping that it would be a happy visit; while Saccie no more than shared my hope. The house when we arrived was rather a surprise since it was really rather large and stood alone in the countryside in about an acre of garden where, although it provided plenty of space for the dog compounds, there appeared to be fewer dogs.

It was an old Georgian house which looked quite grand until closer inspection revealed that it was sorely in need of repair and redecoration. I suspected that Mother might have bought it at a low price, because of its condition, as a speculation maybe to compensate for a failing dog business. Already, she had found an odd-job man to carry out a continuous programme of decoration and repairs on the cheap … as she hoped. Anyway, in spite of Mother still tending to snipe at Saccie, the holiday went quite well for the first few days until Saccie festooned the garden with a line of well-washed white nappies and Mother, that naughty old snob who had never washed a nappy in her life, complained that they were visible from the road and made the place look like a gypsy encampment. Saccie just about contained her anger long enough for us to leave a day later, without outright rancour breaking out between them.

Back to the Air Station at Lee-on-Solent where I flew mostly the dual control Firefly with one or other of the Indian Navy pupils and sometimes with one of the budding young aviators from Dartmouth on the JOAC, the Junior Officers' Air Course. I expected that these instructing tasks would be an easy and gentle form of aviation for me, but it so happened that twice I was nearly written off. The first occasion was when I had to take one of the Indian Navy boys on his initial flight at night in a Firefly. According to his log-book, he had flown in a Harvard at night before so, after I had completed a preliminary circuit and landing to show him the form, I gave him control to taxi back to the end of the runway ready to do his own circuit and landing, which I would supervise from the back cockpit.

It should have been a piece of cake because the aerodrome itself was well marked out with lights and the general area was a blaze of light from all the surrounding houses and street lighting. It was nothing like the almost total blackness as it used to be in wartime and, much as I disliked night-flying, I was quite comfortable with the situation. On his take-off, the Indian boy opened the throttle fully much too quickly and the Firefly started to swing to the right and off the runway. Immediately I spoke on the R/T to tell him 'I have control.' But the wretched boy had panicked and had frozen hard on the controls, so that I had to wrestle with the central column and rudders trying to regain control from him while trying not to shout at him repeating as calmly as I could, 'I have control, I have control, take your hands off.' Meantime the aircraft had gained flying speed and, still low and with the starboard wingtip nearly touching the ground, was turning and hurtling towards the houses to our right. Suddenly, just in time, he let go and I was able to pull up and over with the houses at less than thirty feet below and the engine still roaring at full throttle. I called the control tower for an immediate and emergency landing ... not knowing what the boy might do next, I couldn't get down quick enough!

On the ground, I reported to the CO of the Indian Navy group of pilots that this particular young officer under his command must never be allowed to fly again, which he duly noted and approved. Then I went home to Saccie in our bungalow, which was not far from where I had so nearly hit the houses. I was in rather a bad way with the shakes and in dire need of whisky but, of course, this was the first time that Saccie had ever seen me in this state. I ought really to have gone to the Mess first and consumed my whiskies there without causing her even more worry about my flying, which I knew she hated. But I so badly wanted to be home with her. I seemed to have lost my resilience to twitchy happenings like this one, which had been all too frequent during wartime. The occurrence made me realise too how difficult it may have been at times for the RAF Fighter and Bomber boys, some of whom would return direct from combat to go home to their wives and families living near the aerodrome. It was quite different for aircrew of the Fleet Air Arm, who would return to an entirely masculine environment of their peers, with the Aircraft Carrier as their home base.

The second hairy happening occurred a few days later in a Firefly when I was demonstrating a spin to one of the young potential pilots on the JOAC course. Fortunately I had started at a good height of 12,000 ft because, for some reason unaccountable until later, almost immediately the aircraft went into an inverted spin, a situation I had never experienced before and which was very frightening. I knew the proper action to stop the inverted spin, which should bring it out into a normal spin, from where I could take normal recovery action. But the bloody thing wouldn't come out of its inverted condition and down we went … fast. I was getting panicky and was on the very point of shouting at the pupil to bale out when the Firefly seemed to jerk out of the very uncomfortable inverted flight and started a normal spin. But we had lost a lot of height and I was only just able to stop the spin and to pull out of the ensuing dive so as not to hit the sea below us.

I returned to land at the aerodrome immediately. The face of the boy pupil was white, looking as if he had seen a ghost, as he started to clamber out of the front cockpit almost before I had taxied in to the dispersal. As he was walking away from the aircraft carrying his parachute which, did he but know it he had so nearly had to use, he stopped and turned to me. 'If that's the Fleet Air Arm, sir,' he said, 'then you can stuff it; I never want to go near another aircraft ever again.' Bearing in mind that the purpose of the JOAC course was to encourage young RN officers from Dartmouth to join the FAA, I obviously hadn't done a very good job! Anyway, I had been coming to the conclusion that showing a pupil how to come out of a spin, a hallowed principle of flying training dictated by the Central Flying School of the RAF, was really an unnecessary nonsense. If a chap flew so badly that he went into a spin below about 5000 ft in a modern aircraft, then he was probably going to be dead regardless of what he did. So why bother. I decided that I too had done my last spin.

The end of the story is that a naval test pilot from Farnborough was sent for to see if he could find the cause of the Firefly's inverted spin. To my astonishment, the man who turned up for the job was Ace Bailey, one of my first pupils and best man at our wedding! He had become an experienced test pilot and, after two flights in the Firefly, he established that incorrect weighting at the tail end of the fuselage had caused the trouble. In effect, the airframe rigger had weighted the aircraft as for solo flight, not dual flight.

There had been no reply as yet from their Lordships of the Admiralty to my formal letter asking to be released. I had no idea in what manner or what method these people used to deal with recalcitrant officers who, like me, wrote them cheeky letters; I mean did they have a committee to consider several such problem officers or perhaps one Lordly Admiral on his own would deal with each one, or what? Some two weeks after sending my Admiralty letter and still with trepidation awaiting a reply, I was sitting at the desk in the crew room, smoking and chatting with two other instructors when the telephone rang. Expecting it to be one of the Admiral's staff officers from the main building, who would be hoping to get a flight since it was a nice day, I was alarmed to find that it was the Captain's secretary, to summon me before the Captain and Commander Air on the following morning at 11 a.m. sharp, and he suggested that I wear my best No.1 uniform. To use naval parlance, I was in the rattle.

The next morning, standing to attention in front of the Captain seated at his desk, with Commander Air standing beside him, I was given a formal reprimand for writing directly to the Admiralty without going through the proper channels (i.e. himself) and secondly for implying that the purpose and work of the training squadron, to which I had been appointed, did not justify my recall, or the hardship it had caused me. This severe reprimand would be formally noted on my record. Moreover, as an obvious punishment, I was appointed with immediate effect to RNAS Eglinton in Northern Ireland, as the Instrument Flight examiner, including duties in Air Traffic control. In other words, somebody had contrived a general dogsbody type of job for me in a location as far away in the UK as possible and with the shortest possible pier-head jump, so as to cause difficulty for me and for my young family. I would never know who personally, up there among their Lordships of the Admiralty, had decided upon this punishment, but there was malice in it. It appeared that the malice, of which the Admiralty was capable towards insubordinate junior officers, had remained unabated since their infamous treatment of the young Lord Cochrane in the 1800s.

In response to all this, I made the point that I had accepted my recall without complaint and I had shown that I was fully prepared to fly in war conditions but now, with a family to keep, I was not prepared to take flying risks for the sake of a peacetime activity such as I had been allocated. I considered that I had the right, under these circumstances, to refuse to fly and thus, I would be of no further use to the Service and should be allowed to leave it. After I had gulped out this challenge, for it was nothing less, there were several moments of silence before the Captain spoke slowly and deliberately, 'Mister Adlam, you have been trained for service in the Royal Navy as a pilot, you are fully fit to fly medically and, if you were so foolish as to refuse to fly, it would be tantamount to refusal to obey a direct order. You would be under a Court Martial and would receive the severest sentence commensurate with refusal of a direct order. Please let me advise you formally not to even contemplate anything so foolish.'

After I had left the Captain's office, his secretary outside told me to wait because I was to see the Captain again on his own and informally. The Captain, about to retire as a Commodore I had been told, proved at our second and informal chat to be a most kind and sympathetic man who evidently understood how hard I had been hit by the recall. The gist of his advice was to grin and bear it because for me to cause any more unpleasantness would merely ruin the good record of all my previous service, and get me absolutely nowhere. He was right, of course, and I realised that I should accept his advice. I really had no wish to leave the Royal Navy nursing a sense of grievance for, after all, it had been my life for the eleven years of my adult development and, despite some of its bad leadership of the Fleet Air Arm during the war, I owed it respect and appreciation for the experience it had given me.

Saccie knew that I had been seriously in the rattle and was waiting anxiously for me late that afternoon. I gave her the bad news first; that we were going to Northern Ireland and I would have to report there within a week. She was aghast. 'Presumably it means that I shall have to stay here and join you in Ireland with the children, as soon as I can give notice to leave this bungalow. Then I shall have to pack up all our accumulated belongings, get them crated and send them by sea. It will be ages before we can join you and will cost a fortune. This bloody cruel Navy,' she said, and more, 'Why did we ever serve in it?'

'Shush,' I said 'now let me tell you the good news, which is that I have already given our notice to leave the bungalow and have had to pay no more than an agreed two weeks' final rent. Furthermore, I have decided that we shall travel all the way to Eglinton by taxi, in which we can cram all our accumulated bits and pieces. Going there by taxi means that you won't have to languish here with the children on your own.' Saccie told me not to be daft and that this was not the time to make fun out of a serious situation by talking of taking a taxi four hundred miles across the sea to Ireland. And then, enjoying the bombshell I was about to drop, I explained that I had been inspired to buy an old London taxi, which I had seen earlier, mouldering in our local garage. I had been able to buy it for £30 and had sold our boring little saloon car for £80! 'In the words of the song,' said Saccie, 'Little man, you certainly have had a busy day. And I love you for the silly, daft, impetuous things you do. When can I see the taxi?'

The next day, we looked at the taxi together and Saccie loved it immediately. It was an Austin, probably made prewar, with an immensely strong chassis and able to take a huge weight of luggage and having masses of room for us all. This time, Hank had done good!

Only two days later, in the very early morning, we set off on our epic journey to Northern Ireland in our taxi, packed tight with all our baggage. Saccie travelled in the back with the two children and was almost buried behind cases and clothes with the children's potties on top. She held a long stick with which she could tap the driver's window behind me if she wanted to communicate. Alongside me in the open front of the cab was the pram and heavy luggage. There were two happenings on that first day of the journey to reach Liverpool; the first was sickening when, having stopped at a pub for lunch and nappy changes, I carelessly slammed the heavy door of the taxi so that it crunched on and trapped the little finger of Aza's tiny hand. After an initial screech, the child was just sobbing quietly with shock we thought and we expected to find the bones of the finger smashed and broken. Nothing of the sort had happened; so very young was the child that apparently the bones had not yet formed sufficiently to be broken. Saccie cuddled the resilient little thing, which very soon was gurgling happily up at us again. Saccie had coped, but I had felt quite sick at my carelessness and at the thought of the damage I might have caused to my child, maybe for her lifetime.

Insufficiently careful with my children, yes, but also typically careless about my money too because, as we approached the city of Liverpool in the dark late that evening, after such a long and tiring day, I shouted to Saccie in the back, 'To hell with looking for a Bed and Breakfast place, we are going to a decent Hotel.' I had seen that we were about to pass a large Hotel and I turned Fred (as we now called our taxi) straight into the drive which led to the well-lit, grand and imposing Hotel entrance. But there were a number of other

London-type taxis in front of us, queuing to disgorge their passengers at the entrance. So Fred queued up behind the other taxis. It was very evidently party night because, as the uniformed Doorman opened the door of each taxi in front of us, so emerged ladies in their long party dresses and men in their dinner jackets to disappear slowly into the grand portals of the Hotel. As I drove up level with the entrance, there was no way of avoiding the embarrassment to come, as the Doorman stepped forward and, opening the door of our taxi with a flourish, upset the balance of the baggage inside, so that Jeremy's potty toppled straight off the top and clattered noisily onto the entrance porch, where all those beautifully-dressed people were waiting to enter the Hotel. The best that can be said of the situation was that, at least, the potty was empty. The Doorman appeared totally dumbfounded, until I shouted at him to get a porter to take our suitcases out and up to a room for the night. I had to explain that my family was due to catch the boat for Ireland in the morning. Actually, I had rather enjoyed the situation, which seemed to me then, and still does, hilariously funny. It all got sorted out; we were given a room unusually quickly and I locked Fred away in the hotel garage among the Jaguars and Mercedes. Saccie, not unnaturally, had been embarrassed to arrive in such a ridiculous manner at a smart hotel and it wasn't until, after putting the children to bed, we were sitting down to a good dinner and bottle of wine that she relaxed enough to forgive me and to laugh about it all.

The next day Fred, our taxi with all our belongings locked inside, was hoisted on board the ferry and thereafter we enjoyed a quiet and calm crossing of the Irish Sea. On arrival at the docks in Belfast on the Sunday morning, we had to wait until Fred was unloaded onto the quay by which time the whole docks seemed to be deserted. I urgently needed to find a petrol station because, foolishly, I had followed the boarding instruction to use up as much petrol as possible before loading the taxi onto the ferry. Now I was stuck on an empty quayside with hardly any fuel and no idea where to find a petrol station.

The only person around was the driver of a local taxi, just a normal saloon car. Hitherto, our old London taxi had caused mild amusement in England, mainly, I guess, because it was so big, ugly, noisy and ancient. But I was to find that the people here in Ulster thought Fred was an absolute hoot, since there was no vehicle remotely similar to it on their roads. This taxi driver was no exception and roared with laughter, but he was kindness itself and not only led us to the nearest open petrol station, but stayed with us to lead us right through Belfast on to the north road. He wouldn't take a penny in payment and Saccie, banging with her stick on the window at my back, called out to me, 'If this is Ireland then I like it and its people already.' It was our first experience of much Ulster hospitality to come in the future.

We arrived at Castle Rock, a delightful seaside village on the north coast, and took a room at the small and only hotel. It was about fifteen miles from the Naval Air Station at Eglinton and obviously we must find a place to rent much nearer. But, while searching for accommodation, how much we enjoyed staying at that little hotel, run by the Potts-Harpers, and what fun we had with them and their friends the McDermotts. However, this sort of life was not good; we must be serious and start taking life grimly and earnestly again like grown-up people. It was essential that we get away from such cheerful drinking companions.

Saccie and I had a serious talk with each other. There was no job to which I could return at the Rootes Group since, in reply to a letter I had sent, they confirmed with regret that they could not offer me any guarantee of work once the Korean War was over. This was not surprising because neither their Humber nor their Hillman cars were selling well. Once we had found somewhere to live near the Air Station, I intended to concentrate on job hunting all over again. I proposed to take as little part as possible in Navy life at the Air Station and thereby save as much of my officer's pay as I could. I promised myself and Saccie that I would do my flying job as reasonably well as I could while taking the least risk. If the weather was bad, for example, then no longer would I force myself into it. Pride in myself and my aviation skills would come a poor second, in future, to the more important need to take care of my family. To put it bluntly, the Royal Navy had taken as much out of me already as it was going to get. This pier-head jump to the furthest part of the UK, for yet another unimportant job, at such an obviously difficult time for me, smacked of pure malice on the part of my masters, the Admiralty, in their response to my letter.

I had made my number at the Air Station where I found that I would be working on my own as an Instrument Flight examiner, using a dual Firefly, and be available for the squadron pilots or whomever, whenever their certificate came up for renewal. When there was no flying demand, I would assist in the air traffic control room. I reported to Commander Air that I had not settled my family into accommodation and that it would take a few days yet to do so.

Meantime, we found a tiny little cottage to rent which was located on the hills above the small town of Limavady, about seven miles from the aerodrome. The rent was four shillings per week and, as the low rental implied, the cottage was somewhat squalid consisting of one and a half rooms down with one and a half rooms above, reached by a rickety stairway. Lighting was by means of candles and Tilley paraffin lamps, as was the cooking including hot water from a kettle. The lavatory was a thunderbox located in the far corner of a large adjacent barn. I used it as infrequently as I could manage, as I resented having to share the place with scores of rats, which could be heard scuttling around in the darkness of the barn around me. Our nearest neighbours were in tenant cottages scattered around but none any closer than a mile, unless you counted a huge boar kept in another barn opposite. Every three days, John, a morose old farm labourer, would arrive to clean the beast and feed it. And so we named it 'Piggy Cottage'. As I have described it, life at the cottage should have been highly unpleasant and so it probably was, but yet we and the children were happy. I can't explain it.

Our way of life at Piggy Cottage may best be described by these three little stories:

One day the boar bashed its way out of its barn. I returned from the aerodrome to find Saccie and the children, having been barricaded indoors all day, gesticulating at me through the window trying to point at the boar, which was behind me. I shot back into the taxi like a rabbit and left fast to fetch old John who, with another two farmhands, pushed the huge beast back safely into its barn. Beer all round and then I taxied them back to their cottages.

Another, when a large and strange teenage boy, whom we had seen lurking around several times and, we thought, possibly had a mental problem, just walked into the cottage and ran off with my silver cigarette lighter. Saccie, on her own, saw him and, plonking the two children into the old pram, began to chase furiously after him across the fields. He stopped, frightened by her anger, and gave back the lighter.

In my ignorance, I had thought that a nearby ditch seemed to be a suitable place to dig a hole for the contents of the thunderbox. Two weeks later this prompted the first visit from our neighbours who all turned up to complain that we had used an underground stream and that our disinfected ullage had poisoned their cows and made them ill. We could only apologise for our ignorance and stupidity. We poured glasses of beer all round but they weren't much mollified, and who could blame them? Perhaps they had hoped for a fiver all round, but that I couldn't afford.

My job at Eglinton was nondescript without a great deal to do and I was satisfied that it should be so; I was just marking time until I could leave the Navy and used every opportunity to hunt for a job outside, while saving my pay. But I couldn't help noticing, from the control tower, how low was the standard of flying of the two Firefly squadrons, whose Commanding Officers were Lt/Cdrs, RN; new boys without any wartime experience. Commander Air, Torrens-Spence, one of the old guard of top-class Navy pilots for whom I had great respect, overheard me comment that all the skills and knowledge we had learned in wartime seemed to have been discarded by these two Firefly squadrons. They appeared not to know the essential procedure we had established, particularly in the Pacific, for forming up from Aircraft Carriers after take-off. 'They were,' I was overheard to say scathingly, 'fluttering around the aerodrome like farmyard hens being chased by a fox.' The upshot was that the Commander Air, having heard me explain my views, arranged for me to give a briefing to the squadron pilots and their commanders.

For the first time in my Navy career, I found myself to be rather unpopular in the wardroom mess and around the bar there. It was not altogether due to my scathing opinions of their flying, because most of the squadron pilots had appreciated their value, but nevertheless not many would drink with me at the bar and, if they did so, not for long. It took me a time to realise that our daily life at Piggy Cottage, sitting under the Tilley lamps which emitted paraffin fumes, using paraffin to cook and heat water and with the shortage of washing facilities, caused me to stink like a polecat! I was really rather cross with Saccie for not telling me that I stank but, as she pointed out, everything in the cottage stank anyway, and I was just another item in it. However, using kettles of hot water all day, she had managed to keep herself, the children and their clothes comparatively odourless. Belatedly, I took to using the shower and washing facilities at the Air Station every day.

As winter approached, I had some good luck in being able to secure accommodation in one of the limited number of cottages owned by the Navy near to the aerodrome. The Navy rent was minimal for an attractive cottage with a real kitchen and cooking stove, a sitting room with a log fireplace, two bedrooms upstairs and a flush loo. It was absolute paradise in comparison and we were particularly thankful because we had been worried about how on earth we would keep the children warm during winter in Piggy Cottage. I believe that my good luck had something to do with the support I received from the Commander Air. Christmas of 1951 in the new cottage was an unexpected joy and we were able to entertain Bobby and Gill McDermott, the particular friends we had made at Castle Rock. Bless their hearts, they had suffered an invitation to 'dinner' with us at the previous cottage when the roast chicken, cooked in a biscuit tin over a paraffin stove, had proved to be a burnt disaster tasting entirely of oily paraffin. It was a poor return for the many hot baths and good meals we had received from them when we had badly needed their hospitality.

At the beginning of the year, at work in the Control Tower, I received a private telephone call from a solicitor in London. His name was Baker and he had been acting for my Father for many years past; he rang now to tell me of the death of my Father. I learned for the first time that he had been ill for quite a long period and had died two weeks earlier at a Nursing Home in Switzerland. He had been in the sole company of a Mrs Betty Abbott, who had made all the arrangements out there for his funeral and had been the only one to attend it.

Father had never written to me throughout the war and my last contact with him had been in late 1943, shortly before I had left for the Far East. I was to learn that Mother had written to him, entirely without my knowledge, to tell him that I was destitute and unable to find a job since leaving the Navy and could he help? His letter in reply, which I kept for too many years, said that I had been a damn fool to leave the Navy and, since I had no training, I had better take a job as a car salesman since I was unfit for anything else. I realised that Father had rather enjoyed referring to me as his son in the Royal Navy and was disappointed with me, therefore, for leaving it. But the kindest I could suppose was that this despicable letter had been written perhaps during a period when he was ill.

Father by all accounts had loved his son Leslie, my half-brother killed in action as a naval fighter pilot over the Somme in September 1917, and yet apparently had little love for me, his son and also a naval fighter pilot. Perhaps that I had been lucky enough, unlike Leslie, to survive my war may have had something to do with it? But I think mainly it was because he hardly knew me. He had been too old and set in his ways to have affection for a boy of fourteen, as I was when we had made our first real contact in 1935.

Nevertheless, I felt that it had been a sad ending that Father had been so ill and had died without any family with him. He had been obsessed always with the conviction that family and friends were only 'after his money,' with the result, maybe, that many of his friends became fewer. For my part, I had vowed never on any account to ask Father for money and, as an adult, I had not done so even during my worst period in Salisbury when I had been so desperate to find work.

After the telephone call from Baker, I sat quietly by the fire after supper that evening to recall my memories of Father and to wonder whether, in any one of them, there was any indication that he had wanted to make a closer and perhaps even loving contact with me his son, when I was a boy? And had I, as an immature boy, failed to recognise and respond to those advances? But then surely, a boy already in awe of a him as a stranger could hardly be expected to initiate such a relationship, much as he yearned for it? It was for surely for Father, had he wanted to do so, to form a normal father and son relationship.

My memories of Father go back to when I was a boy of ten years old, living with my Mother in Barnes ………

CHAPTER FIVE

In the Beginning

THE FATHERS

When I was ten years old I used to be confused between God and my Father and which was which. Both of them, as it seemed to me, were equally remote. One, I knew from my bible class at school and from my infrequent attendance at school Chapel, was reckoned to be a very good thing and an all powerful being who would look down benignly on me and my troubles down here on earth, provided I behaved nicely. But it was the other, my Father who had retired to the South of France, who appeared to me as more positively godlike since he so obviously governed the major events of my life, from almost equally afar. For instance, I had once asked 'Our Father who art in Heaven' to help me win my colours for the first Eleven football team at school. It took Him a bit of time, two years, but he got them for me. But when I desperately wanted a new Hercules bike I saved up two pounds from my pocket money and wrote to ask 'My Father who art in France' for the other two pounds and he replied curtly that I must save up the rest.

Mother, divorced from my Father, now lived with me, my sister and with Maddie, our one-time nurse and now Mother's companion, in a nice middle-class sort of house in Ranelagh Road on the edge of Barnes Common. Mother had been well and truly seen off by Father's expensive and clever solicitors at the divorce court and had been left with an eight-year old son, a six-year old daughter and me at two years old plus £600 in the Bank and a small fixed annual income of £400. Oh yes, and she had three Bull Terriers which Father had given her earlier in the hope that exercising them would keep her weight down. These dogs were to play an important role in our lives. Father, then Chairman of George Adlam & Sons, his own large engineering company, earned a huge income and must have been very pleased at the comparative pittance of an allowance the Court had decreed he should pay to Mother.

In the Beginning

The last time I had seen Father had been two years ago when he had descended on us at our then house at the far end of Kensington near Hammersmith. At the time I was attending a small private school nearby where, without any great effort or stress, I learned to read, to repeat my arithmetic tables and to remember bits and pieces of geography and English history. It was a happy place for young children to learn.

But Father's descent among us had put an end to all that and I was sent the very next term to Colet Court, a huge rumbustious preparatory school in Hammersmith with over four hundred boys there, nearly all day-boys. I hated it; possibly because I found it difficult to establish my own identity amongst such large numbers.

The bus from school stopped opposite Ranelagh Road. I jumped off and started to run fast down the road, satchel flapping against my bottom as I ran, for I had arranged a game of cricket with my friends from the local secondary school who would be waiting for me on the Common opposite our house. As I ran I could see the figure of a man walking along the pavement ahead of me and I slowed down as it dawned on me that the figure was Father. Although I had seen him rarely, there had been just two brief holidays with him in Weston-super-Mare three and four years ago which had enabled me to fix his appearance clearly in my young mind.

He was easily recognisable. Always immaculately dressed in an expensive suit with a bow tie, he was now walking along in front of me on the other side of the road swinging a silver topped cane in his right hand in time with his leisured pace. He appeared to be looking with interest at the type of houses in the road and their numbers and I could see his face clearly, with its trimmed and pointed beard, topped with a panama hat set at a jaunty angle on his head. He was slim and very upright and even then, as a young boy, the thought occurred to me that he was a handsome-looking old gentleman. I wished rather wistfully that he could be more like a real Father and that I wasn't in such awe of him.

I held back; it was no good catching him up, if I did so what on earth would I say to him? We were not like real people together so that I could rush up to him and shout 'Hullo, Dad, here I am!' For one thing, I remembered that he liked to be called 'Father' and somehow I found that word rather difficult. And so I turned off to my left onto the common and kind of tracked him along behind the hedges like a Red Indian until he reached our house, entered the porch and rang the bell. The door was opened by Annie, our kennel maid but dressed up reasonably smartly for the occasion as a housemaid, so evidently Mother had been expecting him.

I didn't want to go in so I walked a little way to where my friends would be playing about waiting for me. I would not get a welcome from them because I owned the best of our two bats and the wickets but I did not intend to go into our house to fetch them. My five friends grumbled at me but, as boys did in those days, we adapted to the one bat and ball and soon contrived a different sort of game. I wondered how long Father would be in the house and whether I would have to meet him as I would soon have to go in for my tea.

As we played my mind was not on the game. I was thinking about Father and worrying about the purpose of his visit because I didn't think he would come all that journey just to see us his children. For one thing he had seen Phoebe, my sister and now a pretty fourteen-year old girl, only last Easter when she had visited him for the first time at his villa in France. As for me, I never knew what to say to him and he must have dismissed me as a boring little boy only interested in sport, which he disliked. Michael, my elder brother now sixteen, lived at Wickwar near Bristol with Mrs Handoll who at one time had been the family Nanny. I understood only vaguely that he was not well. Actually, I was not exclusively interested in sport and I had another friend, a boy of the same age called Gordon, with whom I played highly imaginative games in which we could see ourselves as marvellously brave soldiers or as cowboys and Indians with me as the Indian running around in my underpants. Much as I enjoyed these games, I was secretly ashamed of their childishness and kept Gordon well apart from my other cricket and football friends.

But it was Father who paid the school fees and he no doubt considered that it was his right to dictate where we went to school since he paid for our education. Was his visit to do with our schooling and, if so, what was he going to do? I was soon to find out because, although Father had already left in a taxi by the time I came in for my tea, my Mother called me in to the sitting-room immediately to talk about Father's visit. He had decided, she said, to send me to a boarding school called Cottesmore in Sussex and she had argued with him being absolutely convinced for some reason that boys were always being beaten at a boarding school. Father had also decided that Phoebe should go to a boarding school near Reading instead of attending Kensington High School as a day-girl.

Father had more or less convinced Mother, however, that Cottesmore was a famous and very expensive preparatory school with a high standard of education where boys were sent before going on to major public schools. He had left a copy of the prospectus and it certainly did look a lovely place with lots of sports grounds and a good reputation for winning against other schools at football and cricket, all of which interested me. I was due to join Cottesmore at the end of the summer holidays in about seven weeks' time and the more I thought about it, the more I liked the idea of going there. After all, I heartily disliked my present school.

In the meantime, I had the holiday to enjoy before worrying about the new school and what it would be like to be a boarder. This house at Barnes, where we now lived, was the best of all my Mother's houses in my short life. It had the Common opposite as a playground for me. This was the most important aspect because, as had happened with all the previous houses, the garden at the back had been converted into compounds with kennels for the dogs and I had never had any garden area in which to play.

After the divorce, which had left Mother with so little money, one of the two Bull Terrier bitches had produced a litter of puppies and Mother realised that here was a potential financial asset. And so at a time when dog shows and the breeding of pedigree dogs was fast becoming a popular pastime and hobby in the UK, my Mother set about establishing a business based on the breeding, showing and selling of Bull Terrier dogs. She became financially dependent entirely on whatever success she could make of her dog business. And a success she certainly made of it which is why we had this nice house in Ranelagh Road. By this time she had become one of the best-known breeders of these dogs and we had people coming all the time to the house to buy them. I was very proud of her when she was asked to judge at many of the big dog shows, including Crufts. It always amused me though, even then as a young boy and in later life, that Mother never openly accepted her doggy activity as a business. She always referred to it as 'My little hobby, dear.'

All my young life, therefore, I had grown up surrounded by these Bull Terriers, some of which roamed round the house, though most of them were kept on the ground floor rooms at the back of the house or in kennels and compounds in the garden. I had an utter loathing of them, the smell of them, the smell of their food cooking, the messes they made, their incessant barking, the conversion of the garden into dog compounds and the consequent impossibility of asking school friends home to play, but above all, the fear of the appalling dog fight which could ensue if the wrong door or gate was opened at the wrong time. I feared them and, understandably so, since at the age of six I had been nearly savaged by a male Bull Terrier. Dear Maddie had rescued me by beating the dog off with a heavy broom as I had clung screaming to the wire of the dog compound. Bless her, she had probably been as frightened as I was of the horrible, savage animal.

I could not understand at that young age but in later life I realised how hard Mother had worked to build up this doggy business and that it had been the only means she knew to provide a home for us two children. I remember that she used to spend every day writing letters and on the telephone making her business arrangements, even when we were on holiday. She employed a tall, good-looking girl called Annie as her kennel maid who was a natural in her good relationship with and care of the dogs. Annie was good-natured enough to put on a pinny and silly cap to masquerade as a housemaid and serve at table when we had visitors.

We also had Robert, a bogus 'chauffeur,' who in reality was just a chap to drive the car occasionally and to help as a kennel man. A lot of his time was spent delivering or collecting dogs from the railway station. Mother's ménage of three was completed by Maddie who was her companion and friend and did most of the cooking for us all. As far as I was concerned though, Maddie was a second Mother to me and I loved her dearly.

To buy my new school clothes, I suggested that we travel down to the nominated shop in Brighton to fit me out with the corduroy grey shorts, grey shirts and blue jumpers which, together with the sports kit, was the uniform needed for Cottesmore. At the same time, we could have a peek at the school from the outside. I liked the look of the school; a large pleasant building not a bit grim and with sports fields in front and back. Even my Mother seemed reluctantly impressed and so we drove back home to Barnes feeling more relaxed about the future.

COTTESMORE

The first week at Cottesmore was full of shocks. I woke up at dawn on the first morning to find myself in a large dormitory with nineteen other boys having the twenty beds head-to-head in the middle of the room. It was freezing cold as all the windows opposite each bed were partly open. I snuggled down into the bedclothes and thought about the events of yesterday.

IN THE BEGINNING 57

It had started as a disaster with Mother throwing one of her 'weepies' when she met the Headmaster on arrival. Apparently, I learned from Maddie later, she had begged the Headmaster never to beat me and he, sensible man, had told her to realise that her son would not wish to be treated any differently to the other boys. By that time, thankfully, I had been led away by another boy to be told and shown all the things I would need to know. Having taken all this in as best I could, I had been given supper and then shown to this little iron bed in the middle of the dormitory where, with my head in a whirl of new faces and places, I had eventually fallen asleep.

As I dozed with the bedclothes right up to my chin and looking up at the white ceiling of the dormitory, a very loud clanging bell rang and startled me wide awake. All round me boys were getting up out of bed and taking off their pyjama tops. Under every window opposite each bed was a wash-stand and, on top of the stand, a large bowl with a jug full of cold water and a poe on the shelf below. I hadn't needed to use mine during the night, thank goodness. Already the other boys had shut their windows and started washing in the cold water. The cold water wash on that first morning in the cold air of the dormitory was my first shock. I started to dress and realised that all the other boys were somehow miraculously completely clothed already and were lining up by the door at the end of the room. The secret of their speed was quite simple. At night they took off the vest, shirt and jumper as a single unit and then the underpants and shorts together as the second unit. Thus, in the morning two swift actions and they were dressed, needing only stockings and shoes to be fully ready.

What were the boys queuing up for at the dormitory door? It was the Matron standing there at the doorway to examine all our open mouths to ensure that we had cleaned our teeth properly and, of course, in all my hurry and confusion I had not done so. Blushing furiously, I was sent back to clean them again before going down to breakfast. It was difficult for me because I was the only new boy in the dormitory. At breakfast, I was sat at the end of the table nearest to the master in charge where he could keep an eye on me and on my unknown manners as a new boy. The typical fare was lumpy porridge and prefabricated scrambled eggs on buttered bread; thus presaging the coming wartime breakfast by several years.

How quickly, as a young boy, I adapted to this new life and came to love the orderliness of it. I learned not to mind the bad food, the lack of privacy, the stark school furniture and even the strict discipline because these were shared with all the other boys, many of whom were my friends, and very few of us were unhappy. The Headmaster and owner of the school, Mr Forster, was both feared and liked by us boys; he could be very stern and strict especially about certain forms of bad behaviour but always fair in his judgements or punishments. He was a superb teacher with the gift of making his classes fun and interesting.

During that first year at Cottesmore, from being rather a shy child I became quite boisterous and noisy and even had to be spanked with a gym shoe by the Headmaster for minor offences such as talking too much and at the wrong time. Only he or his deputy, Mr Montauban, were permitted to punish boys in that way or with the cane, whereas the other masters could either give a boy detention and lines or send him to the Head for punishment. Detention or lines, typical punishments so beloved by the modern day do-gooders, seemed to boys then as I am sure they do now to be such silly punishments. They merely made the boy feel intensely irritated by the waste of precious time and caused him to feel thoroughly bolshie and bad-tempered for days afterwards.

To be caned was a different matter; the fearful anticipation on being sent to the Headmaster was nearly always very much the worse part of it and never to be forgotten. And then the pain of the actual experience was made just sufficient that a boy would make certain not to repeat his bad behaviour again. It was soon over and school life would go on as before without ill-feelings from anyone concerned.

The dormitory had a life of its own. The good part was the general chat called out from one bed to another which went on during the half hour before lights out at 9.30 p.m. Sometimes one of the boys would tell a story, either one he had made up or perhaps about some adventure he had experienced on holiday. I discovered that I was quite good at storytelling and the other boys would ask me to tell them one. I cheated because on holiday I had bought a book entitled *One Hundred Mystery Stories* and I had mugged up on these and used them as a basis for my own more imaginary stories to tell in the dormitory. I much enjoyed the tense and absolute silence as I worked up to what I hoped would be the exciting climax to the story.

The other part of dormitory life that began to develop was our sexual interests which, once started, became more open. At ages between eleven and thirteen in the dormitory, our sexual urges were beginning to become quite strong. Our activities did not amount to very much really; no more than an experimental feeling of each others what we called 'wobbly bits' and bottoms. But we knew that what we were doing would be regarded as very wrong indeed and would incur the full anger of the Headmaster, should he ever find out. That knowledge made it even more exciting somehow. Not all the boys took part in this naughtiness and, inevitably, somebody blew the whistle on us.

One afternoon instead of games the school assembled in Chapel while the Headmaster, with no other masters present, first of all read a passage from the Bible. He finished and looked down on us all for some two minutes in complete silence before he started to speak vehemently about the sin of sexual activity, which he knew had taken place between boys. He spoke of the evil of such things and how, like a plague, it could spread throughout the school and affect the lives and the future of each one of us. Then we knelt while he prayed for us. We were told to return to the main Hall and to sit down in our usual places. There he read out the names of eight boys, all from my dormitory and with whom I had been naughty. I was gasping with fear and shame expecting my name to be called with the others; but he did not call me. The Headmaster told these boys that he would not cane them; what they had done was too serious for such punishment. They were to stand up in front of the rest of the school in silence for the next five minutes. At the end of the five minutes, we all filed silently to our classrooms.

What a performance by the Headmaster and how effective it had been. I was to enjoy another two years at Cottesmore after that and never again was there the slightest sign of sexual activity. I guessed that the boy who had blown the whistle on us in the dormitory was the one whose bed was head to head with mine. He was a serious boy, strongly religious but I liked him and we got on quite well together although not as special friends. He must have seen me with the other boys but had not included me in his sneaky report.

Since that first term when I had been under-confident and shy, I had become rather a cheeky boy and the several spankings I had to undergo I could take in my stride. But I had to be caned twice. The first time because I couldn't seem to stop talking in class and, after three warnings, was sent trembling in fear to the Headmaster. He listened gravely while I told why I had been sent to him and then he gave me just two strokes with the cane as I bent over.

The second offence was treated differently. For the first time Cottesmore had a Mistress teacher whose subject was Art. All of us in class could see how nervous she was and I, in particular, was enjoying showing off and asking stupid questions. I was being a very unpleasant boy. Eventually, she wrote on a piece of paper, called me to the desk and told me to take it to the Headmaster. He read the paper and I could see that he was very, very angry. He bent me tight over the arm of his big armchair and gave me six strokes with the cane, so severe that I yelled and blubbed. I returned, as he instructed me, to the classroom and clutching my bottom and still crying, said I was very sorry to the Mistress. I never misbehaved in class again.

Football at Cottesmore was a revelation to me. The coach was Mr Montauban who was enormously enthusiastic and very knowledgeable about the game. For the first time the tactics of the game were explained to me. I was shown how and where to pass the ball and how to position and make space for myself on the pitch. I loved the practice games almost every afternoon and, as I evidently had ball skills from playing football on Barnes Common, I was selected for the school second eleven in my first term. What a joy which was only exceeded when, in my second year, I made it to the first eleven and, as had been promised by 'My Father who art in Heaven' two years earlier, was awarded my colours! In all fairness I should also have been thanking my other 'Father who art in France' for sending me to Cottesmore.

Cricket in the summer took place on the large field in the front of the main buildings and the setting for the game was beautiful, with three sides of the green field surrounded by large trees and the figures in white of the boys playing on the two pitches. Even as a schoolboy, I was conscious of the beauty and absorbed it. On the right-hand side were the two cradles for slip catching practice and the cricket nets from where every evening came the lovely sound of bat on ball and the voices of the boys mingling with those of the masters coaching them.

On a games afternoon of that first summer term, the Headmaster at the nets where I was bowling called to me, 'Put on the pads, young Adlam, and let's see what you can do with the bat.' He and the others bowled to me and I concentrated on using the correct batting strokes, which I had learned at a cricketing academy where Mother had sent me during the Easter holiday, rather than trying to hit the ball hard. My correct style, even when I missed the ball, must have impressed them because I was put into the senior game with a chance to get into the second eleven. No doubt about it, I thought, style is everything in cricket and never mind the runs!

Summer again a year later and, as an established player in the cricket second eleven, I was hoping for a trial in the first team and life for me at school was good. Too good; I was enjoying life too much. But the clouds were gathering on my horizon due to the low standard of my work in class. The truth was that I had not worked hard enough to overcome the poor teaching of the previous school and I had never caught up with the standard of the other boys. Father apparently had already entered me for Harrow but my reports indicated that I might not be able to pass the entrance exams and I was beginning to realise that these were only one year ahead.

One Saturday afternoon in the middle of the summer term, quite unexpectedly as far as I was concerned, Father arrived at Cottesmore. It was already a very big day for me because I had squeaked for the first time into the first Eleven and we were playing at home against another preparatory school. I was fielding on the boundary and, between overs, looked towards the Pavilion where the Headmaster was sitting with …. Good Heavens; was that Father sitting next to him? Sure enough it was and I could hardly concentrate on the game wondering what Father was doing there and excited to think of his unexpected visit. Why had he come? Could it be that he had come to see me play cricket for the first Eleven?

The opposing team declared at tea time and the Headmaster beckoned me over to join him and Father. I was so proud to be on the team and hoped Father would realise what an honour it was and perhaps congratulate me and make a bit of a fuss. I so hoped that he would see me bat if I got the chance; I was in at number seven and he might have to wait if the earlier batsmen did well. Oh dear; not a bit of it. Father had come down to talk to the Headmaster about my bad classroom reports. He hardly spoke to me at all, just a distant greeting and said that he would have to go very soon as he had arranged for a car to take him back to London. Meantime he motioned me away so that he could continue his talk with Mr Forster. I found soon afterwards that he had arranged for special tuition for me, especially in maths. After he had gone, not even pressing a ten-bob note into my hand or, for that matter, any other gesture of affection from him, I went into bat and scored two. What a disastrous day and what a disappointment my 'Dad's' visit had been, I thought as I wept silently into my pillow that night in Dormitory.

The other side of the coin was that, during three quiet evenings each week, I was given private tuition by Mr Bull the maths teacher. What a fine teacher he was too; I grasped for the first time the, to me, awful complexities of Algebra and Geometry. Moreover, Father had also arranged for me to spend nearly all of the coming summer holidays with Mr Montauban, the deputy Head, in his house where I was to be given lessons in English, History and French. I enjoyed it. I enjoyed getting a grasp of these subjects and being for the first time ahead of the game, so to speak, instead of floundering at the bottom of the class trying to catch up with the other boys. In fact, I was learning how to learn.

But I also enjoyed living with the Montaubans, who were quite well off as he was a partner in the school and they lived in quite a gracious style. Living with them, and particularly under Mr Montauban's direction and correction, I learned better manners too. Correction, once when I was casual and rude to Mrs Montauban, took the form of being sent straight to bed and, with my pyjamas down, a beating on my bottom with a gym shoe. But I liked him, perhaps because I felt the need for a father figure in my life but also because he was interested in me and in the things I liked. He took me to county cricket matches and later to watch professional football, all of which we enjoyed together. And yet, I realise now as I write, my own Father had been interested enough in me to come over to England and take action on seeing how far I had fallen behind in my class work.

During that summer holiday, while I was living with the Montaubans, Mother moved from Barnes to a larger house just outside Brighton. She had quite a lot of friends in the area and I suppose that visits to me at school on the occasional Sunday reminded her that she liked the area. The new house was quite a bit larger with a much bigger garden so that only a part of it needed to be adapted as dog compounds and it had a really big garage at the end of a driveway alongside the house. I guessed that Mother had become even more successful with her dog business.

Phoebe, my sister, had been expelled from her boarding school for writing what she called love stories in her exercise books, one of which was found. Knowing Phoebe as I did, for we were good chums, I think she left the book to be found on purpose. At home in the holidays, I had thought this to be fun and exciting but Mother did an enormous 'weepie' and Father was very cross indeed. I remember that Phoebe was thoroughly cheerful throughout. However, this was another reason for Mother's move to Brighton because Phoebe was to attend a secretarial school there.

At the end of my working holiday with the Montaubans, I started in September on my last year at Cottesmore; I was now aged twelve and a bit. It was a very good final year for me, the happiest of all my schooldays. I was a senior member of the first Eleven football team with my colours from the previous year. In the summer I gained my first Eleven colours at cricket. My class work improved considerably and I started actually to enjoy classes – well some of them. I did not have to be spanked with the gym shoe or caned all that year but, in spite of my new angelic behaviour, I was not considered responsible enough to be made a Monitor. Towards the end I took the entrance examination for Harrow and passed comfortably enough although without distinction.

Cottesmore was very certainly an 'up' in my life. It transformed my character from that of a shy rather introvert child to that of a more normal, reasonably boisterous, average boy. The school gave me the confidence I had previously lacked. Apart from all that, I loved the place and was happy there. I made many friends and it was easy to ignore the minor hardships of school life of that period when one could laugh and joke about them with such friends. The success of the Headmaster and his teaching staff stemmed, I think, from their genuine interest in each boy, because nothing inspires a boy more than the feeling that, whether he succeeds or fails in whatever he is attempting, it really matters to his teacher.

Because of Cottesmore, I enjoyed life at boarding school and, although slightly nervous of going to a new school, I felt no real trepidation at entering Harrow next term.

HARROW

Gieves, famous since the late eighteenth century as naval tailors, was the shop which had been nominated for many years past by Harrow school as its outfitters. They had a big shop on the Hill at Harrow as well as on the corner of Savile Row in London, where Mother and I duly presented ourselves to buy my school clothes. We were shown upstairs where a young salesman with a grand manner measured me and produced for our inspection a series of outfits I would need.

For Sundays and special occasions there was a black bum-freezer jacket and waistcoat with dark grey trousers to go with a white shirt and large stiff white collar topped, quite literally, with an absurd silk top hat. Apart from the silly hat, it was a smart outfit for a boy. I warmed to the young salesman when he repudiated Mother's suggestion that, in view of the cost of this expensive outfit, perhaps the trousers and jacket could be made large enough for me to grow in to them? 'That would be most inadvisable, Madam,' he said. 'It is regarded as correct at Harrow for these to be close fitted.' Poor Mother, she was beginning to blanch at the cost. For normal weekdays we bought long grey flannel trousers and blue jackets but, then again, these sensible-looking clothes were made ridiculous by a flat straw hat which looked exactly like a large, bright yellow upturned soup plate. Apparently this hard flat plate was to be held firm by an elastic band round the back of the head.

The first days at Harrow passed in a haze. Nobody in particular was detailed to help a new boy and he just had to ask whoever was nearest for information. On the first evening five of us new boys were told to report to the study of a monitor who was the Head of House. Large and pompous for his age of eighteen, he kept a disdainful expression on his face while telling us that we would have eight days in which to learn exactly where all the different buildings and the other Houses were located and, in particular, the initials of each housemaster since (for some obscure reason) each House was known not by its name but by these initials. We must learn to dress correctly. For instance, all three buttons of our blue jackets must be done up until, after one year, we would be allowed to leave one button undone.

The day started at 7 a.m. when everybody, except the seniors, had to rush down to the ground floor to take a cold shower every morning. During the next half-hour we queued up in a passageway to be given a mug of cocoa and a biscuit before making our way outside, in the dark and cold during winter, to our classroom which could be in any one of a dozen buildings scattered on the Hill. The first class of the day started at 7.40 a.m. and breakfast back at the House was at 8.30 a.m. We became accustomed to carrying our books from classrooms at one end of the Hill to the other, striving to arrive at each classroom on time.

After games in the afternoon, there was little time to run up the steep hill back to the House in time to take an early place at the queue for one of the baths, or 'toshes' as they were called. There was only enough hot water to fill each bath once so usually all the baths were, not only tepid, but full of dirty muddy water from the earlier boys. A cold shower afterwards might be necessary to clean the dirty water off. Then upstairs at a run to dress and to hurtle downstairs again to the dining-room to make the toast ready for the leisurely arrival of the monitors. With luck there might be some toast left over, to be swallowed down before having to attend two more classes in the evening.

After a simple supper there would be time, provided there was no Boycall, to collect books ready for the supervised prep which was held downstairs again in the dining room. We could then go up to our study to bed, but it was important to 'get comfortable' first because, being on the top floor, the only lavatories were four flights downstairs in the basement. And so, once back in the study and having pulled the bed out from its wardrobe enclosure, I could sink into it at 9.30 p.m. Lights out for juniors was at 10 p.m. So ended the day. Washing in the morning was with a jug of cold water and a basin as at Cottesmore.

The worst of every day was having to respond to a monitor's call of 'Boy, Boy, Boy!' At that call by any one of the house monitors at the top of his voice, every junior in the house had to drop whatever he was doing and rush pell-mell along the passages, hurtle down those stone, narrow steps at break-neck speed to stop breathless with the others in front of the monitor. The last boy to arrive, regardless of anything else he should be doing, would be given some trivial errand or job to be done immediately. The fagging, either under this Boycall procedure or as part of the weekly roster of duty boys, was the major cause of my misery as a young boy. I did not really mind too much doing the errands or jobs and I could even have borne the beastly waste of my private time in doing them. No; it was the loss of privacy; the loss of any quiet time to myself. I could never relax having one ear perpetually cocked, waiting for that damn Boycall. It invaded my privacy and prevented any enjoyment in quietly reading or writing or even working in my study. How I loathed and dreaded that call.

The allocation of study bedrooms was undertaken by the housemaster, presumably in the holidays, because before a boy left for his holidays at the end of each term he was permitted to nominate another boy with whom he would like to share a study next term. Housemasters and their wives would mull over these requests very carefully to ensure, from their knowledge of the boys in their House, that suitable sharing arrangements were made.

But our housemaster at Druries would have had a problem since he didn't know many of the junior boys in his House. He was a bachelor without a wife to help him with the younger boys. He spoke to me four times in my first two years; the last time to ask my name yet again. However nondescript a boy I had become at Druries, there is no excusing him for that.

I shared a study bedroom for the first term with an older boy who was also a Scholar and as such was excused all fagging duties. How he loved watching me having to run like an idiot in response to the boy calls. It would be difficult to put together two such different types of pupil as him and me. We were like oil and water sloshing about in that study.

He was a well-read, clever boy genuinely interested in his work, and he absolutely detested all games. He loved to hob-nob with the senior boys and would recount to me with relish how he had spoken with some monitor or other. I was in a much lower form and my only pleasure at the school was playing the various games, particularly Rackets and Squash. My cheerful self-confidence acquired at Cottesmore had been squeezed out of me by my misery at Harrow. Probably I was a wretched companion for him.

Throughout my second year my study mate was Thomas, a cheerful boy, taller than me and half a year older, who had put in a request to share a study with me. His main reason for doing so became apparent fairly soon as he evidently had a 'pash' on me, as it was then called at Harrow. But I doubt if I was all that much fun or responsive to him in the way he wanted, probably because I was still influenced by the strict views of my previous Headmaster at Cottesmore, which had made me rather a prude. Despite some differences between us on such matters, Thomas and I remained good friends and I enjoyed sharing the study with him. Bearing in mind that boys in their mid-teens are beginning the full flood of their sexual drive, it would be naïve not to realise that such activity sometimes took place at boarding schools. It is reprehensible, of course, but perhaps has more normality under the circumstances than children of both sexes these days in the twenty-first century who, resulting from three decades of a do-gooder society, are known to have intercourse together from the age of twelve onwards. Anyway, later that year, I was about to be introduced to the company of girls and, after that, such sexual interest that I shared with other boys faded.

But in the meantime, I was driven by my loathing of the Boycalls to cultivate the interest of a senior boy who was due to be a monitor next term. It was evident in various ways that I had attracted his attention and I decided to make the best of the situation. I had in mind that each monitor was allowed to select his own 'boy' as a personal fag to keep his study clean, shine his shoes, brush his clothes and run occasional errands. The boy chosen by the monitor for these personal tasks was thereafter excused other forms of fagging, including having to respond to the dreaded Boycalls. With this last factor very much in mind, I went to see the senior boy in his single study and asked him outright, 'Please may I be your study fag next term when you become a monitor?' 'Well,' he said, 'I had not made up my mind yet whether to accept a boring monitorship but, when a pleasant child like you offers to fag for me, I can see that it has advantages. If you are my study boy you will get a good tip when you earn one, or a good beating when you deserve it, and this would be directly from me and not from the Head of House. Do you accept that?' It was against the rules of the House for a monitor to beat his study fag, but I had no hesitation in accepting the terms gladly.

He was a character and I liked him and his casual attitude towards the House and all its rules. When he had been a junior boy he had established a reputation as a rebel and, despite being punished frequently, had laughed his way through to his present seniority. He was openly rich and generous, as I was to find. Indeed, when he was pleased with me or my work, he would hand me sometimes as much as a ten-shilling note, which was a lot of money in those days and would buy me and my friends any number of meals in the 'Grubber', our local shop on the Hill. He was equally generous with his beatings, which he did with a long-handled clothes brush. I did not mind unduly since he was reasonably moderate about it and I could see that he was obviously enjoying it. It was a very small price to pay for the utter relief of evading those Boycalls. I admired him and I was happy to do the chores he gave me as best I could.

That second year at Harrow was not so bad. Firstly I was happy sharing a study with Thomas who became a good friend and secondly because now, as a study fag to a monitor, I had successfully contrived to avoid the Boycalls which had so spoilt my first year.

Also I had made a number of other friends at Harrow, although these were mostly from outside my own House. I played Rackets, my favourite game, until the end of that second year when Father suddenly woke up to how expensive a game it was and stopped me. It was a great disappointment, I had so hoped to play for the second school 'pair' if not for the first before I left Harrow and, moreover, Rackets was the main focus of my life at the school and the source of most of my friendship with other boys. His decision was a bitter blow for me. But Father had never even heard of the game and could not understand how it could have any importance in my life.

At cricket I had developed into quite a good medium pace spin bowler and played for the House torpids (under sixteen) Eleven which won all the inter-house matches that year: the first tournament Druries had won for years. I played for the House torpids at rugby, but I would never make the school Elevens at the game being a bit of a funk at tackling, as my unblemished white shorts at the end of the game usually indicated.

The quality of teaching at Harrow was high for the scholars, but it seemed that the masters lacked interest in the less able pupils and there was no impetus from them to raise their standards. In those days, after all, pupils normally bought their way into university provided that they could achieve School Certificate. The intense competition now for places into university did not prevail at that time and I suspect that this reflected on the masters who were not under any great pressure to obtain results. Some masters coached the boys in sporting activities but, even so, many of the teaching staff appeared aloof from the boys and uninvolved with them. For example, I was interested in the English classes and enjoyed writing the essays sometimes set for us as 'prep'. But the English master, whom I remember as a tall, dark, bald-headed young man, showed little response to the fifteen-year old schoolboys in his class. The perpetually disdainful expression on his face gave the impression that he found us to be rather smelly and, indeed, we probably were since we only had a clean hot bath (or 'tosh' as it was called) in an evening once a week. Other than that, after rugby games in the afternoon, boys could opt either to share the same muddy and tepid bathwater, or scrimp at washing themselves under a cold shower. Neither of these alternatives was conducive to clean-smelling young bodies.

As I write now in the year 2009, I have no doubt, judging from what I know of it and the boys that I have met in recent years, that Harrow is currently the best independent boys' school in all the UK. For one reason, the Governors had the good sense to keep it as a boys' school, while many of the other famous independent schools made the mistake of becoming co-educational. But Harrow in my time was not a good school. It had a Headmaster who appeared to most of the boys as a tailor's dummy rather than a man of significance, as he paraded each day on the Hill in his wing collars, cravats and morning suits. He had appointed one entirely unsuitable housemaster at Druries and, therefore, may have made equally unsuitable appointments in other houses. Was it really unavoidable at Druries that the food was so bad; that there should be inadequate hot water for baths; that there was not a single lavatory or wash basin on each floor? That there was no means of fire escape from the upper floors other than down the narrow single curving staircase, which would have formed a funnel for the rising smoke fumes? The onus for such aspects of thoroughly bad management lay with the Bursar and the school Governors. But the housemaster of a boarding house is the one who should demand improvements as well as setting the character and style of the house. He should create an atmosphere in which the boys will be happy in the house and take pride in it. The bachelor housemaster at Druries in my time had little contact with the boys, other than lunching with the monitors at a separate table each day. As regards the bad management of the school at that time, a book published many years later, in its review of the school's history and its finances, implied that from 1938-1942, Harrow came close to bankruptcy.

I never really integrated with Harrow. The divorce of my parents may have been a factor as there was a degree of social stigma about divorce in those days and, rightly or not, I felt it to be so. Moreover, my moderate life style living with Mother was different to that of the majority of boys whose home life was very much more grand. I was good at games but not good enough for the first school teams. I preferred the minor sports of Rackets, Squash and Lawn Tennis but at that time Harrow did not compete at either Squash or Tennis and Father had prevented any possibility of my playing Rackets for the school. Despite all that, I made a number of friends there, but by ill chance, few of them survived the war. Perhaps I should have stayed on longer at Harrow because I missed the pleasure which other old boys of public schools seem to have derived from their final years there. They seem to forget how bloody awful it was when they started there as junior boys!

HOLIDAYS

But the most pleasurable aspect of boarding school for me, whether being happy at Cottesmore or rather miserable at Harrow, was always the prospect of the school holidays. I suppose, as with most boarding school boys, it was the feeling of freedom when at home which made life seem so good. Moreover, in my early teens, Mother tended to spoil me and she would somehow provide sufficient pocket-money for me to do, within reason, what I wanted.

I was just thirteen years old, on holiday from Cottesmore, and had saved up five pounds from my pocket money and intended to buy myself a new bike. With Robert driving the Austin, Mother and I were on our way into Brighton where we thought we might look around for a suitable bicycle shop while shopping. But, just as we were driving past a scrap dealers' yard, I spotted a 'for sale' notice over a battered-looking little two-seater car parked in the yard and, on an impulse, immediately asked Mother if we could stop to look at it. The car was a 1926 Singer two-seater with an extra 'dickie' seat at the back and a canvas hood. It looked battered and derelict in the yard but I loved it on sight.

The next day, having paid £4 and ten shillings in cash for the car, I could hardly sit still on the seat as Robert drove us home in it. I was the owner of a real car! Almost every morning of that summer holiday I spent dismantling the engine and learning how to put it back together again. I bashed the metal part of the car body into better shape and, with Maddie's help, repaired much of the hood. Then came the day when joy of joys I drove, gently at first, up and down the drive.

Phoebe, my sister, was supposed to be studying at a secretarial school in Brighton during the mornings; I think it was intended to be a sort of penance after the fracas of her expulsion from boarding school. If so, it was poor thinking by Father because she was certainly not the type of seventeen-year old girl who would knuckle down to anything so prosaic as secretarial work. She was an exciting elder sister, gay and fun-loving, always thinking of something interesting to do and she would involve me in most of her activities in the afternoons. We went skating at the rink often, to the pictures whenever there was a good film, and sometimes even to the theatre. But the best of all for me was the tennis we played at the local club but more often on the municipal courts at the sea front.

Of all the many boy-friends Phoebe acquired in Brighton, her favourite by far was Mike who was the Irish tennis professional at the municipal courts. He could hardly be described as a 'boy' friend since he was probably over thirty years old. Tennis and skating were for Phoebe a means of dressing in the appropriate outfit since she was no earthly good at any sport but she was well aware that she looked very attractive in short skirts or shorts and tight sweaters. Mike was a good-looking man too, full of Irish charm, who was understandably entranced with my vivacious sister. For her sake he went to considerable trouble to give me free tennis coaching and, when not coaching me himself, he arranged for me to play with good, mature players so that my standard of match play for a boy of thirteen became unusually high. I liked Mike as he was a companionable man.

IN THE BEGINNING

In spite of their age difference, I like to think that he was genuinely in love with my sister.

Then all hell was let loose when Phoebe announced that she was going to get married to Mike, the tennis professional! Her young brother, who knew her better by far than either of her parents did, very much doubted any such intention. But Mother immediately panicked and telephoned Father in France. He, a decisive man and a go-getter when action was needed, flew to England straight away and in no uncertain terms told Phoebe not to be so stupid. But she put on a superb act of 'loving that man'. In desperation to get her away from the tennis professional, Father booked a three-month tour round the world for them both on a liner. And off they both went with Phoebe laughing happily.

Even with Phoebe gone, that was a very happy holiday for me. Mainly I drove the car up and down the drive all the mornings, endlessly as it must have seemed to the neighbours, until they could stand the noise no longer and complained to my Mother. I was told to stop but I couldn't bear it and so I started getting up very early in the mornings and driving for short journeys on the empty local roads. I grew more ambitious and one late evening I took the car out onto the main road to London. I had meant to go just a little way but I became enthralled with the drive and went on and on until, inevitably, the lights began to fail since the generator was defunct and could not charge the battery.

Hours later I crept back home, almost without lights at all on the car, to find my Mother with Maddie absolutely distraught with worry. When she saw me at last, safely back, my Mother was angrier than I had ever known her. She was justifiably furious with me and did something I would never have thought her likely or capable of doing; she telephoned Brigadier Vivian Hollander, a wartime hero with a DSO, a close friend she had known for many years. She told him about my escapade and the appalling worry it had caused her and asked him to come and deal with me as if he were my father. I don't think Mother had really thought what that would entail but she could hardly go back on it when the Brigadier arrived next morning looking extremely grim and stern and carrying a short army cane.

I was upstairs and watched him arrive from my bedroom window and I went half-way down the stairs to hear what was going on. I felt very nervous and I could hear him in the sitting-room talking earnestly to Mother who was crying. He came out, saw me and told me to go back to my room where he followed me with the cane in his hand. There was a strong kitchen-type table at the side of the bedroom and he told me to bend over at one end of it. Then he spoke at some length to tell me what a thoroughly bad and selfish boy I had been to cause so much worry for my Mother. Meantime I lay across the table fearful of the beating to come.

He gave me eight strokes of the cane with long deliberate pauses between each one. I was crying by the time he had finished. It wasn't any more painful than being caned at school but that it should happen in my own home environment affected me considerably. It meant that home was no longer a sanctuary. The Brigadier left me to lie on the bed nursing my bottom and later I came down to my Mother to tell her how really sorry I was and we shed more tears together. It was an extraordinary experience; it was quite out of character for my Mother to take that sort of action and somehow it was worse than being punished at school.

Some two days later, old Vivian Hollander visited us again and said to me, 'Come on my boy, I will drive and we will have a last run in the car together before we take it back to the scrap merchant.' He drove first to a nice pub where he bought us a very good lunch and a large whisky for himself, which, under all the circumstances, he probably thoroughly deserved.

I bore him no ill-will and recognised that he was a nice old man doing as he thought best for me and my Mother. He certainly made me realise how stupid and selfish I had been. My first term at Harrow was due at the end of the holiday and preparing myself for it, including trips to London for new clothes at Gieves, kept me occupied for the remaining days.

The experience with the little Singer car during that summer holiday was not wasted, as it happened, because less than a year later Robert left our employment as our sometimes 'chauffeur' so that Mother had to resort to either hiring a driver or a car for her various requirements. I had been driving cars, not only the Singer, in driveways and occasionally on country roads ever since I was eleven and so I made the suggestion, absurd as it may seem now, that I could get a licence and so drive our Austin car for her during school holidays. At the time we were starting the Easter holiday at Tankerton in Kent where Mother had bought a small holiday cottage. Bless her heart, she hadn't a clue and gave no thought to the likelihood that an illegal driving licence would also invalidate the car insurance policy. Such thoughts simply never occurred to people in those days.

I applied for a licence giving my age as seventeen when in fact I had only just had my fourteenth birthday. I was given a provisional licence enabling me to drive accompanied by an experienced driver until passing my driving test in due course. The test at that time in 1936 was still a recent law, an unknown quantity to most, and I don't recall that there were such things as driving schools, the source of much television humour these days. Instead, Mother paid a very nice elderly retired and very experienced chauffeur to accompany me in the car and to advise me. I wish I could remember his name: he was first-class and showed me how to drive as a chauffeur drives to ensure that the car always moves smoothly, without any jerking or rapid accelerations or decelerations. I still wanted to drive like the clappers, as any boy would want to do, but I was also intrigued with the art and skill of driving with total smoothness. Later on in my life, incidentally, I found in rally-driving competitions that smoothness is also part of the skill in driving fast.

And so, just fourteen years old and wearing a brown trilby hat bought specially for the occasion and dressed in the customary grey trousers and tweed jacket which all teenage boys wore in those days, I presented myself at the office of the driving examiner in Canterbury.

What on earth must he have thought when he saw this skinny young boy, not very tall and wearing that absurd trilby hat? At least, thank heavens, I had discarded the pipe, which I had bought in order to appear older; on a trial smoke with it on the previous day I had been sick. The examiner must have considered marching me round to the nearest police station but he must have thought, surely no underage boy would dare actually to apply for a licence; it was unheard of. He evidently decided to see if I could drive first before taking any action. Well, need I write, I passed the test without any adverse comment whatsoever from the examiner.

Being the possessor of a driving licence gave me huge pleasure. It had to be kept absolutely secret, of course, but I hugged the secret to myself and it helped me through the unpleasant life at Harrow when I returned to school. What a secret joy it was to overhear the senior boys and monitors discussing earnestly how they hoped to be taking their driving tests soon. Meantime, during the holidays, it was fun driving Mother for shopping in Brighton and in London too. The one snag was having to drive to dog shows with my Mother sitting alongside making fizzing noises whenever I exceeded thirty-five mph and Annie, the kennel maid, in the back with three Bull Terriers panting and farting all the way there.

Towards the end of that Easter holiday, Father came to London on business with the intention too of viewing a hotel in Weybridge where, if he liked it, he proposed to stay in the summer for several weeks. Apparently, he considered the South of France to be too hot in summer.

I drove with Mother to his hotel in London to pick him up and, to his astonishment, drove all three of us to Weybridge. During lunch at that super Hotel, which I could see had every possible sports facility for young people, Father complimented me on my smooth and competent driving. I was quite overwhelmed and blushed furiously; Father was actually talking to me and saying very nice things. He went on to confirm that he would book the hotel and invited Mother, Phoebe and me to stay there for the summer holiday.

But that was not all. He went on to ask me if I would be able and prepared to drive his Buick car across France to England at the start of the subsequent summer holiday? It was a prospect almost too wonderful for me to believe; of course I would love to do it. He too was obviously quite ignorant and unconcerned about any insurance aspects of my driving and none of us ever gave it a thought. His idea was that I would take the famous Blue Train from Waterloo via Paris to Monaco and spend two weeks with him at his villa in Roquebrune. I could become used to driving the Buick, and then drive him up and over the mountain roads to Grenoble, through Paris and so onto the boat to England. Could any boy of fourteen have a more wonderfully exciting prospect than that? How lucky I was that Father was not just a bad driver but had recognised the fact. He would have been very nervous at the prospect of having to undertake the journey by himself.

At that lunch in Weybridge, I began to lose some of my awe of Father and to like him but, yet, in the years ahead I was never able to become close to him and to have easy communication with him. He, on his part, had little understanding of children and indeed may have been nervous of becoming involved with them. He was a man of considerable intellect and artistry while I was a boy whose only interests at that age were sports. It was difficult to find any common ground.

I shall never forget waking up in the early morning as the Blue Train, after travelling fast through the night, reached the Côte d'Azur and I could feel the heat and smell the heavy scents as the train trundled comparatively slowly along the coast from Marseilles to Monaco. It seemed to me to be a magical journey from the cold grey of Paris suddenly in the early morning to arrive at the heat, the colour and the smell of southern France. Subsequent journeys never lost that magic and excitement for me.

Father was waiting for me at Monaco station with the Buick, a large saloon car, to drive me out of Monte Carlo along the Corniche road and up the hill to his villa below the village of Roquebrune. Villa La Quieta was a comfortable size of house on the side of the mountain, not over ostentatious, which Father had bought some five years earlier as a strong structure but having a derelict interior. He had spent two years redesigning and arranging to rebuild the interior, using Italian craftsmen from across the border, and on the lines and in the proportions of an English Georgian house. The ground floor with its large sitting-room and dining room and marble staircase leading from the entrance hall was particularly lovely, rather grand really. The whole interior was beautifully furnished with his many paintings and ornaments. The house had five bedrooms with bathrooms and a basement flat for Lucien and Lucie; the butler and his wife, who was famous locally as a cook. Under the patio was a large wine cellar in which Father could indulge his hobby of acquiring and storing rare and good wines. It was a very nice set-up indeed for a retired single gentleman who liked to entertain his friends and, quite often, his mistresses.

I had a bedroom with a balcony overlooking the coast and the blue sea about a mile below me. It was all very exciting but what was I to do, as I didn't know anybody and couldn't at that time even speak French? Father and I had lunch together at the end of a huge dining table and it was evident that he too had been thinking about me and what I should do during the next two weeks before we drove to England. With the help of one of his favourites, Estelle Gastrell, he had arranged for me to join the Monte Carlo lawn tennis club where her son Peter, who was my age and also at Harrow, was already a member. They would come and collect me the next morning. I ought to add that these arrangements were not entirely thoughtful kindness, Father had been worried on his own behalf what to do with a young boy hanging around in the house or outside in the garden because he certainly didn't want to be involved in looking after me.

But that afternoon after his snooze, I was to drive the Buick and he would accompany me to show me the areas of Menton, Monte Carlo and the local roads. Not to forget either, he warned, that I would be driving on the right-hand side of the road. The Buick started up easily and the engine sort of hummed gently. Father explained that he liked American cars because they were so much quieter than English cars and I forbore to point out that this was merely due to extra exhaust baffles. I was beginning to grow up and I realised that a boy had to learn tact and must not be so stupid as to correct his Father; especially when we were getting on so well. The steering on the car proved to be nice and light which was a relief as I had rather feared it might be too heavy for me in this big car. It was a 'soft' ride, I thought, and I would have to be careful on the mountain roads when we drove to Grenoble. We both enjoyed that test drive and neither of us had any fears about the forthcoming journey to England.

I spent the two weeks before we were due to leave playing tennis and swimming in the pool at the Club. Well, to be honest sitting and lying in the sun around the pool because I could hardly swim at all, usually only with one toe touching the floor of the pool. Peter, whom I had not much liked before, proved to be a good companion and he knew lots of other young teenagers to whom he introduced me. I met a new species of creature which was quite strange to me. This species was called 'Girls' and they were wonderfully exciting creatures although I felt rather nervous of them. I wanted to touch them but dared not do so and also, for some reason, they always seemed to be laughing at me. Oh, except when I was playing tennis; they didn't laugh at me then because I was usually the best player on the court. There was no time to get to know and understand any of these girls before Father and I were off on what was for me an epic journey across France. But I so much hoped Father would invite me to his Villa again next year as I wanted to find out more about these new young things, these 'Girls'; there was something very attractive about them outside all my previous experience.

The journey across France was easily accomplished over two days and I enjoyed not just driving the car, particularly over the mountains and through Paris, but staying at very expensive Hotels and having lovely meals. It should have been an opportunity for Father and son to make better contact but somehow neither of us seemed able to break the barrier of the disparity in our ages and interests. I remember at dinner in a super hotel near Versailles, feeling boyishly hungry and longing to start the meal, but having to wait impatiently while Father discussed interminably with the wine waiter the best wines to accompany the menu. To him, the wine was by far the most important aspect of the meal.

We arrived at Oatlands Park Hotel in Weybridge to find Mother and Phoebe already there and enjoying its comfort and facilities. All four of us stayed for three weeks at the hotel and we must have appeared very like a real, normal family on holiday, which was a new experience for me and I realised what a happy feeling it gave me. It seemed to me such a pity that we were not a complete family including Michael, my elder brother. By this time, of course, I knew why he had been sent to live with the ex-Nanny near Bristol. He was mentally retarded, so I was told, in that his mind had reached by now no more than age about fourteen whereas he was in fact twenty years old, and he was unlikely to develop further. Moreover, his troubles had been compounded when, as a little boy of eight, he had been sent to a small boarding school where he had been abused and beaten frequently. For this reason, Father and Mother had concluded that he should not again be sent to a school but should live with Mrs Handoll. This also explained why my Mother had been so reluctant for me to board at Cottesmore where she feared that I might be similarly ill-treated.

But had it been the right decision for Michael? The result of it was that he had been living the lifestyle of a working-class boy in a small town where, as he grew up, he worked as a junior railway porter. I had seen him only a few times in recent years and, even in my boyhood, I realised that he looked grubby, badly dressed and spoke with a sort of Bristol/Cockney accent with a cigarette almost constantly bobbing about between his lips as he spoke. In consequence, neither of his parents now liked to have him at their home. Certainly not my Father with his high society friends in France. Mother very occasionally had given Michael a holiday at Tankerton but she did not like to introduce him to her doggie friends. Incidentally, it was at Tankerton that Michael had shown astonishing courage in separating four of the bull terriers in the midst of an appalling dog-fight, which resulted in one of the injured dogs having to be put down.

The alternative was to have treated Michael as normally as possible and sent him to a day school where, although he would probably have been teased, he would at least have had a normal and happy home life. Better that, surely I thought, than being ostracised by his family in this way? When I was a young teenager, I found Michael to be a good companion. For one thing we were mentally the same age then and, because he read avidly from a whole range of magazines, technical books and children's books, he was a fund of knowledge and would spout out all sorts of inconsequential facts, figures and silly riddles. He was fun to be with. I never heard him ever say a word of resentment of the treatment by his family but he must have been hurt by it.

It is not surprising that Michael, a heavy smoker all his life, died of lung cancer at the early age of forty-four. He married Mrs Handoll's daughter and fathered two sons, Leslie and Henry, and went to live in London as a postman. I was living in Ulster at the time of his illness but managed to visit him twice in hospital where he was being treated, and where he died. I felt that his life had been an unnecessarily sad one.

I have digressed and I was writing about all of us being on holiday at the Hotel. I suggested to Mother that Michael ought to be with us and she passed the thought on to Father apparently, because the next day they told Phoebe and me that we were to collect Michael in the Austin and take him on a tour of Wales for a week. An obvious and easy sop to their conscience. Phoebe was exceedingly boot-faced but cheered up slightly at the thought of being in charge, particularly of the petrol, restaurant and hotel money. As for me, I was fine since I loved driving and I liked Michael. My only real contribution to Michael's enjoyment of this sad little outing is that, after the first day, I insisted that Michael sit with me in the front seat of the car. I told Phoebe that it was proper for the 'boss' to be reclining in the back seat. Michael seemed to enjoy the week and so it was worthwhile.

Poor Father, he was quite unused to family commitments but 1936 had been a most unusual year of family demands on him. Earlier in the year before our summer together, he had coped with the problem of Phoebe and her tennis professional by taking her away with him on the three-month cruise. He had in fact enjoyed the cruise during which he had picked up a nice widow to play with. Phoebe had enjoyed an absolute ball of a time flirting with the young ship's officers but finally settling apparently on a 'great' Russian Opera Singer who was also on the cruise and employed to sing to the passengers.

Christmas of that year 1936 was enjoyably quiet, as it usually was for me at home with Mother, where it was such a relief to be after a term at Harrow. Except that Phoebe had returned from the cruise and there was an almost constant noise emanating from her bedroom where she played record after record of Boris, the great opera singer, singing lugubrious Russian songs dealing mostly, as far as I could hear, with vulgar boatmen.

Dear Phoebe, all her life, she would attribute to her friends, particularly the men, some magical and wondrous qualities and imagine exciting backgrounds for them when, in fact, they were all quite ordinary and normal people. From her teenage years and all through the rest of her life, Phoebe had a need to glamorise her life and the people around her. Boris was a typical example. She had led me to imagine his deep bass voice as coming from a huge, magnificent looking man with a mass of black hair. When he came to visit her unexpectedly, I came into the room at home to meet him and there he was: a skinny little man of about fifty, with a large, almost bald, head, white complexion and serious sad eyes. Cruel boy that I was, I could hardly get out of the room fast enough before I burst into laughter.

There were so many others like Boris. Such as the dashing Polish cavalryman at Arbroath who, as it turned out, couldn't ride. The film star in London who in reality featured only in adverts for insurance policies. The ace fighter pilot who turned out to be an airline pilot. It was as if she had a childlike need to enhance her life with these imaginary 'glamorous' people whose great qualities would reflect on her. The exception to all such people was Ward, her first husband, a truly fine man whose character matched her every vision of him. And they were immensely happy in their marriage. His early death was a tragedy for her.

Mother seemed unable to settle in any house for long; I never knew whether it was some wandering instinct inherited from distant ancestors or whether it was just the creditors after a bad year with her dogs. At the beginning of 1937, when I became fifteen, we moved from Brighton to a house in Taplow. I took no part in it, thank goodness, and it was a *fait accompli* by the time I finished the term at Harrow and I arrived to a new home. I guess that Mother's house at Brighton may have been rather too ambitious financially for her, also she may not have taken account of some fluctuation in the demand for her bull terriers. Personally, I never understood why there could be any demand at all for those unpleasant animals; I used to describe them as 'all pink balls and bite', the ugly creatures.

The new abode was a pleasant house of five bedrooms. The area at the back once again was only big enough for the dog compounds but there was a reasonable bit of secluded garden in the front. Mother's good, mostly antique, furniture was looking a bit shabby by now with some of it inevitably having been peed against and chewed by the dogs. But on the whole it was a happy if rather untidy household. Phoebe had now gone to live in France with Father who had accepted that she was never going to bother with secretarial or any other training course and at least while she was living with him he could keep an eye on her affairs. For my part, I spent that Easter holiday just settling into the new home.

As Father had indicated might happen, my summer holidays started as before with the journey on the Blue Train to Monaco. The timing corresponded with a Squash Tournament which, despite the summer heat, was being held in new courts at an hotel in Cannes. On the train were some well-known county players who had entered for the Tournament and I was proud that my standard of play had been considered good enough for my entry to be accepted. I had told Father all about it in a letter. The Tournament would start the next day after my arrival and I had assumed that Father would drive me to Cannes.

I should have known him better, because he had other things to do and he had assumed that I would go by bus. Next morning, I went down the three hundred steps to the Corniche road below to catch the bus. It was so crowded that I could only find a seat on the side with the sun blazing down on it. The bright, hot sun was on me for the long journey along the winding road so that I arrived at Cannes nearly three hours later with a blinding headache. There was just time to change before I was on court for my match. Instead of a high quality opponent, I was against a Frenchman, the local tennis professional, who although athletic had little clue as a squash player. I reckoned that normally I would have won comfortably. But I lost in three straight games and in my bad temper blamed Father entirely for my poor performance.

When I eventually arrived back, dinner that evening with Father was a morose occasion.

I was upset and sulky and he was irritated by my manner without any understanding why it should be so. To him, it was just another day when I had played some game or other and had lost. What was the boy's problem? I went up to bed early, still with a slight headache while, unknown to me, Father telephoned Estelle Gastrell and asked her for heaven's sake to bring her son in the morning and take us both for tennis or whatever else boys might want to do.

The next morning, I joined Peter and the boys and girls I had met last year. A year older, now nearly sixteen, I was determined to establish an easier and closer relationship with the girls who, although much the same age, had tended last time to tease me and laugh at me as if I were younger than they were. I would have none of that this year, I determined. In the following days we cavorted around the swimming pool or on the beach at Menton, where I was at a disadvantage because I still couldn't swim properly. But I shone on the tennis court and also at our teenage dances held spontaneously in various Villas. I had been made to learn dancing at preparatory school and Phoebe had shown me the latest steps, so I rather fancied my chances with the girls on the dance floor. These young teenage friends were mostly French with some English and some Italian, whose parents all lived in and around Monaco.

I was particularly entranced by Janine, a French girl a year older than me with a lovely slender figure and light brown, bobbed hair. I watched her on the beach in her swimming costume and tried hard to imagine what she would look like without it; I hadn't much information to go on, only the soft porn magazine pictures sometimes seen at school. In any case there was no possibility that I would dare to touch her to find out. At least, as she lay face down sunning herself on the beach, I could see her bare brown legs and part of her pert little white bottom. I would sit or lie near her whenever I could while pretending total disinterest in her as, sitting all in a group, we gossiped in English or in my improving French about this and that. Time was running out; I would have to return to England with Father and I had not made any impression on Janine who hardly seemed to notice me.

In desperation, I asked Father if I might borrow the Buick for a day to take a party out to Roche Rouge, a beautiful beach beyond Menton, for a picnic. He was holding one of his luncheon bridge parties in two days' time and said I could have the car for that day.

I wasted no time in arranging an expedition for six of us to Roche Rouge; Janine and I, Peter and his girl and Sebastian, an Italian boy, with his girl. I was the only boy able and allowed to drive a car and this, plus my initiative in organising the party, was bound to impress Janine as nothing else could do, so I thought. And I was right because Janine agreed to be my partner at an informal dance for us young people to be held on the following evening at a large villa in Cap Martin on the nearby coast. Spoilt young things that we were, Sebastian's parents would provide a chauffeur-driven car for us to go and return to the dance. This would be my last evening before leaving with Father for England.

Janine looked absolutely gorgeous. She hadn't messed about putting her hair up, as so many girls did for a party. She was wearing a dark blue, knee length, swirly sort of skirt which showed her figure as she moved and a deep v neck top which left her brown arms bare. My mouth was dry; I was about to hold this lovely girl in my arms when we danced. I could hardly believe my luck. After a couple of dances in which I had showed off, I thought, my expertise at the quick step, Janine moved closer to me and breathed into my ear 'Henri, do not jump about so; take leetle steps slowly and hold me nicely, like thees.' She brought her body up against mine and I felt myself shudder with a surge of strong sexual excitement as I felt for the first time a girl in my arms held close to me. My hand was in the curve of her back as we now slowly danced close together and, under the dim lights of the dance floor, I let it slide down to the divide between the little cheeks of her bottom.

At the end of the evening, as we waited in the dark outside for the car, she turned to me to take my head in her two hands and kissed me hard so that my mouth was forced open to receive her moist tongue against mine. 'Goodbye Henri,' she said as she moved away, 'you are a nice sexy boy; one day you may become an interesting man.' I wrote to her many times but she never replied.

Janine acted as a release for me. Until then, the experience at Cottesmore when I ought to have been called to stand up in disgrace with the other eight boys, for being sexually naughty, had made me into rather a prudish boy afraid of sexuality. Poor Thomas, whom I liked and with whom I shared a study in my second year at Harrow, had received weak responses from me to his advances. But after Janine, when I returned to Harrow, I had a better understanding of his desires with the realisation that his feelings for me might be not unlike mine for Janine. I was prepared to make more allowances for what he wanted of me but now, having held a girl like Janine in my arms, I had little desire for physical contact with a boy.

Mother hadn't joined us at Oatlands Park Hotel this time, as she needed to concentrate on her doggie business. On Saturday evenings, the hotel always held a dance with a particularly good dinner beforehand for which the women dressed up and the men wore dinner jackets. I had to wear an ordinary dark grey suit, being not yet sixteen, and anyway Mother couldn't really afford to buy me a dinner jacket for such occasional use. One of the guests at the Hotel was a most striking-looking woman who appeared to be unescorted by anyone. She was foreign, Cypriot we all thought, with long shining black hair swept back into a coil held by a large expensive comb. Nearly every one of the male guests, including the husbands, had attempted to make her acquaintance but she had rebuffed them all, courteously but firmly.

This lady, dressed in a flowing white evening gown, now made an entrance into the already full dining room and the Maitre d'Hôtel showed her to her solitary table. Father, Phoebe and I were already seated at our table when Father said, 'I think we should invite that charming lady to dine with us, rather than on her own.' With that, he rose to his feet and moved purposefully across the room towards the lady's table. Father really did look rather handsome; slim and immaculately dressed in a perfectly fitting dinner jacket with his short beard, iron grey hair, and upright carriage. All eyes were surreptitiously on him and the room quietened as he moved towards her; would he also be rebuffed and in public? He reached her table, spoke to her and she gave him her hand which he bent and kissed in the correct continental manner. He could be seen making a gesture towards our table and she rose immediately for him to follow her to our table. I nearly cheered. To me it was as if Father had gone in to bat and made a most stylish hundred runs on a difficult pitch!

I spent the following Christmas and Easter holidays with my Mother and Maddie at Taplow. The days passed pleasantly tinkering with the car, reading, with visits here and there to Mother's friends or to the pictures. I liked the reduced pace of life and the peace after the hurly burly of Harrow, although, in 1938, I was entering my third year there and would be able, as a senior, to lead a more normal existence with my own study. Father had asked me if I would like to stay at the Villa for most of the forthcoming summer holidays as he did not intend this year to visit England and, of course, I would be glad to do so. I was particularly pleased to feel that Father actually wanted me there, and not just to drive the car.

I arrived in Monaco to find Phoebe involved with members of the Ballet Russe de Monte Carlo who, as usual each year, had started their season in Monaco before dancing in all the major capitals of the world. She was having a distant affair with one of the senior male dancers and I was interested to join her whenever she visited him at the theatre. The life of these dancers was hard work with constant practice and rehearsals and there seemed to be intense internal rivalries as to who should be dancing such and such a part.

I describe Phoebe's relationship with her ballet dancer as distant. As a group of people the dancers had little time for leisure and it was not often that her chap could take time off from rehearsals. When he could he would join us on the beach, not to swim because that used the wrong muscles apparently, but to cavort about exercising and gracefully exhibiting his phenomenal strength. He was not a big man, slim in fact, but he could lift me as if I was a reed of a boy right up in the air with one hand under my bottom and sort of throw me forward. There were several show-off exercises of that type and I didn't like any of them one bit. Neither did Phoebe, as he was obviously keener on chucking me about than her. So she terminated that affair, such as it was, although we continued to watch the ballet performances in the evenings, which were astoundingly good.

It was the custom in those years before the war for the Mediterranean Fleet of the Royal Navy to show itself off at all the major ports, where the officers would hold magnificent parties on board the ships for top local people and most of the ships would also be open to the local public. The Fleet first anchored off Menton and, as Father was to have another bridge party next day, I asked if I could have the Buick to take six of us, three boys and three girls, to see over one of the ships. He gave his permission on the strict condition that I would be back with the car by six p.m. to take some of his guests home, but there was such a crowd of people visiting that there were insufficient boats to get us off the ship. And so we were very late and Father was cross but, surprisingly, forgave me when I told him the reason.

Perhaps he was relaxed because he and Phoebe had been invited to the officers' party aboard the Aircraft Carrier when the Fleet would be anchored off Monte Carlo in two days' time. At that party Phoebe met Lt Ward-Thompson, a Fleet Air Arm observer, a good-looking fine young man, and it seems that there and then they fell in love. As the fleet moved along the coast to Juan, Cannes and Nice staying several days off each port, so Phoebe and Ward met every day. Father held a lunch and a dinner party at his Villa to entertain Ward, whom he liked, and to introduce him to friends. Before the Fleet left the area, Ward and Phoebe announced their engagement and Ward took leave from his ship for them to get married in London. It had been exciting for me too as I was invited on board the Carrier for parties several times and had been able to take a girl with me. How I missed Janine. If only she had been there for me to take on board and to show off, but she and her family had moved to Switzerland. None of the other girls at that time interested me as she had done.

By 1939 I had entered my third year at Harrow and in the comparative peace of such seniority, with my own study, I was happier there and had settled down to serious schoolwork for the first time and passed the Matriculation examinations. There was an air of great anxiety in the United Kingdom as Hitler with his huge and trained army waged war with the smaller countries on the borders of Germany. Harrow, now that I had obtained the Matriculation, seemed such an unimportant and futile place to be at such an anxious time and I wrote to Father asking if he would allow me to leave school at the end of the summer term in July, although I had no clear idea yet of what I wanted to do. Father, living on the continent in France and so much closer to the fear of war with Germany, must have understood and sympathised with my feeling for he agreed without hesitation.

Yet Hitler was moving so fast that Father nearly missed the sudden mass exodus of English people, most of them wealthy, who had lived on the Côte d'Azur. In mid-August Father, joined by Estelle Gastrell and her son, climbed into his Buick and drove to Marseilles where they caught one of the last ships leaving France for England before the French government closed all exits. Father had to leave everything behind in his villa and hoped that Lucien and Lucie would remain in the basement flat and would be able to hide some of the more valuable contents of the house. But, as he left, he realised that he was unlikely to see his antique furniture, his collection of lovely ornaments, his pictures or the contents of his wine cellar ever again. As for the Buick, he had to leave that on the dockside at Marseilles and forget about it.

Where was he to go when he reached England? He telephoned Mother from Dover and she, the wife he had divorced so mercilessly some twelve years ago, immediately offered him accommodation in her house at Taplow. It really was an odd situation. These two had divorced with considerable animosity on both sides all those years ago and yet here they were with Father as a sort of guest in Mother's house. They got on well together probably because Mother had proved herself to be a good businesswoman, and they now found much in common to talk about and enjoyed each other's company.

APPRENTICE

And so there we were on September 3rd in the year 1939, Father, Mother, Maddie and me all listening to Chamberlain on the radio, when he announced that morning that England was now at war with Germany. Mother, inevitably wept and begged Father to arrange a job for me at our engineering company in Bristol to avoid being called up for the forces in due course. At age seventeen there I sat like a dumb ox, while these two arranged my life.

Father and Mother agreed that an apprenticeship at George Adlam & Sons would be best for me. Father considered that the trade of Toolmaker would provide a good start to a future career and, alongside the apprenticeship, he would arrange for me to attend night classes in machine drawing. Neither of them thought to ask what I might want to do. If they had, I could have told them that in spite of my hobby of fiddling about with cars, I had little aptitude for engineering and I had no great interest in it. My inclination, if anything, was towards the law for which I would need to attend university. I let them get on with it and to make the arrangements for the apprenticeship and for my lodgings near the factory.

It made no difference what they arranged because I had already decided to join up just as soon as I would be accepted at eighteen years old next February.

As general engineers, Adlams of Bristol, with some twelve hundred employees at that time, had a wide range of production facilities including brass foundry, iron foundry, a huge assembly shop and an extensive machine shop with every type of machine tool. The factory had largely converted already to the manufacture of war munitions. I moved into my lodgings where I was welcomed by a landlady of fierce appearance wearing hair curlers and with sleeves rolled up to show forearms like Popeye. She warned me straightaway that the front door would remain shut after 10 p.m. every night and that I would not to be allowed in after that time nor would I be allowed visitors in my room.

At the factory my presence as an apprentice raised knowing nods and smiles as everyone on the shop floor reckoned that here was a member of the boss's family dodging the call-up: and of course, they were absolutely right. For a boy straight out of Harrow, speaking inevitably with a plummy accent, with no knowledge or experience as yet of the real world outside school, never before having met or worked with 'working-class' people as they were then called, my life on the shop floor was made damnably difficult and miserable. In post-war Britain, young men and women of different backgrounds have learned to mix as a matter of course. But in those days and in my particular circumstances, it was not at all easy. Without exaggeration, almost every other word in the factory was the F… word so that it was difficult to understand at first what people were saying. The worst were the older men who delighted in telling me the most appallingly filthy sexual and lavatorial stories. My face obviously betrayed my horror at the sheer muck they were speaking and this gave them considerable amusement.

There was an Adlams' football team and the captain of it worked on a lathe in the machine shop and was a fine young man as I remember him. He was pleased when I asked if there was any chance of a game. It was a gamble for me, and more so for him, but he put me down as right-half for a match the following Saturday. Matches were played on Clifton Downs where we changed in a tiny wooden hut with all eleven of us crammed into it. After the game, there were no showers or even water to get rid of our sweat and mud, so we just towelled ourselves and each other down. I wasn't at all dismayed; after all, it wasn't all that much different from Harrow. I would love to write that I played an outstanding game. But no; this is a real life story and I was pleased simply that I was just about good enough for the team. I didn't shine either when it came to drinking pints of beer at one of the many nearby pubs in Clifton. But thereafter I was accepted by the young men at the factory, if not by the married and older men. And I was asked to turn out again for the team.

Admittedly I had experienced considerable difficulties at Adlams at first but I was given such a variety of jobs around the Works that I became interested. Some of the work, in the iron foundry for instance, was hard physical effort and it did me no harm. It was good to learn too about this business which had been started by my great-grandfather, George Adlam, in 1820 and to see how successfully it had been developed, mainly by Grandfather William and then by my Father. By 1920 it had become the foremost brewers' engineering company in Europe and it was particularly capable of adapting now to the production of war materials, as it had done in the first world war. But from my vantage point on the shop floor, it was alarming to watch how strong and dominant the trade unions became as the war progressed. The needs of our fighting services were so desperately urgent that the management, to ensure continuous production, could only submit in negotiations to whatever demands the unions might make. And the advantages and ascendancy the unions achieved in the UK from that wartime situation were to be maintained during the next forty years.

On February 17th 1940, aged eighteen at last, I presented myself at the recruitment office of the Royal Air Force in Bristol and applied to join up as a pilot; just like that. I was sent away and told that in due course, in company with several hundred other young men, I would receive a notice to attend for interview. So back I went to the shop floor. I hadn't told either of my parents yet what I was doing. It was two months later before I was called to Cardington where aircrew interviews took place. I sat before a table full of very senior Air Force officers and answered their questions suitably well apparently since they told me I was accepted subject to passing the medical ... but the doctors failed me! I could not believe it. I never found out what was wrong, I was simply told to try the medical again in three months' time. So back I went to the shop floor.

I was better organised by now having bought a motor-bike so that I could return home as often as possible rather than suffer the monotony of the lodgings. Also with the motor-bike I was able from time to time to visit my brother Michael at Wickwar where he liked to show me over his railway station, and we could meet his friends and go to his local pub.

In the meantime, Father had gathered together his finances and bought an attractive cottage called 'The Old Well House' in the village of Coffinswell in Devon. He and Mother had been getting along so well together that he made the astonishing suggestion that we all, Maddie included, move into the cottage and live together as a family. A purely platonic arrangement, of course, as far as he and Mother were concerned. And so, surprisingly, it was agreed. But my Mother, wise old bird, made sure of an escape hatch in case it all went wrong by retaining her house at Taplow and paying one of her doggie friends to help Annie manage the kennels. Thus also she continued to obtain an income from her dog business. As far as the village was concerned we were a nice normal family who had just moved in.

In escaping from France, Father was delighted that he had managed also to escape from Estelle Gastrell who had been his favourite and close mistress in France for many years. She was a woman about ten years younger than Father with a face rather like a frog, although it might have been attractive when she was younger, and she had a good sexy figure which she dressed beautifully and very expensively. In fact, she was the widow of a very rich man. She was very jealous and liable to erupt into a fury with Father when he strayed towards other women and, since she had a temper like a fishwife when roused, Father dreaded and feared her. He might as well have been married, except he reckoned that his money was safer with a mistress than with a wife. He would never forget how his third wife had given him his come-uppance the moment he strayed and had taken a massive capital sum from him at their divorce. Happily, when coming off the boat at Dover and hiring a car to Taplow, Father had managed to give Estelle the slip and she had lost him. Father very much wanted to keep it that way.

The village of Coffinswell although picturesque was mostly full of middle-aged rather up-market type of people in place of the original farmers. However, soon after the Adlams appeared as a normal and entirely respectable family of Father, Mother and son living amongst them, the rural tranquillity was broken by the arrival of Mrs Estelle Gastrell, who had at last found where Father was hiding out.

On a lovely sunny Sunday morning when most of the people were drifting towards the village church and talking quietly amongst themselves, the peace of it all suddenly was shattered by the Gastrell woman screeching foul language at the top of her voice directed at poor Father who, aghast at her unexpected arrival, had been trying to explain that their relationship was over. If that was the case, she shouted, then she would be glad to be shot of him; he had become old, ugly and no good in bed anyway, she yelled.

What added to the oddness of the scene was that this screeching woman, who sounded exactly like the proverbial fishwife, was beautifully dressed in the height of fashion and had evidently arrived driving an expensive car. All this to the unholy delight of the village people who were definitely going to be very late for church that Sunday.

Meantime, Mother and I had funked the whole thing and were peering out from behind the window curtains and being no help at all to 'Poor dear Father' in his awful trouble and embarrassment.

It was a most unfortunate scene and affair because, until then, there was a chance that Father, Mother and I might have settled successfully as a normal-looking family into the village. But we now felt awkward, to say the least, and Father became tetchy. I had a row with him about the use of the petrol coupons and the car, which I considered to be Mother's and mine, forgetting that we were supposed to be sharing as a real family would do. Only eighteen, I should never have been rude to him as I was. Mother, who had been used to running her own show for many years, became uppity at no longer being head of her household and the whole ménage began to disintegrate. So many rows went on that I renamed the cottage 'The Old Hell House'. Mother returned to her house in Taplow, which she had been sensible and realistic enough to keep, while I went back to my Gorgon landlady in Bristol.

My social boredom at Bristol wouldn't have been so bad if only I had known how to chase a girl or two; but I did not seem able to just go up to them in a pub or wherever and chat. I had met Janine when I was part of a group of young people all talking together and, even then, I had been frightened of being rebuffed and laughed at. But mainly I was fed up with the blooming Royal Air Force doctors as I had heard nothing more from them. At this time the war had fully erupted and, after the shattering retreat of our Army from France, the Germans were being held at bay in the air by our Spitfire and Hurricane pilots. Fed up as I was, I felt I could wait no longer before joining the forces and taking some part in the fight for our country, for that is how I saw it. To hell with the factory, I thought, and I walked down to the recruiting office of the Royal Navy to join up as a junior rating, an ordinary sailor. Again I was told to wait until I was sent for.

I said goodbye to my landlady, who wasn't half so bad as she had looked, and arrived home to tell Mother I had joined up. She did not make any fuss; she knew my voluntary call-up was right and she just gave me a resigned, tearful hug and that was that. Everybody was aware that the Germans were massed on the other side of the channel, revelling in their might and looking forward to their successful invasion of England. Meantime, they bombed our cities.

I had expected to have to wait a week or two but, in the end, it was more like two months before I was called up to report at Portsmouth barracks in December. The first morning was spent selecting the right size of 'square-rig' uniform and then learning how to put it on. By tradition the blue jumper and trousers had to be tight so putting on the whole rig, with its big blue collar and ribbons, was complicated. Training was mostly drill which we called 'square-bashing' and we attended classes to teach us the parts of ship, Morse Code and knots. In the first week I read on the notice board that suitably qualified applicants (School Certificate at least) were required urgently as aircrew for the Fleet Air Arm. Fed up with square bashing and remembering my visits to the Aircraft Carrier in the previous year, I wasted not a moment in applying. But, of course, I made no mention of having already applied to the RAF and having failed their medical.

My application must have hit just the right time to accord with the date of the Interview Board because, only a week later, I was summoned to report for the interview at HMS *St Vincent* in Gosport. This time I didn't have to pass a medical since, being already in the service, I was presumed fit. There were about ten other young men waiting for interview, all civilians in their smart suits, and I was the only sailor in my uniform as immaculate as I could get it. I was called last. Leaving my cap on the chair for I didn't know whether it was correct to wear it or not, I was ushered into the room where, sitting behind a long table, were six senior naval officers wearing lots of gold braid. They were all wingless except the most junior of them, who had pilot's wings on his left sleeve.

I knew enough to stand rigidly at attention in front of them until I was told to be at ease and to sit down. Among other questions, I was asked why the Fleet Air Arm? To this obviously expected question, I gave my rehearsed reply of how impressed I had been when I visited an Aircraft Carrier in a Mediterranean port and I let drop in my reply that I had been there as a guest of the Wardroom. It all seemed to go well and, when the senior officer terminated the interview and told me to wait outside, I stood up at attention again, did a smart about turn without falling over and marched myself out. My short experience in the Navy had evidently helped me to conduct myself in a manner they liked and, except to an abstruse maths question, I had made the right sort of replies. I was given Christmas leave and told to report to HMS *St Vincent* for Number 23 Pilots' Course next January 5th 1941.

I went home on leave feeling very pleased with myself and to show off my uniform to my Mother, Maddie and to our neighbours. Next door to us lived Howard, an apparently retired man of about fifty, with his much younger wife who taught ballroom and tap dancing in their front room. Philippa must have been about thirty-five, quite nice-looking in spite of her age, I thought, with the supple, taut figure of a dancer.

While I had been waiting to be called up, she had been anxious to teach me to dance better and we had several sessions of dancing together to her gramophone music. I felt that she rather fancied me when she so often used to hold my stomach in with her left hand while firmly pressing my bottom in with her right, saying that I must improve my posture. And I liked holding her when we danced. Her husband, Howard, although cheerful and always pleasant to me, was a big powerful man and I did not want to upset him. In consequence I dared not let the possibility of our little romance develop any further than the dance floor. And anyway, it would be absurd - she was so old! But I was highly pleased when she said how handsome I looked in my uniform as a sailor.

That was a pleasant Christmas at home with Mother and Maddie and we enjoyed it quietly being aware that the years ahead of us were full of the uncertainty and menace of war with Germany. As for me, there was excitement in the very uncertainty of the new experiences ahead of me. I was not to know or realise then how lucky I would be to survive five years of war as a naval fighter pilot, flying from aircraft carriers against the Japanese as well as the Germans.

CHAPTER SIX

My Father's Will

I woke up in the cottage at Eglinton, shivering and feeling chilled, as the log fire had all but gone out while I had sat there in front of it, recalling the memories of my teenage and boyhood. I had hoped that my memories, particularly as they related to Father, would have led me to understand him better and to see if I could find some reason, looking, back, why he and I had failed to reach a good father and son relationship. There had been so many opportunities to do so, but the truth is that Father had died still a stranger to me and it was too late now, in 1952, to rectify it.

The next day, before I drove to the Naval Airfield at Eglinton, I telephoned Baker the solicitor in London. He suggested that I contact Phoebe, who was already in France, to arrange with her for the Villa and contents to be listed and valued. All he knew at that stage was that Father had left capital in a trust fund in America to be shared by all three children, with the Villa being left for Phoebe. I was surprised because I had not expected that either Michael or I would benefit from Father's Will, since he had so little awareness of either of us, whereas he had always been proud of Phoebe and understandably very fond of her, as his attractive daughter. Meanwhile, it was easy enough for me to get compassionate leave; after all I was not doing anything of any importance at Eglinton anyway. And so, expensive as it was, I travelled to France to meet Phoebe at the Villa since it seemed the right thing to do even though it was too late for the funeral.

By the time I arrived, Phoebe had been busy already in arranging for an agent to list and value the contents of the Villa and also consulting an expensive lawyer in Monte Carlo about the Will. Through him and his contacts in America, she had obtained confirmation that there was indeed a trust fund for the benefit of all three of us while the Villa and contents would be solely for Phoebe. I was entirely happy with the situation and could not see why Phoebe did not simply leave it to old Baker, back in London, to sort it all out quietly with his expenses and fees paid for from the Trust. But no, she was particularly incensed because Mrs Betty Abbott, being the only person Father had wanted with him during the last days of his life, had been left under his Will a very nice flat in Monte Carlo, together with quite a substantial annuity from the Trust. Betty had been presumably not only his mistress, but obviously also a very good friend and, as far as I was concerned, it was 'good on her' as my New Zealand friends would say. I reckoned that the benefits she was to receive under his Will were only right and proper, particularly since she had looked after him all through his last years and during his final illness.

Phoebe's purpose of employing the clever French lawyer was apparently to see if this part of the Will which benefited Betty Abbott could be contested. Phoebe had invited Betty to the Villa for lunch and I didn't quite catch on to the situation and Phoebe's intention to thwart that part of the Will, if she could, until that little lunch meeting. I found Betty to be an elderly lady, obviously a good-looker in her youth, and an entirely charming and kind person who had loved my Father. She was different from most of his mistresses who tended usually to be moneyed women and sometimes just a little bit loud. I believe that Betty was as astonished as I was when she realised that Phoebe proposed to contest the Will and hoped to buy Betty off with an offer of an immediate but much lesser sum. It was a ridiculous situation and I sided with Betty on the matter, once I understood it, much to Phoebe's anger. Indeed, I was embarrassed and irritated by Phoebe, who had been well provided for by Father's legacy, and should have been well content.

Until this time, I had seen very little of Phoebe. After the double tragedy of losing her husband Ward, killed as an Observer in the Fleet Air Arm in 1941, followed by the death of her fiancé, Pat Humphreys, killed in action also as an Observer in late 1942, she had married Johnnie Lowder. Johnnie had been a colleague and fellow pilot in my fighter squadron when we had been stationed for a short period at Donibristle in Scotland. This was just before the squadron was appointed to HMS *Illustrious* in 1943 and at that time, before we were due to fly onto the ship, I had introduced Johnnie to Phoebe. They got on well together and kept up a correspondence so that, when Johnnie came back from the Pacific in 1945, they were married. But after the war, they were posted to the Naval Air Station at Ford in Sussex whereas my postings had been in Somerset and Cornwall. Hence,

Phoebe and I had rarely been in contact with each other in recent years.

As regards the Villa, and to finish off this rather unsavoury story relating to Father's legacy, I have to tell that Phoebe was intent on selling it as soon as possible while hoping to keep the basement flat, previously used by the butler and his wife, as a pied-à-terre for herself. The only potential immediate buyer, a famous aviator called White, made her an offer for the Villa and the entire contents at £11,000. It was an absurd offer even at that time since, in a matter of a year or two, as Europe continued to recover from the war, the property and contents inevitably would be worth at least ten times that amount, at the very least. But, with her husband Johnnie limited to the pay of a naval Lieutenant, Phoebe lived in constant debt and apparently was desperate to get her hands on the money immediately. In consequence and unbelievably, she accepted the ridiculous offer. Father's interest throughout his life had been the selecting and purchasing of exquisite Georgian furniture and the collection of paintings and beautiful porcelain, but the whole lot, including the lovely Villa, was tossed away for £11,000. I have a note left by my Father which tells that before the war he paid £150 each for the fourteen Chippendale chairs in the dining room and, these, plus the long dining table, the porcelain and the paintings must have made that dining room alone worth the £11,000! Dear Phoebe was never very bright intellectually but, even so, she and Johnnie must have been in an appalling state of debt for her to have made such a bad decision. For instance, why did she not raise a temporary mortgage, to pay off the debts, until the house and its precious lovely furniture reached its proper value.

As for me, not having heard from my Father for nine years since 1943, I was surprised to have been included in the legacy at all and glad to have an income from the trust which in due course might be about £400 annually, about half my naval pay at the time. I was genuinely pleased too that Michael was to receive an equal share from the trust and it seemed that, although Father had not much liked either Michael or me, he had felt some responsibility to us as his sons. Personally, I would have preferred that he had left the family engineering company as a going concern for me to manage, rather than the trust money, but by then, of course, that was not possible.

One exciting occurrence on the evening before I left France was a visit to the Casino in Monte Carlo where I dared to risk all but my fare home at roulette and won the huge sum of £46, much more than sufficient to cover all the expenses of my visit.

Tired from the long train journey back from the south of France, and tired too of the constant harping on about money with Phoebe at the Villa, it was a relief to return to the sanity of Saccie and to the pleasure of being a normal person at home with her and the children. First of all, I plonked the sum of over £40 remaining from my gambling, on the table in front of Saccie and then told her the good news of our future legacy. We agreed that we need not continue in future to be quite so miserly in our mode of living but, as Saccie said, we still had a lot of saving to do before we could buy a house, and I still did not have a job or a career outside the Navy.

Nevertheless, when I settled down to writing job-seeking letters again, I did so with a different feeling of hope and with a prouder attitude in my approach to these heads of companies. Previously, when writing from Salisbury, I had felt so hopeless and degraded considering myself to be a person without any substance, a veritable man of straw. I had gone cringing to look for work, forgetting that I had a background of which I should have been reasonably proud. The effect of having some income to come, instead of being penniless, made all the difference and I believe that my letters had a stronger and better tone to them.

One of the many companies to whom I wrote asking for a job was Short Bros & Harland, the famous aircraft manufacturers who were located at Sydenham aerodrome on the edge of Belfast. I had addressed my letter to Captain St. John Fancourt, DSO, RN, who had been Captain in HMS *Unicorn* when my squadron had been operating from her for a short period in the Far East during 1944. He replied agreeing to interview me at the factory in Belfast and this was about the time in 1952 when the war in Korea was beginning to draw to a close.

But I still had the old taxi and I didn't want to turn up looking desperate for work in quite such an old jalopy. For I was beginning to learn, when job-hunting, it is important to appear as if you were in a sound enough financial situation not to be too concerned if you didn't get the job. Bobby McDermott, my friend in Castle Rock who owned a shirt factory in Coleraine, came to my rescue and loaned me his smart new silver Triumph car for the occasion of my interview. Captain Fancourt in fact did not have much say in company matters, as I was to learn, since his job was merely as host of Rathmoyle, the company VIP guest house for entertaining customers. But he was a close personal friend of the chairman, Sir Matthew Slattery, who was a respected Admiral being one of the very few to have flying experience in the service. Fancourt, evidently suitably impressed by my borrowed car, my manner and my record of service in the Navy, as shown by my Navy 'flimsies' (written reports), arranged that I would be interviewed by Sir Matthew at the London office of the company.

In London at a smart office in the west end, I explained to Sir Matthew that I would be prepared to work hard for a career in management, irrespective of how lowly I might have to start, but I had no interest in promoting and furthering my expertise as a pilot. He understood and appreciated what I wanted but said that I would have to fly for the company for a period of time until some suitable desk job became available.

I would be required to test naval aircraft maintained by Shorts, to be an instructor and the manager of the Newtownards Flying Club owned by Shorts and, occasionally, to ferry refurbished naval aircraft to their aerodromes. Sir Matthew accepted that in any case I would not be able to start work until the Navy released me when the Korean War ended. This was indeed a very fair offer and I was happy to accept it, feeling that I could rely on the Admiral to put me behind a desk as soon as one became available.

With the certainty now of a future career for me with Short Bros & Harland in the aircraft industry, both Saccie and I were content to see out our time at the Naval Air Station, Eglinton and to spread our wings a bit after our austere lifestyle in recent months. I started by selling our dear old taxi to a garage in Limavady and, with some accumulated income from the Trust, bought a second-hand, sporty-looking Alvis saloon car in Belfast at a reasonable price. Typical of me, as soon as there was some money in my pocket, I had to spend it.

Having a decent car again enabled us to travel around Northern Ireland, to make new friends and to learn something about Ulster for the first time. We had arrived knowing absolutely nothing about the political and sectarian situation in Belfast and the County and, during all that time in Piggy Cottage, we had remained blissfully unaware of the antagonism between the Protestant and Catholic people. But then, no-one else at the naval air station seemed to be aware of the situation either, and I don't recall any officer in the mess ever discussing it. Certainly at that time, it never apparently occurred to the Royal Navy to brief any of the personnel about the politics of the place before they were sent to Ulster. Perhaps it was a naval policy not to do so.

I first became aware of the situation when a decision was made to have an open day and air display at Eglinton, our naval air station only a few miles from Londonderry, where the majority of the community were Catholics. Because I had been involved in organising an air display at Yeovilton in earlier years, I was commandeered to organise the PR, advertising and travel arrangements for this display. And I set about it enthusiastically.

After arranging publicity and advertising with the cinemas and newspapers in Belfast and Coleraine, and organising bus and coach services from those cities, I turned my attention to Londonderry thinking that there would be no difficulty in making similar arrangements there.

The editor of the Londonderry newspaper had not seemed particularly happy at the idea of advertising and promoting the air display but, with a reluctance which I couldn't comprehend at the time, had agreed to do so. But the manager of the cinema in Londonderry, when I asked him to display an advert for the Eglinton open day on his screen, hooted with incredulous laughter. 'Are you quite mad?' he asked. 'Don't you know that there are large factions of people in Northern Ireland, particularly here in Londonderry, who regard you in the British services as an army of invasion? If I were to put your advertisement up on the screen, they would probably wreck my cinema.' I felt a right idiot for being so uninformed and, on return to the Air Station, reported to the Commander my fears for the security of the aerodrome and its aircraft on a day open to the general public. 'You may leave the security to me, Mr Adlam,' said the rather pompous Commander of the Air Station. 'Your job is to get as many people as possible to visit us on the day.'

He was one of that old guard of the Royal Navy who tended to address junior officers, not by rank or name, but as 'Mister,' which I had found disconcerting at first but, on reflection, I thought there was something rather quaint and charming about this old traditional form of address from the Nelson era and I did not resent it. Anyway, that first Open Day at Eglinton went quite well with some four thousand visitors to it, mostly from the south, and without any aggravation or sabotage taking place. This may have been due to the closure of the hangars to the public, and to those aircraft on view on the ground being surrounded by security guards. But visitors seemed to enjoy the air display itself, if little else.

CHAPTER SEVEN

Civilian Life

In 1952 I was released from the Royal Navy and, as had been promised by Admiral Slattery, took up my appointment with Shorts, to commence flying for the company and to operate the Flying Club it owned at Newtownards, about ten miles from Belfast. For the first time since our marriage Saccie and I were so to speak, really in the money, with a decent salary from Shorts for my flying job plus the income from the trust fund. We used it to obtain a mortgage which, with some accumulated capital, enabled us to buy a small but very attractive and modern new house in Cloverhill Park, a newly-made road on the edge of Belfast which bounded the grand and imposing new Government building at Stormont only a few hundred yards from the house.

This was a most joyful period of our lives. The children were a constant delight and my memories of them playing together and with Saccie at that time, in the garden or in the adjacent fields, are of the happiest. Jeremy was about five years old by then and Aza nearly four, but she was so agile and forward that they seemed to be about the same age and Jeremy never resented it whenever Aza could do something better than him.

They were great pals and companions together and this companionship and love for each other never left them. The only blot on the children's landscape at Cloverhill Park were the 'Pushings', two slightly older children who lived close by and were so called by our family because of their tendency to bully and push Jeremy and Aza about. Saccie and I kept a watch on the situation but felt that our children must learn to look after themselves and so we rarely interfered. In this Nanny State of the UK in the twenty-first century, young parents would make a fuss about such minor bullying behaviour.

The house at Cloverhill Park was so new that the garden area around it was still just so much rough ground. This was the opportunity for Saccie to find out how really good a gardener she was because, up to then, gardening for her had been under the dominant eye of Alice, her mother. But now she found great pleasure in designing the layout of the plants, shrubs and flowers, which we bought, and in the work of planting them around the new grass, which had been laid according to her plan. She worked hard at it and the garden began to look not fussy or ornate, but lovely in its simplicity and naturalness. It was evident that Saccie was a natural and gifted gardener.

As an example of different attitudes and lifestyles to ours in that suburb of Belfast, one summer Sunday afternoon we were all in the front garden with the children playing. As for me, I was just sitting in a deckchair lazily watching them while Saccie was happily working hard doing something or other to the garden. These idyllic activities were interrupted by two very smart-looking old ladies, both wearing large ornate hats who, looking over the fence, complimented Saccie on her new garden and on how well it was looking. 'But,' they said, 'what a pity that she was working on it on a Sunday, and that the children were not attending the bible class at the church that afternoon.' We were rather shocked; in our experience people did not criticise complete strangers about their activities. On the other hand, it was indicative of the community life, which existed so strongly in Ulster, where people tended to grow up together from their schooldays, remaining as neighbours in the same area for most of their lives. Hence, there was an interest in any new family moving into the neighbourhood and local people were forthright in their approach towards newcomers, although always offering friendship, if they were of similar religion.

And there were other differences. For instance, the parents of the Pushings, a nice-enough couple, strongly Protestant and quite a bit older than Saccie and I, invited us to their nearby home for the evening and we found their lifestyle to be vastly different from ours. We didn't have a drink before we left, since our customary friends would have plied us with too much during the forthcoming evening anyway. But on that evening with the Pushings' parents, the hours wore on with rather difficult small talk because our backgrounds had little in common, and eventually it wasn't until after nine p.m. that we were offered a small sweet sherry. Then, instead of dinner or supper, the wife wheeled in two trolleys absolutely groaning with the weight of magnificent-looking cream, chocolate and lemon cakes. She must have been cooking like mad all day to have created such a display of culinary art. It was their kindest and highest form of hospitality, but vastly different from anything we had ever experienced before. Saccie, who was never keen on cooking anyway, didn't intend to try emulating the wife's standard of cakes in return, and instead invited them to dinner for the following week. However, the Pushing parents regretted politely that they never ate full meals in the evenings. And so that really was that. Later, when we moved to the seaside town of Bangor, we found the same strong sense of community but in a much more relaxed style.

My flying job at Shorts was not onerous and was pleasantly varied. The Chief Test Pilot was Tom Brooke-Smith and there were three other test pilots, all of whom were busy. Tom was involved in the appallingly dangerous task of prototype-testing an aircraft of Shorts' design with three variable sweepback configurations of the wings, and really with hardly enough thrust from the comparatively small jet engine to get it airborne in any one of them. He had recently been testing the SC1, the first vertical take-off aircraft having eight small vertical jets and one for forward flight. They don't give gongs to test pilots of such dangerous prototype aircraft, but Tom's courage and skill should have earned him something more than just his salary from Shorts. The other pilots were testing the new Shorts Sealand, an amphibious commercial seaplane, and types of other aircraft which Shorts had under contract for refurbishing, such as the Canberra for the RAF and Fireflies, Sea Furies and Seafires for the Admiralty. Although I had not done an MTP course (Maintenance Test Pilot), I occasionally had to test one of the Fireflies or Seafires, since I knew them so well anyway, but more often my job was to help out with the delivery of them to an air station after testing.

We had a Dominie, better known as a Rapide, being a twin-engined commercial biplane of antique design capable of taking five passengers, which we used for the purpose of fetching our pilots back from the various air stations. Piloting this rather absurd old passenger plane around the UK to pick up the other chaps became an occasional job for me. The pilot sat right in the nose with just the glass canopy-cum windscreen around him to give ideal visibility. It really wasn't powerful enough to climb up above bad weather so that, in such conditions, I would have to bumble along below the clouds flying very low down over the roads and villages to map-read the route to the destination. This was back to the old fashioned style of aviation and very different from the modern method, by then, of flying all the way on instruments in bad weather. But I liked to feel that, in an emergency, I could fly the dear old Dominie just off the stall at around 65 mph and just bump gently, if necessary, into the nearest hillside. Absolute nonsense, of course, but a comforting thought, which I doubt if my passengers would have shared with me!

I do remember one occasion in the Dominie sneaking in from over the sea to arrive on a runway at Lossiemouth Air Station, in truly appalling weather conditions with much of the cloud base almost at ground level. All flying had long since been cancelled and everyone, except the duty crew in the Control tower, had disappeared to the bar in the Wardroom or to the local pubs. After I had landed, the control tower crew had to send a van out onto the aerodrome to find me and lead me with their lights to the dispersal area. How immensely satisfying it was to be greeted in the Wardroom bar by old naval friends, who were astonished when I airily told them that I had just dropped in via Donibristle to pick up a couple of passengers! I could not have been prevented from flying back, as I still had my ticket as an Instrument Flight Examiner, but how thankful I was when both passengers refused absolutely to fly back to Belfast with me in that weather. It was out of the question really, of course, but I put on quite a good show of pretended disappointment at their refusal. More seriously, the truth was that I had frightened myself silly flying in those awful weather conditions in that elderly out-of-date aircraft and, in doing so, had reneged on my promise to Saccie and myself that I would never put myself at risk again in the air. However, as I should have known and would be reminded again later, making such a promise is not practical in the flying business.

My other task, as flying instructor and manager of the very small flying club at Newtownards, was rather more interesting. To start with, I had to spend some few days at a large flying club just outside London to obtain my civilian instructor's licence, since my service qualification, as good as it was, did not automatically qualify me for civilian work. I had to resuscitate and remember the old patter and jargon from my days at the Central Flying School sufficiently well to satisfy the examiner, which I managed to do.

While I was there, I had a good look round their successful flying club and at the latest type of aircraft being used for club instruction and flying. They were nearly all a new type of aircraft, designed and built in America, where people with medium but adequate wealth were accustomed to regard their aircraft much as they did their car. Thus the seating, furnishing and general layout inside these small

American aircraft was very similar to a car, but with a control column and rudder bar instead of a steering wheel.

A very different situation existed back at my own very basic little flying club. The only aircraft we had were two Tiger Moths and an Auster. The Tiger Moth had been the main *ab initio* training aircraft in the RAF for the past twenty years and it was as good as any aircraft could possibly be for learning how to fly properly and to gain an understanding of the basic principles of flight. But it was old hat compared with this new modern type of American aircraft into which, for example, almost total stability had been designed. When stalled, such aircraft could not spin and did not flick over on one side or the other; they merely flopped gently downwards until the airspeed built up again for self-recovery. In consequence, such aircraft were safe and easy to fly, provided that all you wanted was to bumble across the sky from one place to another or, as some club members did, just to do circuits and landings around the airfield. As for the Auster, this was an earlier and not an altogether successful attempt by the British industry to develop a small cabin aircraft suitable for amateur fliers.

It was obvious that our club would need more modern aircraft if it was to prosper but there seemed little possibility of getting them. The club was successful in having quite a large membership of about 120 people but this was the age of the three-guinea annual subscription, which in those days seemed to apply universally to all types of clubs, be they golf, tennis, squash, sailing or even flying clubs. It was a ludicrously low subscription to cover all the high costs of a flying club such as the salary of a flying instructor, wages of a full-time mechanic and the upkeep of the aircraft, airfield and buildings. There was a flight charge of £2 per hour, which was nowhere near enough to cover all this expenditure plus petrol and oil for the flight. The directors of Shorts, who had been supporting the club for some time past, probably regretted their original commitment to subsidise its operation.

In fact, quite a good proportion of the club income came from the bar because it was, if nothing else, a very cheerful social club well run by a committee of which, in future, I would as manager also have to be the chairman. There were only a small number of members who had been keen enough to obtain their Private Pilot's Licence while the expectations of the majority were no higher than eventually to go solo in the Tiger Moth under the instruction of Tubby Lane, the full-time flying instructor. Most members just enjoyed an occasional flight and talking about it in the bar afterwards. The reality was that a cold, wind-blown and bumpy flight at £2 an hour around the local area in a difficult little aircraft like the Tiger Moth was no great incentive for anyone to fly.

It was obvious that the club needed an injection of a new type of aircraft and I made contact with a company, based at Oxford aerodrome, which acted as distributors in the UK of the American Piper aircraft. I learned that a contract could be made to lease such aircraft with an option to buy at the end of the term. But I would appear as a useless wimp to my directors at Shorts if, as my first action as manager of their flying club, I were to ask them for an immediate further subsidy with which to buy or even lease new aircraft. Anyway, their approval was highly unlikely. The only solution that I could see, therefore, was to raise the annual rate of the member's subscription.

And so, after consultation with the Company Secretary of Shorts on the proper procedure, I called an extraordinary general meeting of the club members at which I intended to inform them of an immediate threefold increase in the subscription to £9 annually. It was a proprietary club owned by Shorts for whom I was acting and therefore I had the right to raise the fees. I imagined myself, as chairman of the meeting, explaining lucidly and well to the members all the benefits that would accrue from leasing two new-style American aircraft and of the pleasure members would derive from learning to fly these safe and simple aircraft and how they would, in due course, be able to use them for cross-country flights. Moreover, with the extra income, it would be possible not only to improve the appearance of the club but also its bar, kitchen and leisure facilities. At that time, the club was no more than a converted Nissen hut with a bar at one end and a few chairs and tables scattered around. A second Nissen hut served as a small hangar and as a workshop for the one mechanic.

There was nearly a full turn-out of members at the meeting since, of course, the increase in the subscription was the main item of the agenda. And they were all furiously angry. There was a stony silence at first when I stood up to speak but, as I did so, questions and complaints were called at me and I simply did not have any experience, either as a chairman or as a speaker, to deal with the situation. I was rescued by a member of the committee, a very keen amateur aviator, already the holder of a Private Pilot's Licence, and owner of a small engineering business. He was one of the few people with whom I had discussed my proposals beforehand. He persuaded those at the meeting to give me a hearing, at least, before they resigned *en masse* from the club, as they all threatened to do. I began to speak again and gradually my enthusiasm for the project must have had an effect and sensible discussions took place.

The conclusion of the affair, some weeks later, was that only a few members had resigned and, from the remaining members, we had sufficient extra income for the two new Piper aircraft to be leased and some improvements to be started to the club premises. The two aircraft, rather flimsy-looking low-wing monoplanes, were bottom of the Piper range but they were a start to an altogether more substantial and successful type of flying club. As for me, the best thing was that I had learned lessons which I never forgot in my later business life. The essential lesson was always to consult with those concerned before mooting a new proposal. Also, before a meeting, always to lobby as many members of it as possible to explain individually to each one the proposal. If anyone should disagree, I would at least know his point of view and maybe, by speaking early at the meeting, pre-empt it.

In the days before that meeting and before the new Piper aircraft were obtained, the only lucrative aspect of the club operations had been a contract with the RAF to train their local cadets to Private Pilot's Licence standard. But it had been taking months for Tubby Lane, with other commitments, to teach only one cadet, and there was a danger of losing this valuable annual contract. Most of the cadets lived in and around Belfast, so I decided to bring one of the Tiger Moths up to our main aerodrome at Sydenham during the week-days, because it was nearer and more convenient both for me and for the cadet pupils. This was much better and I started piling up the flying hours enabling all three cadets to obtain their licences within six months. As the result of this successful conclusion, the contract was duly renewed.

There had been one near mishap on the occasion of an engine failure in the Tiger Moth shortly after I had taken off from Sydenham with one of the cadet pupils. It was an absolute rule of flying instruction, written in blood, that in the event of engine failure on take-off, the pilot must never think of turning back to land downwind; almost inevitably the aircraft would stall as the pilot tried to turn without engine power and so crash. The rule was that the pilot must continue straight ahead and put the aircraft down as best he could, wherever he could. And of course, as a trained CFS Instructor, I had always drummed this rule into the heads of my pupils. But this was different, this was me about to bash into the houses in the town of

Holywood just ahead of me and even a slow-flying Tiger Moth would come off badly in such a confrontation: much more important, so would I and my pupil and the unfortunate people in the houses. I had about nine hundred feet height, so I did the wrong thing in stuffing the aircraft nose steeply down to gain sufficient speed enabling me to spiral round and to put the aircraft down safely on the downwind edge of the runway. The problem afterwards was trying to explain to the young cadet, who had been over-impressed by my handling of the situation, why he must never follow my example in similar circumstances.

The variety of aviation which the job at Shorts required of me, was not unduly onerous since, apart from the occasion of landing the Dominie at Lossiemouth, I avoided flying in bad weather conditions, as there was no real need to do so. My working hours were flexible and there were times when I was able to take time off to be with Saccie and the family during the afternoons. But the flying job with Shorts, pleasant enough as it generally was, did not give me much of new interest on which to focus. Most service and ex-service pilots tend to rabbit on throughout their lives about how wonderful it is to fly but, for me, the excitement and joy of flight, which I had certainly experienced as a young pilot, was now a rare feeling for me. Indeed, I hoped to be shot of the whole business of flying as soon as possible.

Meantime, I had heard about a new charitable organisation called 'The Samaritans' which had been first formed in London to deal with and care for those individuals in such deep trouble that they were suicidal. The organisation was proving to be so effective and valuable that many cities, including Belfast, now had a Samaritan office in the centre of the city.

All Samaritans were volunteers but I had to undergo two long interviews with experienced members from the very heart of the organisation before I was accepted. Saccie, who with her natural gift as a confidante would have been so much better than I at such work, advised against my joining saying that I was not the type of character able to stand back objectively and would become too involved with deeply-troubled people. She was absolutely right. I found it impossible to listen to the deep, deep sorrow of another human being on the verge of suicide, to listen and to continue listening, as one had to do, to all of that sorrow and despair and then somehow to dismiss it all from my mind, when I returned home to my own family.

When the time came for me to move from flying to a desk job, it became obvious that I would have more than enough worries on my own plate in trying to make my way in industry and caring for my family, without also trying to cope with Samaritan problems. And so I resigned. However, I still have the letters from both Chad Varah, the founder of the Samaritans, and from the Bishop of Belfast, to thank me for such help as I had gradually learned to give. It had been an experience for me but, at times, a frightening one especially at night when, as was the practice in those days, the office with its two volunteers was open to all comers. It was by no means all work on the telephone, as many would seek our help in the office where a volunteer could listen to their problems in a private room. Sometimes but not often enough, I was able, listening and talking either on the telephone or privately in the office, to persuade a 'case' that the problems being suffered were not entirely insoluble and thus, perhaps, to have given some hope and help. But I never really knew, as there was rarely any feedback from a person who had sought help. The best would be that after time had elapsed, there would be no more contact from that person, implying that he or she had resolved the situation. The worst would be, and thank heaven it didn't happen for me, a newspaper report of a case's suicide.

At home, the children were now attending a nursery school where, as far as we could find out from the children's chatter, the main activity was playing with Plasticine, plus looking at pictures of animals and trees and all that type of activity. Both Jeremy and Aza were disappointed in their expectation that school would provide them with lots of new and interesting things to do. The fees seemed to be an awful waste of money too, especially as Saccie had already started teaching them to read using the well-known *Janet and John* series of books and, although these books have been much derided by modern educationalists, the fact is that both of our children were reading well ahead of others of their age as the result of her teaching and their use.

Moreover, Saccie taught them quite a lot of general knowledge about the countryside and, during our walks with the children, would name the different trees and point out the variety of foliage and all that kind of thing, all of which was as new to me as it was to the children. I had not realised before the extent of her knowledge about the countryside and she told me that it stemmed from the long caravan holidays which her parents took regularly twice every year during her childhood and teenage years. In those days, the early 1930s, the sight of a car-and-caravan was rare indeed and, since there were no special caravan parks, the holiday would be spent in the peace and quiet of a field, probably near a farm from where milk and eggs could be obtained. Her great pleasure was to go for long solitary walks, leaving after breakfast to explore the countryside and probably not returning to the caravan until the afternoon. Neither she or her parents gave any thought, apparently, to the possibility of any harm coming to her and indeed none did in those days but, writing now in this quite different and increasingly violent country of England in the twenty-first century, my fearful mind boggles at the thought of that beautiful young girl wandering alone. Aza, my daughter, has inherited the same strange pleasure in the solitude of long walks by herself in the country, but at least she knows the modern world well enough to arm herself with a mobile phone.

CHAPTER EIGHT

A Desk Job with Shorts and a New Home

In 1953 the Chairman of Shorts, Sir Matthew Slattery, kept his promise and put me to work as a clerk. At last I was flying a desk, albeit a small one, instead of an aircraft. I found myself as an exceedingly junior clerk in the Sales Office, as it was quaintly called, with two ex-members of the drawing office, Jim Dwerryhouse and John Atkinson, both of whom a few years earlier had been transferred from the drawing office to the sales department. The function of this department was to deal with customers, almost entirely by correspondence, and to pass their requirements, such as spare parts, design modifications or whatever, through to the appropriate departments of the factory for action.

Both Jim and John were not far off from their retirement, and they took me as a young upstart into the slow, comfortable fold of their office in the most helpful and kind manner. On the opposite side of the corridor, in his office every bit as big as ours, was our boss, Bill Hambrook, with the title of Sales Controller, and he too had come from the drawing office where he had been a senior designer. An aspect of the set-up, which infuriated both of my senior colleagues, was the bell-ringing apparatus which Hambrook had caused to be installed so that he could summon whichever one of us he wanted into his office. This apparatus was a box of bells hung on the wall and under each bell was a tag with our names on it, which waggled imperiously when rung. The arrangement was as might be found in the kitchen of a large Victorian house and would have been used to summon the butler, the valet or a maid to the master's study.

This was an extraordinarily insensitive and ill-mannered way to summon us into his office and my two colleagues seethed with fury whenever one of the bells rang. But Hambrook, who may have been a nice-enough sort of chap at heart, was altogether too thick and insensitive to realise the hurt this procedure caused to the pride of his two ex-colleagues of the drawing office. For my part, I was only too glad to have my feet under an office desk at last, rather than in an aircraft cockpit, to allow such a minor indignity to concern me. And anyway, I had been accustomed to eat much more humble pie than that in my earlier years as a salesman, lavatory cleaner and factory worker when I had first left the Navy to become a civilian.

Short Bros & Harland Ltd, more usually known as 'Shorts', had been one of the foremost aircraft manufacturers in the world and, during the earlier days of World War II, had produced the Sterling as a moderately successful heavy bomber. But Shorts was particularly famous for designing and building large flying boats, such as the Sunderland, which during the 1930s had created passenger routes to many countries in the Far East and to Australia. There had been expectations after the war that flying boats might become the main means of long-distance air travel because of their size, plus the availability and low cost of waterways for landing. But unfortunately for Shorts it was not to be; the hull configuration of the flying boat and the consequent drag and low speed of it, proved too costly in terms of payload, and flying boats could not compete economically with land-based and faster airliners. Thus the Solent, the latest of the large flying boat on which Shorts had based their main hope for manufacture and sales after the war, was gradually discarded by those few airlines which had based their business on flying boats.

At the time when I joined Shorts in 1953 it was reduced to a labour force of about 8000, engaged mainly on production of aircraft parts and refurbishing of service aircraft under Ministry contracts for the RAF and FAA. Such military contracts were negotiated for Shorts by the Contracts Manager, Mark Howard, and his staff, who were experienced in the specialised contract procedures required by the Ministry.

Although involved in the research, design and construction of three experimental aircraft, Shorts had only one project of its own design in production at that time. This was the Sealand, a twin-engine, small amphibious flying boat with a potential payload equivalent to about six passengers over short distances. It was intended for operations in and out of difficult terrain and waterways around the world. But with the drag of its hull shape and the weight of its undercarriage, it had little payload. Moreover, it was apparently quite tricky to fly on take-off and landing and therefore hardly suitable for difficult situations in rough country abroad, and had a very poor

A Desk Job with Shorts 111

single-engine performance. A forceful and slick sales team would have been needed, if there were to be any possibilities of developing this little amphibian aircraft into a commercial success. But the two nice old codgers who never went outside their sales office and wrote their flowery letters instead, combined with their boss, the aptly-titled 'Sales Controller', were not a team likely to effect many sales. Nevertheless, a number of Sealands had been sold, mainly due to the efforts of the Chairman and the test pilots. Ten were ordered by the Indian Navy, two were sold in Canada, two to a large Indian trading company, four to a small airline in the West Indies and two to an American Missionary Alliance for work in New Guinea.

The sale of two Sealands to the Christian and Missionary Alliance of America is a story worth the telling of the faith and courage of one man. This Alliance, which obtained substantial funds from its many members, needed the Sealand to transport missionaries and equipment to the head-hunters in the jungle hills of New Guinea, to convert them to Christianity. The location of its Mission there necessitated landing and taking off the Sealand from a narrow, fast flowing river, with steep overhanging banks and with a bend in it halfway along the take-off path. Moreover the weather over the mountains where the Mission was located could be very bad. The missionary prepared to undertake this extremely hazardous flying task was the Reverend Lewis who, according to our test pilots who had to fly with him, was a poor pilot and moreover had almost no experience on flying boats. Nevertheless Rev. Lewis, seemingly unaware of his doubtful ability as a seaplane pilot, pressed on with the project.

The first Sealand was dismantled and transported by sea to New Guinea where engineers from Shorts reassembled it and maintained it for a whole month of successful flying operations in those dangerous and difficult conditions. It was reported by the Alliance, our customer, that the head-hunters and their families were converted to Christianity in droves by their wonderment at this marvellous means of transport, so much better than a canoe! It was not to last though, and, as no surprise to our test pilots, the intrepid and courageous Rev. Lewis crashed on taking off from the river, but fortunately without killing himself or any of his naked passengers.

Despite this disaster and shortly after my joining the sales office at Shorts, two Trustees of the Alliance and Rev. Lewis arrived to take delivery of their second Sealand. Having paid for the aircraft and following the inevitable exchange of boring speeches (Ulstermen do so love making a speech) the Trustees returned to America leaving Rev. Lewis on his own in Belfast, where he intended to stay for a few days to watch while his second Sealand was being prepared for transport by sea. It seemed to me that the management treated Rev. Lewis rather casually; they could for instance easily have put him up at Rathmoyle, the company VIP house. Instead they allocated the clerk Adlam to look after him generally and to help him find a hotel and so forth.

In any case I admired the man and, despite his serious and rather austere manner, I liked him. Nothing seemed to faze him; neither his own bad piloting and awful landings in the Sealand nor the lack of hospitality from Shorts and certainly not the dangerous prospect ahead of him in New Guinea. I told Saccie about it and, since we had a spare bedroom, she suggested that we invite him to stay with us for the two days of his visit. Reverend Mark Lewis was delighted to accept, and from the moment he stepped into our house and met the children, he seemed a different man. In appearance he looked to be nearly fifty years old, of medium height with a powerful-looking physique, black hair and moustache and, now in our home, his face and eyes were kindly and smiling at us and the children. He was a widower without children of his own.

We enjoyed his company and, since he had spent many years in the Far East, we were fascinated by the tales he told and the photographs he showed us of that part of the world, and particularly about the head-hunters of New Guinea and their lifestyle. He was a deeply religious man and so dedicated to the conversion of the native tribesmen of New Guinea to Christianity that he had learned to fly, since an aircraft would be the only means of regular transport to the jungle interior of the country. I once questioned him about whether these tribesmen would benefit from such conversion and he described vehemently to me the constant misery that their tribal customs imposed on the people and, once converted, the evident comparative happiness of their lives. His faith in the importance of his work out there and the courage of his determination to undertake truly awful risks for the purpose was impressive. Alas, and almost inevitably as it seemed, Mark Lewis crashed the second Sealand while flying over the mountains in bad weather to the river where the Mission was located. Neither he or any of his passengers survived.

Almost as soon as I had joined Hambrook's sales team, I had also commenced a correspondence course to qualify, I hoped in due course, as a company secretary. Not that I was particularly interested

A Desk Job with Shorts

in that type of job, but I felt that I must obtain some sort of professional qualification and status if I were to get onwards and upwards in business life and such a course would give me both legal and accounting knowledge at the highest level which would boost me in whatever I did. It would be a long period of learning to qualify, but I found the correspondence course to be very professional and so very much better in its teaching and organisation than the night-schools in Salisbury and Coventry had been. Also I was learning all the time from my office work and came to the conclusion that I could cope well and perhaps even rather better than the commercial managers above me, who were basically design engineers with no more commercial training than I had. Indeed, I had begun to correspond with the few potential customers we had and to meet them when they visited the factory. As a mere clerk, probably I was beginning to get a bit cocky and above myself.

Meantime, as regards my home and family life, it had become evident that I had overstepped myself in buying the modern house at Cloverhill Park. Typical of me, I had not thought ahead to realise that my wages for whatever desk job I was given would be a lot less than my salary as a pilot, and I found now that I could no longer afford the mortgage. Moreover my naturally careless attitude towards personal finance, inherited I suppose from a wartime disregard of money as having no importance, was no help either because we were living now beyond our means and particularly so with school fees looming. Cloverhill Park, which I had bought so impetuously, was undoubtedly an attractive modern house and Saccie had made a lovely garden for it, but typically it was not well built in that immediate post-war period and already there was damp in the ground-floor rooms. And so maybe we did quite well to sell it enabling us to buy for £1800 a comfortable house at Waverley Drive in Ballyholme, which was part of the seaside town and harbour of Bangor in County Down, about fifteen miles from my work in Belfast.

In fact, although we had done financially well out of the exchange of houses, there was much more room for us in Waverley Drive where the house of an older style provided a large kitchen-dining room, a big sitting room and three larger bedrooms. As usual I was very pleased with myself for my successful negotiations in the exchange of houses, which had resulted in a substantial reduction in the mortgage payments. And it had provided some capital for me to put on deposit with the bank. The only snag to our new house was that it had only a tiny garden in the front with just a concrete yard at the back, and how sadly therefore Saccie must have missed the beautiful garden she had created at the previous house. However, typical of her character, she accepted the need for the move, but she must have realised, after almost seven years, what an unthinking and impetuous husband she had married. Nevertheless, it seemed that she loved me regardless … and that for her (and me) was what mattered.

Our lives changed quite a lot after we moved to Waverley Drive. Soon after we had moved there, I was promoted as Assistant to the Company Secretary, Bill Woolmer, who was highly-regarded and had long experience in his job. The time had come to train someone as his successor for when he retired and, since it was known that I was working to qualify for the secretarial examinations, and moreover had shown some business aptitude during my time in the sales office, I was selected by the Chairman for the job and provided with a secretary and a small but smart office next to Woolmer. There followed a period of sometimes intense boredom as, for one example, we would engage in long and tedious negotiations with the Harbour Master's Board of Belfast for control of our aerodrome, hitherto part of the harbour. It never seemed to matter how long the Secretary's office might take before the conclusion of matters such as these. On the other hand, discussions with lawyers, architects and building contractors over proposals for new buildings on the aerodrome were more interesting and instructive.

I was earning a fairly decent salary again and, most important of all, learning a great deal from Bill Woolmer and the work he gave me about contract law, employment law, insurance, pensions and negotiation procedures with trade unions, all of which would stand me in good stead for the future. During this period, at home in the evenings, I was slogging away at the correspondence course for the secretarial qualification and after eighteen months managed to pass the intermediate examination papers, being rather more than the half-way stage of the qualification. All the subjects, particularly contract law interested me, and I didn't at all mind the work of learning them, with the exception of accountancy, which I loathed.

Living at Waverley Drive in Bangor, where people were much more relaxed and friendly than those in the Belfast suburb had been, we started to make many friends. I played squash in the senior team for the Craigavad Golf Club which had two squash courts and also played at the Crawfordsburn Country Club where we met all sorts of local people and enjoyed dinner and dancing with groups of them at week-ends. Saccie developed a particular friendship with Dorrie

A Desk Job with Shorts

Nesbit who, with her husband Hubert, lived in a somewhat larger house almost opposite to us, and our immediate neighbours Ron and Liz Irvine were also good friends.

Apart from squash, the other main sporting activities in that area of Ulster were golf and sailing and here I made another bad decision, although I didn't regret it until much later in life, when I opted for sailing rather than golf as my main sporting activity in the summer. Consequently, we joined the Royal Ulster Yacht Club, rather a posh outfit, and the much more actively-sailing Yacht Club at Ballyholme, where in due course I took part in dinghy racing twice a week. To start with I crewed for other members on their yachts, as I was advised that this was the only way to learn sailing, but quickly became bored with not being in charge of the thing and, anyway, I always reckoned that the best way to learn a new activity was to get on and do it. So I bought my own Enterprise dinghy for racing and later, a 20 ft yacht with a small cabin, for local cruising.

The purchase of this second yacht came about thus. At a large party of many club members held at the RUYC, I caught sight of a man at the far end of the crowded room who looked quite extraordinarily like a friend of mine, Buzz Aldwell, whom I had last seen as he was shot down in his Barracuda during an attack on a Japanese-held airfield in Sumatra, and I had watched from the cockpit of my Hellcat as his aircraft crashed into the jungle. He had been officially reported as killed in action since very few aircrew, even if they survived the crash, were likely to live for long after capture by the Japanese. Every gesture, every facial expression of this unknown man reminded me of Buzz Aldwell, whom I knew with absolute certainty to be dead. The man caught sight of me, as I made my way through the crowded room towards him, and his whole face lit up into a delighted smile of welcome. He was indeed Buzz Aldwell, and very much alive! But, to be alive at all, that tough young man somehow had survived nine months of ill treatment and torture at the hands of the Japanese, with their peculiar hatred of enemy aircrew. I would find that Buzz could never say a word about the appalling treatment he had suffered and I would only know about some of it from Elizabeth, his wife. They had only recently moved into the area and Buzz had started a small business selling boats and chandlery. And, of course, I liked the idea of helping him to make a start by buying a small yacht from him.

There was no justification for my buying the second boat, but I had some money in the bank after selling Cloverhill Park and, as would happen throughout my life, some irresponsible peculiarity in my character made it difficult for me to leave money in a bank. Earlier in our marriage, just after leaving the Navy, Saccie and I with our young family to feed had lived for over two years in real poverty, and yet had done so without falling into debt. So I knew only too well how to exercise strict control over my expenditure when necessary. Could it have been a reaction to that period of such strict restraint, which encouraged me now to spend money whenever it became available? Or was it entirely due to the careless attitude towards money which I had developed during the war, when it had been of absolutely no importance to me at all? Whether it was either of these two factors or a combination of them, it was hard luck on Saccie and my family who suffered as the result since, whenever the money was there, I had an irresistible inclination to spend it. Most normal men of my age would regard the accumulation of wealth as a main goal in life, but not I. Although, strangely enough, I would budget stringently with sums of money on behalf of Shorts, or any other company for whom I subsequently worked.

We went on a number of jaunts in the yacht and on the whole as a family we enjoyed them, especially later on when I kept the boat at a mooring in Strangford Lough where there were a variety of small islands, each one of them a bird sanctuary, to be visited for picnics ashore. The truth was that neither Saccie or Aza were too keen on the actual sailing but Saccie, bless her, was prepared to suffer the typical and dreadful discomfort of a small sailing boat both for my sake and for her pleasure in the bird life and surroundings of Strangford. Happily however, Jeremy liked sailing and enjoyed crewing with me, especially to regattas at other sailing clubs. He would put up with and usually giggle at my bossy shouting, the result so very often of too much booze taken at the club bar. Rather as with flying in my wartime days, if the weather was bad, I seemed unable to sail quietly and competently without the assistance of alcohol.

Jeremy was at Rockport School, a small private preparatory school of about ninety boys up to the age of thirteen, half of whom were day-boys. The school was on the route to my work in Belfast, and as the hours in my new job were entirely regular, I was able to take him in to school and fetch him on most days and, if not, some other parent working in Belfast would do so. I like to believe that Jeremy was happy there as a little boy of nearly nine years old at that time, although it was already apparent that he did not like organised school games such as football and cricket and would have much preferred to be at home quietly reading a book. Aza attended Glenlola, a private and popular school for girls which was in the local area of Bangor. She was a cheerful and vivacious little girl, with her hair in long pig-tails, who made friends easily with grown-ups and other children and also, according to the reports, she was doing well at school. Saccie and I were very proud of them both and took photographs of them; Jeremy in the dreary prep-school uniform, customary in those days, of grey shirt and tie with grey jacket and shorts, and Aza in dark blue pinafore dress with white shirt and school tie, and a little beret on top.

Our happiness at Waverley Drive at that time was reduced, gradually and progressively over many months, by a strange disease which Saccie contracted and which sapped her strength and vitality. She became in a state of half-sleep all through each day and was unable to enjoy all the pleasures of that period of childhood with the children. She tried so hard to force herself out for our usual walks with the children or for outings in the car but after months of this dreadful illness she had become almost immobile, capable of little more than lying quietly in a chair for most of each day. It was most desperately worrying, not just for me, but for Jeremy and Aza, who were so anxious about their Mum. In the earlier stages of the illness, my job had enabled me on most days to get home regularly and early enough to look after them, but as the mysterious illness continued, it was apparent that this manner of care for the children at their age was not good enough, particularly as the possibility was emerging that my job might change and involve constant travel. Consequently, after consulting with the Headmistress, I took Aza away from the day-school at Glenlola and sent her across the water, on her own, to stay with her grandparents, Popsie and Grampie as the children called them. As for poor Jeremy, I had to arrange for him to become a boarder at Rockport Preparatory School, which he hated as he so loved the quieter life at home.

After a period of this worsening situation, it was evident that the doctors were at a complete loss to diagnose and treat the illness. I insisted therefore that a top specialist be consulted and that Saccie be taken to hospital for examination. This was done and she came under the care of a Mr Jackson, head consultant of the County Down hospitals, who arranged for a whole series of examinations to take place in Bangor Hospital.

The first thing they found at the hospital was a large internal growth in her womb and this was operated upon immediately. I remember the shock and fright of seeing Saccie, looking so white and ill as she was wheeled out of the operating theatre, and my utter relief as she recovered normally in the ward afterwards. But it transpired that the removal of the growth had not cured the sleeping sickness; in fact it had nothing whatever to do with it. This weird sickness became a challenge to Mr Jackson the consultant, and to the hospital where Saccie consequently was retained for a month while every awful test imaginable was conducted on her. Saccie was extraordinarily cheerful under the circumstances, as she told me that some of these medical examinations were most unpleasant and painful, but she was stoical and happy enough to suffer them in the knowledge that so much trouble was being taken to diagnose this extraordinary illness and the lethargy it caused.

It was a month before there was some sort of breakthrough and Mr Jackson, normally rather a sombre chap but looking justifiably rather pleased with himself, allowed Saccie home for a trial period. Apparently, he had found she had a glandular disease, previously almost unknown, and he prescribed a miraculous drug in pill form, which Saccie had to take daily for the rest of her life. If she forgot to take the pill, then almost immediately she relapsed. The case of Saccie with her disease was featured in the *Lancet*, the medical journal famous for the announcement of new medical discoveries, and this must have been a well-deserved accolade for Mr Jackson. Within a month of her return home, the miracle of this cure enabled Saccie and me to go dancing together again and to take long walks and outings with the children. We were back to normal and it was nothing less than a miracle for all four of us.

CHAPTER NINE

Painting and Promotion

Christmas of 1956 was at the beginning of Saccie's awful illness and, because she made so little fuss, we her family initially assumed that she was just suffering a bad bout of 'flu, which made her not quite her normal self. Or rather, we just hoped secretly inside ourselves that her illness was something normal like 'flu, which we could all understand. Nevertheless, we prepared for Christmas and made or bought presents for each other, which we kept hidden away until the great day. It was our family tradition on Christmas Eve to place the principal presents like a pyramid on the floor near the tree and to hang small surprise presents on the tree or under it, and the children had enormous woolly stockings to rummage in at the crack of dawn, left by a rather tipsy Father Christmas. On the table nearby would be the colourful crèche made by Aza in an earlier year, with realistic figures constructed from cardboard and each one beautifully painted. My surprise present from Saccie that year was a small set of 'painting by numbers' as a kind of joke. But, joke or not, I had a go at using the oil paints anyway and became entranced with the way they could sometimes produce such astonishing effects, even in the hands of a complete amateur.

I might have been interested in painting or drawing earlier had I not been put off it at Harrow, where the Art Master, a bald little martinet of a man, had made us spend most of the voluntary art class learning a rather intricate form of handwriting, before eventually placing a pot of some sort on a tall pedestal for us to draw. Well, as a boy of fourteen, I had absolutely no interest whatsoever in trying to draw such a boring object, whereas, had he put up a model car or aeroplane for us to draw, that would have captured my interest. On my desk was this large foolscap page of thick drawing paper, which to my mind was just asking to be converted into a beautiful flying dart. And convert it I did, to send it flying swiftly and gracefully across the art room as soon as the master's back was turned. It was intended to arrive at the desk of another boy on the other side of the room, but the dart developed an unfortunate steep turn to the right and flew instead straight at the wretched pot and nearly knocked it off its pedestal. The Art Master turned in time to see what had happened and, that humourless little man, was so furious that he went straight to a cupboard, brought out a cane, bade me bend over and proceeded to give me six strokes on the bottom right there and then! After that, I never ever attended another art class anywhere. Now, twenty years later in 1956, how deeply I was regretting that silly decision made as a sulky schoolboy all those years earlier, because now I had a new longing to learn to draw and paint properly.

As soon as that Christmas was over I bought more paints, brushes, linen paper and some canvases and launched myself at learning to paint in oils. My first efforts were ludicrously awful, no better than any child of five could have done. But I kept hard at it and was helped by the particular circumstances of that time since, with Saccie's illness, we could not go out of the house on walks or outings often and, moreover, my work at Shorts as Assistant Secretary was not at all demanding (boring as hell to be honest), so that it didn't really matter much if I was tired each morning from lack of sleep, having painted late into each night. In that early stage, I had a lot of help from our neighbour, Ron Irvine, who was a keen artist, and from Saccie too, who had studied at art school and also inherited much artistic knowledge and ability from her grandfather. Thus, during the long period of Saccie's illness, I divided most of my time at home between studying for the secretarial examinations and painting, continuing the latter often until 2 a.m. in the morning.

I completed so many paintings and at such a rate that their quality was improving fast so that, later on and by the time Saccie had fully recovered, I was able to benefit from our family holidays in Ireland, where I was inspired by the beauty of the rugged seashores and countryside to produce reasonably good paintings. Indeed, I was persuaded by a well-known professional artist, Raymond Piper, to submit a painting to the Royal Ulster Academy annual exhibition. We arrived as a family at the opening of the exhibition to find that already a red dot had been stuck onto the seascape I had submitted and yet, so dim and ignorant were we, that we didn't even realise the significance of the dot. In fact, it was the first painting to be sold at the exhibition and at the price of twenty-one guineas, which was a reasonable sum at that time. However, my joy at this my first sale was diminished when I learned that the purchaser, a grand and imposing lady in a

Painting and Promotion 121

large hat, had bought it for the purpose of presenting it to an old people's home for the blind! Maybe she had reckoned that my somewhat over-enthusiastic style of *impasto* painting would enable them to 'feel' the waves on my marine painting, even if they couldn't see them. Anyway, the kudos of acceptance and sale of one of my paintings at the Royal Ulster Academy resulted in several more subsequent sales.

Meantime, back at work, things were beginning to go rather well for me. Our Chairman, Sir Matthew Slattery, decided that a new organisation was needed to deal with the sale of small aircraft. The amphibian Sealand aircraft had proved to be a busted flush, since we had sold no more than the first batch of twenty-five, but now there was a new aircraft from our design team which was appropriately called the Skyvan. It was a twin-engine, high-wing monoplane with a fuselage built like a box and capable of taking a payload, either of twelve passengers, or of awkward loads, such as a small car or a tractor. These could enter over the large rear door which, when let down, would enable small vehicles to be driven up into the body of the aircraft. The concept of the Skyvan was that it should be a rugged little commercial aircraft, capable of being flown from small airfields and difficult terrain in countries around the world and capable of carrying a wide variety of freight. It was a well-thought-out design with good possibilities and the first prototype flew well when, in due course, it commenced continuous test flights to obtain its Certificate of Airworthiness.

It was decided too that Shorts should undertake the design and marketing of business aircraft similar to those used so extensively by companies and private owners in America. But this type of general aviation, for which there was a huge market in America, was not so well-known in Europe and it would be sensible to test the market in the UK and on the Continent first before designing and starting any production, and thereby determine what size and type of aircraft would be best suited for these areas. Moreover, we needed to learn marketing skills and techniques from America where such aircraft were sold through dealers and main distributors in the same manner as cars were normally sold. With all this in mind, Shorts entered into a main distributorship agreement with the Beechcraft Corporation of America to cover the sale of their aircraft in the UK and would include responsibility for the maintenance and servicing after sale. Beechcraft was famous worldwide for its design and production of private and business aircraft of the highest quality and, in the world of private aviation, it was regarded as the equivalent of Rolls-Royce. Their aircraft ranged from small single engine aeroplanes such as the Musketeer, to twin-engine aircraft such as the Queenair able to carry up to eight passengers in first-class comfort over long distances.

A new Light Aircraft Division was formed which in due course would promote the sale and servicing of the Skyvan when it was ready and to operate the Beechcraft distributorship. Then, oh the blessed joy of it, I was offered the plum appointment as Commercial Manager of the Division. Although I was soon to take the final examinations to qualify as a Company Secretary, I thought to hell with the qualification since, in any case, I had learned some contract law, which interested me more, and was the main subject I would need for my future career in business. So I didn't hesitate a second to accept the offer of this exciting new job opportunity and I was happy to get shot of the rather tedious job as the Assistant Company Secretary, valuable as it had been for my learning curve.

At the same time a new Sales Manager, Doug Scoffham, was appointed and it was intended that he would operate mainly from our offices in the west end of London. Doug was an ex-wartime RAF pilot, a tall fine-looking man of imposing appearance with moustache and iron-grey hair and just the man to put some realistic sales experience and oomph into the hitherto flaccid sales organisation of Shorts. Shorts management had appointed a service manager for light aircraft and also a young pilot as our sales demonstration pilot. The latter was a civilian-trained pilot with some experience in a minor airline, which might have been adequate experience for our purpose, but he saw himself as a super salesman. It became evident that his loud and brash approach, suitable maybe for Beechcraft sales in America, tended to put off our potential British customers. Moreover, I was uneasy flying with him as my instinct, perhaps prompted by my long experience as a flying instructor, sensed that he was not all that confident in the air in bad weather. It was particularly unfortunate that this young man had been foisted on us because his argumentative manner made for unnecessary stress at a time when, with a new business to promote, our team needed to run smoothly together. Scoffham and I, after consultation with Hugh Conway, the new joint Managing Director of Shorts, arranged for him to be replaced with a more mature, quieter and experienced ex-airline pilot. This new pilot also understood that to sell expensive private aircraft in the UK calls for all the intensity of good salesmanship, but tempered with a quiet approach.

It quickly became clear to me that the main works at Belfast was the wrong location for the marketing of business aircraft. Such companies as had the financial means and the need to operate their own business aircraft would want a slick easily-available organisation for the servicing of their aircraft. They would expect comfortable offices, lounges and attractive surroundings at the departure and arrival point for their directors and top managers. It seemed obvious to me that our typically large, noisy and dirty production factory, with a grotty little reception office, hundreds of miles away on the edge of Belfast, was not quite what these people would want. Therefore, I negotiated and reached agreement for the rental of hangar space with appropriate servicing and office facilities at Gatwick, in easy reach from London. The problem now was to convince the members of my main Board at Shorts that, although the rental at Gatwick was very high, the facilities there were absolutely essential, if we were to be successful in the sale of business aircraft.

Sir Matthew Slattery had left Shorts to become Chairman of BOAC but, before he did so, he had arranged with the government shareholders of Shorts for the appointment of Hugh Conway who, with Bob Harvey, was to be joint Managing Director of the company. The general intention was that Conway would be responsible for design and sales at Shorts while Bob Harvey, as the other joint Managing Director, would continue to deal with factory production and general administration. Conway was a large man in every way; quite a young man, but his size, his enthusiasm and his ideas were all large and, above all, he had an easy manner with his working colleagues, whether they were at his level or junior. His arrival at Shorts could be described as not so much a new breeze blowing through the organisation, but more like a force eight gale. However, from my point of view, he arrived absolutely at the right time because he saw immediately the need for the Beechcraft business to move to Gatwick and supported the move so strongly that, within a month, we were operating our business from there.

I would learn from this that an important element in working one's way upward in any large-scale industrial complex is that one needs to come under the influence and patronage of one or other of the top directors in a company. In moving from the company secretarial job, for instance, I had in effect moved from under the influence of Bob Harvey and his administration to the patronage of Hugh Conway, who was in charge of sales. Or, to put it more bluntly, Harvey had been looking after me as one of his team, and now I had, so to speak, transferred my allegiance to Conway. The former was not best pleased and tended to be noticeably short with me whenever we met. But, nauseating as it may seem, this was the way it used to be in the individually competitive world of large industry and it was essential for me to latch on to the top senior man, whose influence was commensurate with the type of work I was doing.

After the move to Gatwick, where we kept almost a full range of Beechcraft in the large rented hangar ready for demonstration flights and, having now the benefit of the excellent new demonstration pilot, there began a very considerable improvement in aircraft sales. Moreover, during this period, interest in the Skyvan was developing, both in America and the Far East. There was too, a useful and quite lucrative contract for the delivery and servicing of military aircraft to Saudi Arabia. Having regard to all this gathering success, it was decided that a subsidiary company be formed with the name Short Bros Air Services Ltd, and I was absolutely delighted with the entirely unexpected appointment to its Board as a Director and Commercial Manager. A 'Company Director': there was magic in the very words! And I took a childish pleasure in writing them into my passport.

The Company Secretary job had been a very quiet but valuable learning period for me but, after I had been promoted to commercial manager of the Light Aircraft Division, my whole lifestyle at work and at home had to change. Although I worked on most days from my office in Belfast, I flew over to Gatwick almost every week, sometimes using the Queenair, which Shorts had bought for its own business use as well as for sales demonstration purposes. I also had to visit the network of dealers around the British Isles which, in company with Doug Scoffham, I had set up as the main means of aircraft sales, very much in the same pattern as car sales are effected. This amount of travelling would have made my working life difficult without Ruth, my middle-aged treasure of a secretary, who held the fort for me in Belfast where she managed my office and correspondence with complete competence. If my return was delayed, I could telephone her from Gatwick, or wherever, dictate the synopsis of what I wanted to say and rely on her to compose it into a decent letter, sign it on my behalf and send it off.

Occasionally, I would myself fly to an aerodrome to take a potential business passenger for a demonstration flight, but these were generally the smaller aircraft while our professional demonstration pilot would be engaged elsewhere demonstrating a larger type of Beechcraft. It was a good selling ploy for me to be flying

Painting and Promotion

the thing, especially later on when I became a director. However, I cut down on such flights after I was badly frightened by a near engine failure over a very cold, rough Irish Sea in bad weather when flying a Musketeer, the smallest of our range of Beechcraft. I looked down from the cabin at that horrible-looking waves below and realised that the little machine I was flying would never withstand the impact of a ditching in that sort of sea, as had the fighter aircraft I had previously ditched. This little commercial aircraft would inevitably break up as soon as it hit the water. Moreover, I would have no Mae-West or dinghy to keep me afloat, even if I could survive the impact of a ditching. How damned stupid and daft of me to take any flying risks at all at this stage of my life. However, my still-ticking brain realised the possibility of carburettor icing at that low temperature and, once I had found the switch for the device to heat the carburettor air intakes, the engine picked up power and I breathed again.

I resolved there and then to give up flying entirely. After all, I no longer had to fly, it was only a form of vanity and I had long ago ceased to get any pleasure from piloting an aircraft. Even though modern aircraft were now so very much safer, with their technical development and modern navigational aids, the truth was that I still disliked having to fly in the wretched things, and even more so if someone else was the pilot. But the job and vanity would keep me flying for a while yet.

Sales presentation shows of Beechcraft were put on at our own Sydenham aerodrome in Belfast and at aerodromes near major cities, such as Newcastle, Manchester and Glasgow. Arrangements for these shows, including radio and television coverage, were made mainly by our Public Relations department but our sales team, consisting of Scoffham, Robert Hayley the demonstration pilot, and me, led by Conway, had to do the selling. My job was to explain to heads of companies that a business aircraft was not just a prestige means of travel for the Chairman, but a business tool of communication with economic advantages for their company. Scoffham would then talk about the types of aircraft and their capability and, thereafter, Hayley would take potential buyers on flights using the full range of aircraft to demonstrate their comfort, safety and speed. Our sales and publicity teams also took part in the major international exhibitions at Farnborough, Paris and Hanover where we promoted the possibilities of our newly designed Skyvan and entertained in our caravan all those airline operators who, during the year, had expressed interest in this unusual little passenger-cum-freight aircraft. At such major international exhibitions as these, however, our top brass of the Chairman, Harvey, Conway, Keith-Lucas and Brooke-Smith would be more involved in promoting our research aircraft and the major project of the Belfast, a huge four-engine, military freight aircraft on which the future of Shorts might depend.

I visited the Beechcraft factory and offices in America on several occasions where I usually stayed at the home of one of the directors, as we got on well together while discussing matters to do with the distributorship. Twice I timed the visit to attend and watch the Beechcraft annual sales conference, which was an absolute hoot. The occasion was of immense importance to their salesmen, every one of whom as distributors and dealers from every part of America would be sure to attend, since the essence of it was the intense competition between them for the highest sales figures during the past year. The razzmattazz of the occasion and the arrangements for it were unbelievable to English eyes. A huge and highly-decorated hall was filled with salesmen seated in rows of chairs and, as each name was called out to receive a prize from the chairman on the stage, an orchestra would blare out music appropriate to the home area of the successful salesman, accompanied by enthusiastic and generous applause from all the other salesmen. Needless to say that I, as a sort of representative of the Shorts distributorship, did not feature at all since our sales figures were paltry compared to those of any of the American distributors. However, I had been received earlier quite graciously by 'Ma' Beechcraft, who was the widow of the founder of the company and was now the formidable Chairman, much feared by the other directors and employees of every rank, to whom every word of this awesomely-splendid old lady was law.

Nevertheless, as the first Beechcraft distributor in the UK, we were doing quite well financially and, at the same time, learning the business of design and marketing this type of aircraft. We had agreed a commission of 22% from the parent company of which we allowed 17% to our sub-dealers if they made a sale. The prices for the various types of Beechcraft ranged from around £30,000 up to £140,000 for the Queenair and so, with an average sale price of, say, £85,000, Shorts was knocking up a turnover in the region of half a million annually. Not a lot of profit in it after the costs of Gatwick and salaries, but not bad. While I was in America mainly on Beechcraft business, I was also in touch with those interested in our prototype Skyvan and it became apparent that there would have been so much more interest in the aircraft had it been powered by American engines rather than French turbo engines. A director of Garrett AiResearch made contact with me to urge that we transfer to an engine of his company, which was simpler than the French turbo and, in my opinion, appeared particularly suitable for the type of rugged operations envisaged for our little freighter aircraft. But Conway would not hear of it. He spoke French like a native and I often wondered whether this was a factor in sticking to his choice of the French engines. Years later, the Skyvan came to be powered by American engines and subsequently sold very well indeed world-wide.

In 1960, on a visit to Beechcraft, they mooted the idea that Shorts might establish a distributorship in Nigeria where, as they pointed out, the same sales organisation could be used to sell the Skyvan although, at that time, it was only flying as a first prototype.

The intention would be that Beechcraft would initiate the distributorship and then Shorts would take it on and manage it. Nigeria was booming with oil and, in such a fast-developing country, there should be good opportunities for the sale of both Beechcraft and Skyvan. Rather to my surprise, the Board at Shorts approved of the idea and authorised me to go ahead and combine with Beechcraft in making the arrangements. My partner in this venture would be Raymond Hartney, an ex-bomber pilot of the US Air Force during the war, and now a demonstration pilot for Beechcraft. A quiet, rather lugubrious sort of chap to be honest, but we got on well enough. While I was in America, we discussed the project together and agreed that the Baron would be the best aircraft for demonstration and for the long flight to Lagos. It was a powerful twin-engine, low-wing monoplane with racy good looks, capable of taking three passengers and with a particularly good single-engine performance in the event of failure by one. In due course, at Gatwick, the rear seats of a demonstration Baron aircraft were removed and replaced with a large extra fuel tank. We calculated that there would be sufficient fuel from all the tanks to take us across the longest part of the flight, across the Sahara from Morocco to Kano, the northernmost aerodrome in Nigeria, and I, for one, wanted to be quite certain that the engines wouldn't conk out over the Sahara for lack of fuel. I had been telling myself for some time now that I would give up flying, but this trip to Nigeria was unusual and really rather exciting; I would be a complete wimp to miss the opportunity of this last flight before I gave up. Also I was content for Raymond to be the boss man since he was much more conversant than I was with flight lane procedures and with the use of the Collins radio and navigation equipment, which was a miniature version of that used by the large airliners. Anyway, the aircraft belonged to Beechcraft, so I could hardly object.

Our first hop was to Bilbao before arriving at Casablanca where we fuelled the Baron to its maximum capacity to take off before dawn the next morning for Kano. We expected the flight to take ten hours and so had stocked the cabin with plenty of drinking water, a medical kit, sandwiches and a bucket for peeing into; anything more serious in the way of lavatorial needs would just have to be regarded as an unavoidable disaster. Although this would be a long flight, Raymond could have managed perfectly well on his own, especially as there was an automatic 'George' fitted, but at least taking it in turn to fly every two hours gave each of us the opportunity to navigate or have a brief kip. And it was a relief we did so because droning along over mostly sparse land was quite tiring. There was not much to look at. We flew at 8000 feet most of the way and underneath was often hazy with just a lot of sand and an occasional small group of dwellings to be seen. The journey was really rather boring and it reinforced the decision I had made, four years earlier, when I had rejected an approach from Aer Lingus to become one of their airline pilots. Marvellous pay, of course, and five days on and off duty, but a boring job as little more than a bus driver. Or so I thought then, but the time would come when, as I grew older and wiser, I was going to kick myself for having rejected the security of that lucrative and comparatively stress-free career as an airline pilot.

On arrival at Kano, we had a good night's sleep before the last stage of the journey to our destination at Lagos. We were met at Lagos aerodrome by our agents, who had been selected and appointed by Beechcraft. They were four Englishmen who, as agents, already represented a number of British and American companies of which the most successful was an air conditioning and cooling company, whose units were selling like ice creams throughout Nigeria at that time. Mike Grainger and his team of agents knew little about aircraft but that didn't matter; what was required of them was to introduce us to people of influence in the business community who might be interested in the purchase of Beechcraft or the Skyvan. We also expected Mike and his team to put us in touch with those Ministers and others in the Nigerian Government who might influence government orders for either of these aircraft, although creating interest in the Skyvan was the more important task from my point of view.

Replacement rear seats for the Baron had been air-freighted from America to Lagos and, as soon as these had been fitted and the Baron washed and polished, we were ready to start chatting up the potential customers and to give them demonstration flights. Mike and his agency which, if all went well, would handle the dealership and act for Shorts in Nigeria, had set up a number of people interested to discuss both the Skyvan and the range of Beechcraft aircraft. And so Raymond and I spent most of the next two weeks giving demonstration flights to wealthy people of Nigeria, some of whom had travelled from other parts of the country outside Lagos.

An amusing situation arose first of all, because Raymond wanted to see how I would demonstrate the Baron in flight. Fair enough, I thought, because it was after all our intention to learn from Beechcraft how to market and sell this type of aircraft. On my final approach to land, I couldn't help noticing that Raymond was fidgeting about and appeared to be uncomfortable. Eventually, he burst out with the question, 'Why the hell do you keep fiddling with the throttles, why can't you just keep a steady throttle setting?'

I realised then that his background of bringing heavy bombers into land on large airfields and mine of juggling a fighter aircraft onto the rising and falling deck of a small moving Aircraft Carrier, for which constant throttle adjustment was essential, made the difference between our landing styles. He was quite right, of course, and I adapted quickly to keeping more or less the same throttle setting on the approach, as would an airline pilot. With aircraft of this type like the Baron a few extra knots of airspeed wouldn't matter and, with a tricycle undercarriage, one simply drove the thing like a car onto the runway anyway.

In between flights in the Baron, I met and entertained in my hotel restaurant a couple of government ministers and a number of other Africans and Europeans, many of them in the building trade, to discuss the possibilities and advantages of the Skyvan. I was glad not to have spent too much time on the ministers because Mike, my silly ass of an agent, had got hold of the wrong chaps, whose responsibilities had nothing at all to do with aircraft procurement. I just hope he hadn't bribed them overmuch to meet and talk to me about Skyvan! There was some degree of interest from these meetings but nothing definite; I doubt if there was enough money about at that time in Nigeria, but I reckoned that I had laid positive seeds for potential future orders, when the financial boom in the country could be expected to develop.

I stayed in Lagos for two weeks and, in that time, managed to take two trips. One was for fun some hundred miles or so into the interior with Mike in his Landrover. He showed me two villages, each of them alongside a river and surrounded by jungle. These village scenes of huts and log-like fishing boats, with children swimming and running about playing, gave me some lovely and exciting ideas for future paintings.

For my second trip, Mike had given me the name of a man in the neighbouring country of Ghana who, he said, had expressed firm interest in the Skyvan. So I did a stupid thing. While Raymond went off on his turn for a fun trip, I flew the Baron with his agreement across to Accra, the capital city of Ghana, where I had arranged by telephone to meet this prospective customer. But I simply could not wait or be bothered to go through the procedure of obtaining a special visa for the visit as I had reckoned to arrive at Accra, meet the guy for lunch at the airport restaurant, and then beetle back to Lagos in the Baron later in the afternoon. It was a disastrous visit because I was stopped as soon as I presented my passport, which was immediately confiscated, and I was marched off between two large, uniformed policemen to stand in front of their Chief Inspector of Police, seated at a large desk in his office. He was an imposing-looking African, very smart, quite young and tall, as he stood up to harangue and question me on the reason for my visit. He reminded me that I had no visa and no prior permission to fly across Ghana or to land at the Accra airport. 'The days when British people like you could lord it over Africa are gone,' he said angrily, 'and you personally are going to learn now to respect the rules and regulations of Ghana, our country.' He told me that I would be kept in an airport room until my aircraft had been thoroughly examined and he was satisfied with my credentials and that I posed no threat to the country. He warned that this examination might take several hours or even several days, to be followed by a heavy penalty or imprisonment if anything suspicious was found. In the face of such anger and threats, my simple story of just taking off to fly across their border to meet a prospective customer appeared very lame. And I felt vulnerable and not a little frightened.

The two guards on either side of me (actually I never knew whether they were police or army), took me to a very small room further along the passage and I heard the door lock behind me. The furniture was simply a wooden bunk, a table and a chair and, thank goodness, a pee bucket which in my fright I badly needed. In reality, it was the equivalent of a prison cell and I spent two of the longest hours of my life in it before the door was opened by the guards, who escorted me out to my Beechcraft Baron, and handed back my passport. I had already paid for the aircraft to be refuelled and now, after asking permission humbly from the Control Tower, I taxied out to the runway and took off back to Lagos as fast as ever I could go. I really had been very foolish because Ghana, with the recent election of its new President Nkruma, had been going through a period of extreme political turmoil. I was highly relieved to get back in time for a good dinner and a bottle of wine at my hotel in Lagos.

A day or two later, I flew back to England and Ulster via a BOAC flight and was thankful to be back at home and to resume normal work. It had been a busted flush as a business trip as nothing of significance had been achieved. Salesmanship was never my line anyway and I was moderately content at having aroused interest in the Skyvan for possible future orders, which is mainly what I had intended to do. But it had all been a bit of fun when, as I would experience more and more in future, there was not much fun to be had in the grimly-competitive and pressurised world of large industry.

CHAPTER TEN

At Home

At home in Waverley Drive, at the time when I was still working at Shorts as the Assistant Company Secretary, it was my turn to become quite seriously ill. Saccie had only just recovered from her long illness when, during a walk with the family, I fell on the ground in a faint. Back at home in bed, our nice family doctor was unable to diagnose my very high temperature, loss of strength and fainting fit and called in another doctor for a second opinion. The upshot of their consultation was that I was ambulanced off to the hospital at Newtownards, where I was put into a single room and stayed there for six weeks. It was an urinary problem of some sort, cystitis I think they thought it to be, but all I knew was that I felt horribly ill and suffered fairly constant aching pain in my back. Looking back on it now and, having had no less than five kidney stones removed during subsequent years, I reckon now that it was just another such stone, or prune as I used to call them. Evidently I am prone to prunes, you might say.

Nevertheless, during those six weeks in hospital, there were some excitements for me.

The first was that I had to be stabbed in my bottom with a syringe every morning by an attractive red-haired nurse. The procedure was that I had to lie across the side of the bed with my pyjama trousers down while the nurse, always the same one, stabbed my bare bottom. I found this quite exciting at first but gradually, as my punctured cheeks became more and more sore from the morning stab, I came to dread it. In the afternoons, I was able to go up onto the roof of the hospital and lie out alone up there in the sun of that hot summer and my body became as brown as if I had spent those weeks in the south of France and, for a man in hospital, I must have looked absurdly healthy. Sometimes, when off duty, the red-haired nurse would join me on the roof to read her book or we would talk quietly together, mostly about her boy-friend problems. Something sexy would occasionally cross my mind – but I had no wish to take this friendship further, or to hurt Saccie in any way.

Every week some different medical test would be perpetrated on me. I think that the worst was one morning when a very young doctor bounced into the room, smiling most cheerfully, and carrying a sort of balloon with a thin rubber pipe coming out of it. 'Just going to do a little test on your bladder,' he announced, 'so please drop your trousers down and lie still on your back in the bed.' Whereupon he seized my penis and proceeded, although as gently as he could, to insert the long rubber tube into it. I almost hit the ceiling as I arched up with the agonising pain of it. I know now that the test is called cystoscopy, because I have just had one done in hospital here sixty years later and, although uncomfortable, it didn't hurt a bit. So at least something has changed for the better in the UK since those days.

During those six weeks of the hottest summer I have ever known in Ulster, Saccie visited me several times every week, having come all the way by bus from Bangor because she didn't drive at that time, accompanied often in the evenings by Jeremy and Aza. She was a bit off-hand with my red haired nurse at first but they were quite good friends by the time I was discharged. My boss at Shorts, Woolmer, insisted that I take a month's leave to recuperate, and so we took the car across the water to Swanage where Stuart, Saccie's father, had had a very nice house of local Purbeck stone built for his retirement.

The change in my type of work, when I started the new job as commercial manager, also prompted changes to our family lifestyle at home. For one thing, it was inevitable I was going to be away in England or abroad quite often and, more significantly, I was now earning quite a good salary. At our present home in Waverley Drive we all missed the availability of a nice garden and I reckoned we could afford to look around for another house. It need not be any bigger or grander, just so long as it had a decent garden for us all to enjoy. We found what we wanted in Groomsport Road, only about five hundred yards away, much the same size and style of house but with a good long garden at the back and a big wooden greenhouse, full of grapes and tomatoes and things, all of which delighted Saccie. So I bought it and we moved in.

Jeremy was now nearly eleven and Aza eight and the time had come to think again about their schooling. Aza seemed to be happy and settled at Glenlola, although the period during Saccie's illness, when she had been away staying with Grampie and Popsie at Swanage, had affected her classroom work, and her reports were not as good as before when she had been nearly top of her class. However, we reckoned that she was bright enough and would soon recover from the set-back of that temporary absence from school. She was cheerful and had lots of friends, which was the more important aspect for a girl of her age.

We were concerned about Jeremy. Well, it was I who was more concerned than Saccie. Jeremy was an unusually quiet boy who didn't like games such as football and cricket. For instance, he never just enjoyed kicking a football about with other boys on the nearby park area or any other activities of that sort, as I would have done. He loved reading and also could spend hours just peering at the ground intently watching ants and other insects. I understood that he didn't like organised ball games since, after all, neither did his Mother. But it seemed unusual to me, if not to Saccie, that he was so very quiet, especially in my presence. The truly awful thought percolated into my mind that he might be frightened of me. Could that be possible? The fact was that, in taking on this new job as commercial manager, I had bitten off rather more than I could at first chew. I had to function now for the first time as a business manager, making my own business decisions and fighting my corner in making them effective. Moreover, at the outset I had to deal with the unpleasant salesman-pilot, who was backed by the Beechcraft organisation to whom he seemed their ideal salesman. It was all too obvious that he very much wanted my job as manager. Hence, I was so stressed and worried with the fear of failure and the consequent loss of my job, that I may have been bad-tempered and nasty to my family at times when I came home. Saccie was marvellous in coping with me in that condition, but to the children I may have appeared as a fearful old ogre. All the more important then, during this period, were the annual holidays we so enjoyed together as a solitary family on the lonely beaches of the lovely west coast of Ireland.

Remembering how happy I had been as a boarder at Cottesmore, a really good preparatory school, I persuaded Saccie that boarding at a similar school could be what Jeremy needed to bring him out more. In consequence, we visited Headfort School located at Kells, half way down the eastern side of Ireland, where we met the Headmaster, Mr Wild, and some of his staff. The school had taken over the beautiful house and grounds of the Headfort family some ten years earlier and had established a good reputation, resulting in attendance of about one hundred and sixty boarding boys between the ages of eight and thirteen. I have made so many cock-up decisions in my life that it is nice to record that this time it seemed that I had done right in sending Jeremy to Headfort. He developed well at the school, gaining confidence and establishing many friendships with the other boys, which he kept for most of his life. He never came to enjoy organised games but there were other things for him to do, such as sailing and swimming in the large lake near Headfort and enjoying the gardens and grounds of the house. I had been worried that, as a day-boy at Rockport, he had been so very well behaved and quiet but now, boarding at Headfort, he became cheerful and sufficiently naughty (I was relieved to learn) that he had to have his bottom stung with a gym shoe a couple of times.

In the early terms, we would allocate a whole Sunday to taking Jeremy out for the day accompanied by either one or two of his special friends. The pattern of these visits was nearly always the same; Saccie and I would arrive on the previous Saturday evening at the Headfort Hotel in the village where a boozy party would take place with other parents, who were also staying at the hotel. The next morning, slightly hung-over, we must not arrive at the school any later than 9 a.m. when Jeremy, with his friend or friends, would be hopping about impatiently waiting for us. Lunch was nearly always at the horribly expensive airport restaurant outside Dublin and, in the afternoon, we sometimes broke the school rules to take them to the cinema in Dublin, where we would invariably see other parents with their boys. After returning the tired boys back to school, we had to make our own weary way back, across the Irish border, to Bangor and home. I came to realise that this expensive day out was, in effect, adding another twenty-five pounds onto the school fees each term and I could not afford it. Subsequently, we tried driving down to Headfort early on the Sunday morning and having a picnic lunch with Jeremy on his own without his friends. Aza, who had usually been left behind with our friends in Bangor on these jaunts because we couldn't afford to take her to the hotel, came with us on these picnics and her close friendship with Jeremy helped to overcome his disappointment and to give him a happy day out.

Another story about Jeremy at Headfort is more about me really. I had been invited to play cricket for the Fathers against the school first eleven and, although Jeremy wasn't playing of course, I think he was rather pleased that I was on the Fathers' team and had told all his schoolfriends that his Dad could be expected to score lots of runs. And, as for me, I had no doubt at all that I would fulfil his expectations. It was a hot afternoon in the lovely environment of the cricket ground and we were sitting amongst the other families in deckchairs, under the shade of the trees, while enjoying a picnic tea of strawberries and cream. The boys' team had made a good score and the opening batsmen for the Fathers were scoring well too, when I murmured to Jeremy, Saccie and Aza that I would wander over to the scorer to check at what number I would be batting, with the expectation that I would be in at number five. By the time I arrived at the scorer's hut, two Fathers had suddenly been bowled out and I had to rush to put on a pair of pads and make myself ready as I was in next. The next idiot Father was out almost immediately and now it was up to me to go in to bat and stop the rot. I arrived at the crease, pedantically took careful guard from the umpire at the other end, looked slowly and carefully round to note the position of the opposing fielders and confidently faced the bowler ready for his first ball at me. This wretched, good-looking blond boy of about thirteen, tall for his age, took a long run and hurtled a perfect length ball at me which whistled between my pad and bat and knocked my middle stump flying. Out first ball! I made a pitiful little grimace of a sporting smile and thought, as I walked back to the scorer's hut, of how I would love to throttle that beastly boy who had bowled me out so easily. So I walked slowly back to where my family was sitting, all three still chatting as I had left them, and Jeremy looked up at me and asked, 'When will you be going in to bat, Dad?'

This last story which I am writing about Jeremy at Headfort is the most significant of all for me, since it tells of his astonishing nerve and courage as an eleven year old boy. Near to Headfort there is a large lake about a mile long, and half a mile across. A boat was available for use by the boys under the supervision of a young master, Mr Macaleese, who normally taught English lessons but who also took responsibility for the sailing activities. In fact, as it transpired, this young man had very little sailing experience but he was enthusiastic in his relationship with the pupils and so, when asked to take on the responsibility, agreed to supervise and care for those boys who were interested in sailing. This arrangement was satisfactory normally, but the reality is that he had not the experience to recognise dangerous weather conditions. Thus, one afternoon it was arranged that he would take three boys, including Jeremy, out sailing on the lake in the school dinghy, which was in fact a solid, clinker built open fishing boat, about sixteen feet long, with gaffe-rig sails. It was a good safe boat, therefore, able to take up to four people. When Macaleese, Jeremy and the other two boys arrived that afternoon at the little wooden pier where the boat was tied, the weather conditions were ominous with dark clouds and increasingly high wind. But Mr Macaleese was apparently pressing on regardless and, when Jeremy ventured to suggest rather too timidly that perhaps it was not a suitable day for sailing, Macaleese looked up at the darkening sky and said, 'Oh yes, it doesn't look too good does it, so we will just sail ten minutes close to the shore, to give us some experience in this stronger wind, before we come straight back to the pier.'

Easier said than done, however, because by the time they had got the old gaffe sail up, having tried and failed to reef it down, the wind had become very much stronger and, no sooner had they let go from the pier, than the boat was driven fast by the force of the wind out towards the middle of the lake. Macaleese tried to go about, but the boat keeled over alarmingly and would not be turned into that strong gusting wind and driving rain. At this point Jeremy, who had amassed quite a lot of earlier experience while sailing with his Dad, shouted that they ought to take the main sail down quickly and use just the small jib sail to get them to the nearest shore. Macaleese, foolish man, took no notice of this sensible and correct advice from an eleven-year old boy and, the stupidest of all things, attempted to gybe or wear round the other way. Fortunately he had warned the boys to keep their heads down, otherwise the mainsail and its boom, which rocketed round with the full force of the gale, would have cracked their heads off. Tough little boat though it was, it could not stand up to that by now ferocious wind and keeled right over as the full force hit the mainsail and deposited all the three boys and the schoolmaster into the lake as it capsized. The nearest shore was still the pier from whence they had come and the schoolmaster shouted to the boys that they were to swim with him to this nearest shore. But it was some hundred yards or more back and receding fast as the wind and waves were pushing the boat and the boys further away from it. Jeremy, who was a good swimmer and better than the other two boys, just knew it was the wrong decision; they would never make it back to the pier against the high waves and wind against them from that direction. 'No,' he shouted, 'we must all stay with the boat, keep hold of it and push it along with the wind and waves, swimming with our legs to help push!'

To the other two boys this must have seemed madness because the further shore was several hundred yards away, but fortunately Macaleese recognised the good sense of it and, 'He's right,' he shouted. 'Everybody get round to the windward side of the boat, hold onto it and swim with it.' The gunwale on the upper side of the boat was high enough out of the water for the wind to catch it and force the capsized boat along and Jeremy, seeing this, swam round to the bow to turn the hull further at a right angle to the wind. Some fifty minutes later the boat ground against the shore and they could all stand up and stagger, wet and shivering with cold, towards the nearest house alongside the lake, where Macaleese was able to obtain help (hot drinks was the priority) and phone for transport back to school.

How do I know so much detail of this story, you may well ask? Well, not much from Jeremy, I have to answer, except for his description of the boat. But the first I knew of this adventure was the long closely handwritten letter I received from Mr Macaleese in which he described the whole incident in detail and acknowledged that, in his opinion, he and the two other boys owed their lives to Jeremy and his cool-headed courage. Saccie and I were immensely chuffed with such a letter and so proud of Jeremy. I still am. Actually, on a later occasion, I met Ginger, one of the two other boys, who confirmed the whole story to me. And there was a kind letter from the Headmaster, Mr Wild, about it also.

I returned home to Groomsport Road from work one evening to find Saccie very worried about her father, Stuart Leaman. When she had telephoned him as she usually did every month, he had been incomprehensible with difficulty in speaking. Saccie told me that she had already booked an early morning flight to London for the next day and intended to travel down to Swanage to find out what was the matter with him. Her mother, Alice, never used or answered a telephone. The following evening, Saccie phoned from Swanage to give me the bad news that her father had suffered a stroke and she would have to stay while she sorted out what was to be done. Apparently the old boy had collapsed while relaying a path in the garden at his wife's insistence, having already spent an hour mowing the lawns. It never seemed to occur to the daft woman that Stuart was too old now for so much physical effort.

There followed three weeks of hard and hectic work for Saccie in Swanage where Stuart, under her care and with the opportunity of complete rest, recovered well enough to travel, although his left leg was semi-paralysed and his speech remained slurred.

Saccie had been able to convince her parents that the only answer was for them to sell their house, which overlooked Swanage, and move to Bangor where we could look after them. Well, there really was no alternative, as I couldn't leave my job in Ulster. The most awkward problem, that of selling their house within a reasonable time period, resolved itself in the most absurd and ridiculous manner. Alice, that daft old lady, made such a fuss about strangers, potential buyers, looking over her house and seeing all her private bits and pieces of furniture, pictures and photos, that Stuart, who should have had more sense, agreed to sell that lovely house, plus much of the furniture, at factually half the proper price to a retired ex-member of his comparatively junior staff from Salisbury. They would both come to regret this idiotic decision when they were short of money in later years but, right then, it made an early move for them to Bangor possible.

In the meantime, as there was no spare room at Groomsport Road, I had booked a nice bedroom for them on the ground floor at the Ballyholme Hotel, which was a pleasant little hotel near our house. This would give them time to settle in and to look for a bungalow, or whatever, to buy in the area. Saccie, still at Swanage, hired a large car with chauffeur to take them all with their luggage to Heathrow and made special arrangements with the airline for both Stuart and Alice to have special care and wheelchairs to take them on and off the aircraft for the flight to Belfast. She also arranged for their remaining furniture to be collected and stored until they were ready to move. What a kerfuffle it all was, but Saccie made all the arrangements without fuss and with total competence. Surprisingly, because it must have been a hugely traumatic time for such elderly people, both of Saccie's parents coped well with this upheaval of their lives. I think that Stuart must have been so grateful that Saccie was there to organise them and the relief enabled him to begin a good recovery from his stroke.

By this time in our lives, I had bought a small second car for Saccie to drive and this proved to be essential in looking after her parents and driving them around the area to find a suitable new home for them in Ballyholme. This search seemed to go on forever as none of the bungalows they looked at seemed to be what they wanted. Eventually, Stuart came up with a most surprising suggestion.

One of the properties which Stuart and Alice had been to view with Saccie was a huge and very attractive-looking bungalow, right on the sea front at Ballyholme overlooking the beach itself, and having lovely gardens both at the back and front of it which were surrounded by a white wall about five feet high. Stuart's idea was that I should sell our house at Groomsport Road and that he and I should then share the cost of purchasing this large very upmarket-looking property which, in fact, was more of a house than a bungalow since it had a partial second floor. When I went to look at the so-called bungalow with Saccie, the idea seemed entirely sensible, provided that Stuart and we between us could afford the price. It was a huge place, with a complete 'Granny Annex' of bedroom, sitting room, bathroom and kitchen and all of these of a decent size to accommodate Stuart and Alice very comfortably. I think that the bungalow may have been used as a holiday home for a large and wealthy family because, including the granny annex, it had nine bedrooms and four bathrooms, three living rooms and, of course two kitchens. In addition to all this, it had a double garage, a boathouse and a sort of tower sticking up on one side which could be used as a studio, all this and a full-length enclosed glass patio overlooking the sea. I was entranced with Stuart's idea since the property was very upmarket and posh, well beyond my normal dreams, and would be a beautiful home for us all to live in, enabling Saccie and me more easily to look after her elderly parents. So I arranged the sale of the Groomsport house and, between us, Stuart and I knocked up the purchase price of £7,000 and bought it. House prices in Ulster were always much lower than on the mainland, but it is astonishing now to recall that in the year 1960 one could buy such a property in the UK for so little money.

Of course the house turned out not to be perfect, but then nothing ever is. There was no central heating and the only means of combating the almost constant cold wind from off the sea just fifty yards away from the front of the house were paltry little electric fires. Except for Stuart and Alice in their smaller annex, my family spent the winter evenings huddled and frozen around an electric fire in the smaller living room next to the comparative warmth of the kitchen. We never used the large living room, in which we put our smarter furniture, except in the height of summer for an occasional party. Jeremy and Aza had the choice of five bedrooms and two bathrooms on the upper floor, while Saccie and I had a large, en-suite (as I believe is the correct description) bedroom, bathroom and dressing room on the ground floor, and all the rooms, up or downstairs, were equally freezing.

Jeremy was coming up to his thirteenth birthday and the time had come to do something positive about the next stage of schooling for him, and not just to be thinking about it, as we had been doing. In spite of my experience of working and mixing with all classes of people, which should have given me a broad outlook on education, it simply never entered my mind to have Jeremy educated at anything other than a private school. Somehow my mind had become bunged up with the certainty that I would not be fulfilling my responsibility to Jeremy unless I paid for his education. So certain was I about this, that I never looked at the first-class education immediately available for him on our doorstep at the Bangor Grammar school, which had a superb academic reputation. I can see so easily now in hindsight that it would have been ideal for Jeremy, who loved home life with his family and wanted nothing more than to read and work quietly at home. What a clot I was.

Instead, without so much as a glance at the first-class local school, I set about finding a suitable 'Public School' for Jeremy, accompanied by Saccie, whose reluctance about the whole project I feigned not to notice. There were a number of factors involved in choosing a school; firstly that I did not have much income to apply towards a good private education for Jeremy, and paying the fares to send him across the water to England and back for three school terms a year would be even more difficult. Secondly, although he had enjoyed his time at Headfort, his work in class had not been good and he was unlikely to pass the entrance exams for any of the better schools in England. Well, that left only two possibilities, really, either Campbell College in Belfast or St Columba's College, a Protestant boarding school for boys just outside Dublin. I had an old-fashioned and absurd opinion that life at a boarding school for boys at the later stages of their schooling, however unpleasant it might be, was good for a boy's strength of character and independence and, to be fair, this had proved to be so for Jeremy while boarding at Headfort. But I ruled out Campbell College because for a boy to be boarding at a school only a few miles from his home seemed pointless and unfair. Moreover, Jeremy's academic standard might not be good enough to pass their high standard of entrance exam, and I didn't want him to suffer failure. This left St Columba's College as the best possibility.

In due course, therefore, Saccie and I motored down to Dublin to have a look at the school and to meet the Headmaster, Dr. Argyle, who called himself 'The Warden.' He was a tall, well-built and most imposing-looking man of about fifty with a mane of white hair, who greeted us affably enough in the sitting room of his large Georgian house, and I gathered that he was the owner, as well as Headmaster, of this private school. In the years to come, as the Bursar of probably the largest independent school in the UK, I would know just about everything there is to know about independent schools but, at that time, I hadn't a clue about what to look for or what questions to ask before sending my son to be educated at such a place. We learned that there were five boarding houses for a total of about 300 boys in the school, of which some forty were day boys from Dublin. These boarding houses and the classrooms were situated in buildings around the main house, with the playing fields and the farm just outside. It was therefore quite a big complex.

True to form at minor private schools, we were shown the best and recently modernised boarding house and, although we didn't meet the housemaster, we were quite impressed with the standard of the facilities and the dormitory accommodation. Aware of Jeremy's dislike of organised games, I made a point of asking what other activities were provided for the boys and we were shown quite an interesting radio and electrical workshop, a small carpentry workshop and then an art studio, but Argyle was keen also to emphasize the value of the school farm as an additional interest for the boys. It all seemed rather good value and Saccie, who had preferred the possibility of the school in Belfast, was reassured.

There were two other factors about the school which clinched my choice of it.

The first was a government subsidy of the fees (not a lot, but helpful) for those boys who undertook to learn Irish, and this was no problem as Jeremy was keen to do so. But by far the more important factor was the almost certain *entrée* which Jeremy would have from the school into Trinity College Dublin. I knew that Jeremy was no fool, but he was a dreamer and, unless particularly interested in a subject, more than a little lazy. I knew that it was going to be very difficult indeed to get him into a university anywhere in the UK, when the time came for his examinations. But, coming from the local St. Columba's College, Jeremy could be reasonably sure of being accepted by Trinity in due course, so long as he didn't make a complete cock of the examinations. I was obsessively concerned about this last factor, because I didn't want Jeremy ever to suffer the same huge disadvantage, as I had in my life, of having no qualifications of any sort such as a university degree and thus having constantly to compete against others who had been able to qualify and train for a profession. An added consideration in favour of Columba's was that a number of Jeremy's friends from Headfort would be going there in the same September term.

And so Jeremy entered St Columba's College at the age of thirteen and a half. I wanted so much to take him down for his first term and to see him settled in but I could not avoid business in England and so

Saccie drove her car to Dublin with Jeremy, who was very nervous indeed of the unknown life ahead of him at a new boarding school, and settled him into his dormitory. While doing so, she established a very good and lasting friendship with the mother of another new boy, who was to be in the next bed. He was Antony Patey and he and Jeremy were to have a friendship lasting all their lives. On arrival at the school, Saccie found that Jeremy had been allocated to quite a different boarding house than the modernised one that she and I had been shown on our initial visit (a procedural cheating which was par for the course at minor private schools). The green slime on dripping wet walls in the changing room and lavatories was highly unpleasant, but it would not have been sensible for Saccie to make a fuss at that stage without making life difficult for Jeremy. Moreover, as regards the voluntary school activities, there were no masters able to take voluntary classes for the radio or carpentry workshops, so that both of these facilities were in reality non-existent. The farm was real but, being essential for the provision of vegetables and meat for school meals, was run professionally and such boys as worked on it did little more than dig potatoes. To be fair, my eventual impression was that the quality of teaching at Columba's was quite good but, as it would appear from his end of term reports, Jeremy didn't take sufficient interest in any subjects other than biology, English and Irish; the latter being of little practical use to him.

Rugby was the main sporting activity at Columba's during winter, with hockey and cricket during summer, all of which Jeremy absolutely loathed. The only pleasure he derived from having to play any of them was by his development of a powerful whistle through his teeth, which sounded uncannily and precisely like a referee's whistle. Apparently, as I learned later, he could cause absolute havoc at rugby games, since none of the players could tell the difference between his whistle and that of the referee. However, Jeremy sensed his Father's disappointment that he was no games player and, for love of his Dad, took up boxing which he most certainly didn't want to do either but, after all, it did not require any ability to hit or catch a ball and was just a matter of being bashed and bashing back. And so, bless him, he had the guts to be good at it and was selected for the boxing team as a light-middleweight, and won three of his five fights for the school in his first year at this so-called sport.

Jeremy's reward for taking up boxing came in the form of a great and long-lasting friendship with Chris Pearson, a huge young man and the heavyweight captain of the boxing team. On the occasion of an unauthorised afternoon visit to Dublin, Jeremy was attacked by a gang of four teenagers and, on his return to school with his face battered, Chris was so angry he insisted on visiting the same area and dealing with the gang. Accordingly, a couple of days later, the powerful Chris, wielding a heavy stick and with Jeremy in support, returned to Dublin where they found and confronted the same gang. The pair of them were altogether too much of a handful for the gang, which was only too glad to beat a bloodied retreat. In later years, Chris was best man at Jeremy's wedding and the two of them never lost contact even though eventually Chris, as a successful doctor, emigrated to America. Thinking back on Jeremy's time at both Headfort and Columba's, I guess that the most significant aspect was his emerging ability to make firm and lasting friendships in life. Indeed, he may have been a poor and rather lazy scholar but, if a man is judged by the strength of his friendships and the quality of his friends then ... he did all right.

Meantime, as Jeremy was adapting to boarding school life at Columba's, so Aza was still at Glenlola school in Ballyholme ... but only just! There was a problem with the standard of her work in class, and I believe that it stemmed from the period of two months when, because Saccie had been so ill, she had stayed with the grandparents in Swanage when I had been unable to cope adequately both with work and with looking after the children. Up until then, Aza had been doing well at school and had been near the top of her class in most subjects but, after her short absence from school, she was failing to keep up with the other girls, except in art and games at both of which she excelled. There were all sorts of excuses, including a minor bout of glandular fever, but the probable truth is that in terms of general character Aza liked to be at the top and, once there, would always strive to stay there, but she was not so strong at competing and forcing her way up from the bottom of a class. Anyway, as parents, we were shocked to receive a letter from the Headmistress to suggest, if that is the right word, that Aza would do better at some other school because she was unable to attain the standard of class work required at Glenlola. It was, in effect, a kindly worded expulsion from the school. I was furious and frightened for the sake of Aza's future, so I fired back a pompous letter to the effect that it was the school which had the responsibility to bring Aza back up to her earlier standard, and it was the school which had failed, rather than the girl. This resulted in an interview with the Headmistress who reluctantly

At Home 145

agreed that Aza could remain at Glenlola for another term, on probation so to speak, to see if she could improve.

Well, this was a relief from the dreaded alternative of apparent expulsion and, moreover, might fit in with Aza's very recently expressed desire to attend a boarding school. She was particularly keen on Methodist College near Belfast (known as Methody), a co-education boarding and day school justly famous for the high standard of its boys' rugby. Being normal parents, we were not as totally half-baked and foolish as our children liked to regard us, and so we were aware that Aza, coming up to age thirteen at the time, was much more interested in the prospect of co-education with boys than with the need to settle down to a new start at work. It could be, I thought naively, that competing with boys in class might act as a spur for her to work harder. How little I knew in those days about education because, of course, inevitably the presence of boys had the opposite effect. At first, because she made friends easily with either sex, Aza seemed happy at Methody and appeared to find the life of a boarder to be rather fun, but it all too soon began to pall and we received telephone calls during each week from this anxious little voice asking if it could come home for the week-end. This was the inevitable result, in my view, of attending a boarding school so near to home.

There were some occasional bright spots among Aza's school reports from Methody, but clearly there was not going to be some dramatic break through into the upper echelons of the class, and this worried Saccie and me because we both reckoned she was bright and intelligent enough to do so much better. Saccie I know did her best to encourage Aza at her work and it was my job to do something about the situation, such as maybe finding another school for her. In particular, we both felt that something ought to be done about Aza's undoubtedly high artistic ability but, from our enquiries, there was no school of art for her to attend. Moreover, at that time, I was intensely involved in getting to grips with an entirely new type of job as commercial manager, and having to work hard and learning as I worked. And so Aza would have to press on at Methody, much as she now apparently disliked it, even though she had asked to go there.

Happiness is a feeling which, in my opinion, people rarely recognise at the time and only do so when they look back upon it. Thus I believe that, with Saccie as the foundation, we were on the whole a happy family, particularly at that time. Jeremy was coping with his life during each term at Columba's and Aza was soldering on more as a day-girl than a boarder with her friends both at Ballyholme and at Methody, and all four of us enjoying life together in the holiday periods, which were often spent caravanning in the south of Ireland. Life was particularly good to me personally because, as well as the pleasure my family gave me, I was getting to grips with my job and was having the rare experience in my lifetime of enjoying my work. In addition, my playtime as a member of two yacht clubs, two squash clubs, a golf club and attending frequent dinner-dances and other social occasions with Saccie was … well, about as good as it can get. As a natural-born worrier, however, I didn't entirely recognise or realise our happy state at the time.

Then came the shock of a telephone call from Camilla, my niece, to say that my sister Phoebe had committed suicide. I don't know but I suspect her suicide was for two reasons; massive debts, mainly to all those dress shops in London, without any possibility of paying them off; secondly and more pertinently, she may have believed that her youth and attractiveness to men were failing, and that in particular she could not bear.

I had known Phoebe so well, when we were younger, as a wilful attractive girl who had the gift of being able to bring fun and excitement into the lives of those around her. Her marriage to Ward-Thompson had been a good one. She had loved him profoundly. He in turn adored her, and was justly proud of this vivacious girl who became his wife and mother of his two children. Ward was fun to be with but a strong character and Phoebe, with him as a partner, would have led a happy life. But he was killed in 1941 while undertaking a secret and dangerous task in a naval aircraft.

Ward's death was enormously bad luck and devastating for Phoebe, as it was for so very many other war widows of aircrew in the Fleet Air Arm. They all had to cope somehow, but it seems that Phoebe found it more difficult than most. Her way of doing so at first was to remain with the Navy at Arbroath and continue in the company of those who had been Ward's peers. She particularly liked Pat Humphreys, who was the holder of the George Cross for outstanding valour. They became engaged but, shortly before their marriage, Pat too was killed in action.

I came on the scene when my squadron was posted to the Air Station at Donibristle, not far from Arbroath, prior to joining another Aircraft Carrier, HMS *Illustrious*. I telephoned Phoebe who was glad to stay at a small hotel near Donibristle and to join me and the other pilots in my squadron at our various parties. She met Johnnie Lowder, a new pilot in our squadron who, during the course of the next three years of war, became one of our best fighter pilots. Johnnie, with his good looks and his careless outlook and wildness, appealed to Phoebe immediately. And she attracted him, perhaps for the same reasons. At the end of the war, we came back from the Pacific and Phoebe and Johnnie were married. It was a disastrous marriage. They both tended to be financially irresponsible and Johnnie, having left the Navy, tried to promote and run various businesses of his own but, having neither knowledge or experience of business, he failed in them all. They ran into further debt despite, by this time, Phoebe's legacy from Father.

After divorce from Johnnie, Phoebe met and married Michael Rouse, ex-army and an attractive and initially wealthy man with a nice mews house in the west end of London. When he worked, which he rarely did in the early period of the marriage, he was an impresario who promoted theatre entertainments in the UK with well-known, indeed famous, singers, music groups and comedians. As his wealth gradually ran out, he had to work harder at these promotions which, in their very nature, were financially rather risky.

During those earlier years of her third marriage, I had met Phoebe a number of times, usually without Saccie, when I was on business in London. Her lifestyle seemed to be one of dressing for the theatre or parties and for meeting friends at pubs and restaurants. I urged her to write, remembering her early efforts to do so as a girl, or indeed to do something, anything, which would give her some focus in life, now that her children were teenagers.

I regret that our last meeting at her flat in London was a bitter and sad one. I had called in unexpectedly and became very angry to find her just about to leave for the Bahamas, for the second time apparently, where some man was waiting for her. Phoebe told me, quite bluntly, she meant to stay with this 'wonderful' man for as long as he would have her and she was sorry, but it was just bad luck on Michael and the children. I was utterly shocked by her attitude. I could not understand how Phoebe, with a foundation and background to her life of four fine, real men of substance and character, Ward, Pat, Johnnie and Michael, could now descend to cohabiting with a total bounder. For that old-fashioned, Edwardian word bounder was the only one, I told her, that I could think of to describe and fit someone whose intention was to seduce a middle-aged married woman away from her husband and family for the sake of a sexual relationship, a relationship which most probably would be financed by her and her husband's money. In the event, I believe that she only stayed with the man for six months. The money had run out or, to put it perhaps more accurately, Michael's money had run out.

As her young brother, I loved Phoebe. And I did so and admired her all through our childhood and the teenage years and through the war years. But gradually in her later years she appeared to me as a pathetic and sad figure. And I could do nothing about it. Heaven knows and this biography will show that I made enough cock-ups in my own life but always I had Heather, my much-loved Saccie, to rely on and to hold me. Phoebe lost Ward, her support, too early.

Apart from the sudden shock of Phoebe's death, my life and that of my family was going well, particularly for me at my work, which had become progressively more interesting and even exciting as I became experienced in management and business. At that time, there were really only a few managers at Shorts of my age now at forty years old, with apparent potential for appointment to the main Board and I was, so to speak, poised for such an appointment. Indeed, I realised that some of the tasks I was given were to test my suitability for board level.

But then out of the blue, so to speak, but more precisely from the Bristol-based BAE, which was in fact the foremost company in the UK for the design and manufacture of aircraft and guided weapons, came their interest in offering me a senior appointment. It came about because already some of our top people at Shorts had been head-hunted by that huge company and two of them, George Gedge and Eric Hyde, had become directors and now wanted me to join them. The plan was that first of all I should have a quiet meeting and discussion in Bristol with their Commercial Director and, if I impressed him, I would be offered the job as a senior man in his department. And so it happened that in due course, after a second and more formal interview, I received the offer of appointment with the company in Bristol.

It would be madness, on the face of it, even to contemplate leaving Shorts at that time with so much going for me in that company, and with a seemingly assured future on the Board. Furthermore, we would have to move not only ourselves but Stuart and Alice as well, which would mean finding and buying a house for them near us in England and moving them again. Also at that time, house prices were very much higher in England than in Ulster, which was another important factor to consider.

On the other hand, there were a number of reasons which favoured such a move to BAE. Firstly, I was flattered at being head-hunted by such a famous company. Secondly, I was travelling so frequently to England anyway. Thirdly, we were beginning to become worried by the political-cum-religious 'troubles' in Ulster and the increasing violence. Fourthly, Saccie and I were aware of the tendency for the children of those Englishmen who had come from the mainland to work at Shorts to gravitate back to the mainland as they grew older and thus, as had happened in their case, we might become separated from our children. And fifth, although I had this very good career mapped out for me at Shorts, I had the thought that the grass might be just as green or even greener in the huge aircraft company of BAE which had factories in London, Bristol and the North.

And there were other factors to consider. Much as we loved the Ulster people for their forthright honesty, kindness and friendliness, they were a very close community, having attended the same schools together and, after their schooling, tending to live in the same area and among the friends of their childhood. It was easier for me, as a man, to join in and enter into the Ulster community life with the contacts at my work-place and the contacts formed from my particular interests of playing squash, golf and sailing. But it was not so easy for Saccie, despite her attractively gentle and easy manner, to make more than a few close and good friends among the wives in the community. Although she put no pressure on me whatever, I sensed that Saccie wanted to be back in England. Nevertheless, this was not a deciding factor because I, such a stupid man, had already made the decision to accept the job at Bristol. This was the second significant decision of my life so far, the first having been to remain in the Navy after the war ended back in 1945. Both of these decisions were almost equally disastrous at their time.

CHAPTER ELEVEN

Back to the Mainland

In large-scale industry, such as BAE, the top management tends to form itself into a pattern of stars and satellites; or to put it more simply, each star man at director level will establish his own team of supportive, satellite senior managers, all of whom will fight his corner for him at the various inter-departmental meetings which so constantly take place in large industry. I had been appointed as a commercial manager to work under an older and experienced director of BAE, this large aircraft-manufacturing company. He had head-hunted me to be one of his supporting managers on the advice of two other people from Shorts, both of whom were now in very senior positions at BAE. All should have been well as I expected to rise in due course under this man's star. However, I had hardly arrived and settled into my quite grand office at the works in Bristol when the bombshell landed on me. There was to be a takeover of the commercial division of the BAE factory at Weybridge and my man, my particular star, was moved to Weybridge together with most of his original entourage. Under these takeover arrangements, so recently made, there was nothing left here in Bristol for me to do. My job had been made redundant, even before I arrived to start working at it.

There was no help from anyone. There was no job and I sat there like a prune in that office with no work, no papers, no communication, nothing. I was regarded as an interloper and, "ard luck on you mate', my director had left me in the lurch with virtually nothing to do. My two friends from Shorts urged me to stick it out and the Managing Director himself promised that he would find an alternative position for me. Meantime, I tried to probe around for something I could get my teeth into; some fault in the system I could rectify. Certainly there were plenty of faulty contract procedures, particularly in the purchasing department but, not unexpectedly, my offers to examine and redraft some of the standard form of sub-contracts was rebuffed by those departmental heads already in

Chapter 1

Heather Adlam (Saccie) outside the Watch House, Coverack ▶

Coverack, Cornwall

Saccie and Jeremy, 1949

Chapters 2 and 3

Stuart Leaman with Saccie, Salisbury

Saccie and Alice, with Aza and Jeremy, 1950

Alice and Stuart Leaman (Popsie and Grampie), 1960s

Chapter 4

Piggy Cottage

Hank, Aza and Jeremy outside Piggy Cottage

Chapter 5

Crete Hill, Bristol, where Hank was born

Mother, Phoebe, Hank, Michael

Maddie with Bull Terrier

Hank in the First XI at Cottesmore, 1934 (front right) and when at Harrow (above)

Chapter 6

Villa La Quieta, Roquebrune ▶

A corner of the dining room at Villa La Quieta

Phoebe, aged 16, with Bunty ▼

Chapters 7 and 8

Left, Jeremy and Aza outside Cloverhill Park, Belfast
Below, Hank and Saccie in the TR2

Left and below, Jeremy and Aza

7, Waverley Drive, Bangor, above and right. Saccie with Popsie and Grampie during her illness ▶

Chapter 8 continued

Beechcraft Baron at Lagos in Nigeria

Sales presentations for Beechcraft at Shorts when Hank was Commercial Manager ▼ ▶

Jeremy in his Rockport uniform, left, and, right, at Waverley Drive, reading – his favourite occupation

Hank's first daubs

Ballyholme Road, Bangor

Chapter 9

Saccie hoisting the jib on Strangford Lough

Chapter 11

Aza with her ice dance partner, Mick Baker, at Richmond ice rink

Chapters 13 to 16

Saccie with boys, Clifton College

*The Old San, above and left
Hank with boys and their friends*

Below, a Rugby match on the Close

The Bursar and his wife at a College wedding

Left, the opening of the Coulson Centre

Below, Terry Whatley (back left) and Hank (back, second from right) with one of the Squash teams

Chapter 16

Opening a new Sports Pavilion at Beggars Bush

Saccie with John and Ruth Bush

Above, the Bursar's house at 24, College Road, Clifton, and right, Saccie in the kitchen with boys

Chapter 17

Above, deck hockey on SS Uganda, *April 1982, and right, Hank carrying Ben Howe through Venice*

Chapter 18

The cottage garden in Herefordshire, before Saccie started work, above, and right, after she had begun to make it over

Chapter 19

Alice, aged 3, with Saccie, Ross on Wye

Jeremy, Atauea, Alice and Kate

The family together in Monmouth, during the 50th wedding anniversary celebrations, 1998

Saccie in the Market Place, Ross on Wye

Chapter 19 continued

The Chantry, outside the sherry shed, and right, Saccie in her garden

Chapters 21 and 22

At the care home, Hank with Hazel

Captain Leahy DSC, RN and Hank at the hanging of his painting, photograph by kind permission of the Bath and County Club

Baroness Thatcher admiring a painting by Hank, photograph by kind permission of the Victory Services Club

A view from Hank's flat overlooking Bristol docks

charge. As was to be expected, I was soon shunted into a small office and given the sort of minor jobs which nobody else wanted to deal with and for which there would be no credit.

I was in the worst state of despair that I had ever suffered before. Even during the period just after leaving the Navy there had been hope, because I had been at the very bottom of life and knew I could only go upwards. This time I had relinquished a position at Shorts as a director and top manager and had lost it all in one stupid decision to change jobs. I couldn't sleep and felt physically sick as each day I contemplated the mess I had made of my career and the resultant precarious future now for my family. Saccie, with a much more realistic attitude to the awful situation, wanted me to ignore the advice of George and Eric, my two genuine friends from Shorts, who were still urging me to stick it out at BAE until a real job could be found for me. Far better, Saccie advised, to get the hell out of BAE, where I had lost status and respect because of the situation created there, and make a new start elsewhere. She pointed out that as we had some savings, this would buy time for me to get cracking and look for another job. I thought hard about what she was urging, and realised that she was absolutely right. The whole arrangement with BAE had become a busted flush and, to moulder on there hoping like Mr. Micawber for something to turn up could only drag me further down. This meant leaving BAE immediately. And I did so on the basis that, since they had created my redundancy, then at least I was due three months' salary and, indeed, they could hardly argue with that.

And so yet again I started the process of searching for work, reading the appointment columns in the newspapers and writing in response to those offering work at top management level. I didn't want to start by aiming low although, after a time, I became desperate enough to lower my sights considerably. The great difficulty was to maintain the impression that I was still a high-powered executive, so necessary if I was to obtain the standard of job I wanted. Meantime, while we tried to maintain the impression that all was well, Saccie had cut down on our house and living expenses. We had to pay the school fees to keep Jeremy at school in Ireland and for Aza, who was now at a second-rate but expensive private school for girls in Bristol, as if life was normal. I had hoped to get her into the excellent Clifton High School but their entry standards were too high. They were both too young, I thought, for us to explain how worried we were and why. But, as I look back, I guess that Saccie probably had sensibly explained the situation to them and comforted them that I would soon get a job and all would be well.

At that time, we were living in a very pleasant modern house in Dennyview Road at Abbots Leigh, a village just outside Bristol, and I didn't want to panic into selling it until I knew where my next job, if and when I could get one, was to come from. Moreover, I had a good-quality car, which it was important for me to keep for the sake of appearances at such interviews as I might obtain, although Saccie sold her little car as soon as she could. My many letters over a long period of weeks had produced eventually seven short-listed interviews, at all of which I failed to secure a job. It became evident that my business background, solely in the aviation industry, was the problem because it was so commercially specialised and different from those industries I was seeking to enter.

Two interviews stick in my mind; one was at the highest level with the financial director of Ford cars in the UK and I had been able to achieve the interview by referring to my employment at one time with the Rootes Group of car manufacturers. I thought briefly that I might be about to be offered a top job, until he detected that I had been no more than a trainee with the Group. At another interview, I had my first encounter with a Personnel Manager, one of a new breed of increasingly influential executives emerging at that time in industry, and he was insistent that I write my answers to a kind of questionnaire paper before I was permitted an actual interview. I am absolutely hopeless at that type of questionnaire so, in answer, I became heavily pompous and told him that, at my level, I expected to be interviewed by a director of their company only, and not to waste my time with childish trick questions. It worked because within half an hour I was taken to meet the Chairman with whom I got on well but, sadly, in discussion it became evident that my experience in the aircraft industry was not commensurate with the job he had in mind.

Eventually, I was offered and accepted the appointment as an Appeals Secretary of the Spastics Society. I kidded myself that I was interested in this major charity, which certainly did most valuable work. Although I would be based at an office in London, I would have to travel around the UK and therefore it would be sensible for Saccie to remain in our house in Bristol, from where Aza could continue to attend the same school. The salary was a huge drop from my earlier earnings. The charity, I found, was constituted of a number of regional committees in England, from which was formed the main committee which met in London every two months. This main committee was composed almost entirely of voluntary Ladies in large Hats, whose knowledge of management was nil and yet who had the authority to make the final decisions. Many of the people employed by the charity were second-rate failures from commerce or industry and I, very appropriately, had become one of them.

As well as carrying out fundraising projects around the country, I tried to introduce two main new sources of charity income; one from industry through agreement with the TGWU trade union and the other, again in industry, using a stamp system. At a large meeting of the Hats, I asked for a period of nine months without interference to allow these quite complicated projects time to work. They agreed, and yet at their next meeting two months later, the Hats, having had all sorts of second thoughts, couldn't resist interfering with the arrangements I had made. It was hopeless. Moreover, although it was not my 'part of ship', it seemed to me that the building projects, from the funds raised, tended to be over-ambitious and expensive. While I continued to do my best to promote more funds, I started to look for other employment. Apart from my disillusionment with the charity, it was difficult to return home as often as I needed, to see Saccie and to have the support which she never failed to give me. It was not easy for her on her own either, filled with worry, as she tried to keep the house comfortable for the family. She found occasional work at a dress shop in Bristol but, as Saccie herself admitted, she tended to be a lousy saleswoman, unable to resist telling a customer frankly if a dress was unsuitable, rather than secure a sale.

Among the many advertisements in the financial newspapers, one appeared at last which might fit my aviation background. It was for a Commercial Manager with one of the Plessey companies dealing with aircraft radar and surveillance systems. I applied and in due course was interviewed by a director who, as I found after I was appointed, was probably on his way out and was desperate to find a strong supporter to help him hold onto his position. I was intended to fill that role. But, as a commercial manager, I had to deal in the entirely new, to me, ball-game of the booming electronic industry of which, frankly, I had no knowledge. The pricing of these new surveillance systems, for instance, astounded me. Our technical estimators would apply massive percentage increases to cover the uncertainty of design and production costs of each project, plus I was expected to apply high contingencies on every commercial aspect of the contract and, on top of all this, I was to add a very high profit margin. It was a brand-new industry and neither our Ministry of Defence nor other foreign government customers had sufficient knowledge to question our estimates or our prices effectively. How I loathed working for Plessey; although it produced vital and valuable electronic equipment, there was no satisfaction or honour in the commercial aspect of working for it. Time and again I was instructed to give way in negotiating a difficult commercial provision in a contract, which I had regarded as important. But since there was such an enormous leeway in our overall price, what did it really matter after all if I had to yield on some aspect of the contract I was negotiating?

The directors were nearly all young, clever and practical ex-servicing engineers who, having gained their expertise out in the field installing these newly developed electronic systems and making them work on site, were now paramount in this industry and particularly so in our company. I well remember the young Managing Director of our division arriving at morning 'prayers', as we termed the regular meeting of managers at 9 a.m. every morning, to throw a large package on the table and say, 'There's a complete copy of the tender to the Ministry submitted by our main competitor. Make sure that we keep below their price levels.' And so I learned that it was considered normal practice to pay for spies to steal the technical secrets and commercial terms of competitive companies. Nevertheless, I was shocked when I found cause to suspect my own secretary, a sweet-looking middle-aged old biddy, of being a spy. I reckoned that she was regularly sending copies of my contract tender documents to a competitor company, although I never actually caught her doing it.

Once I had begun to suspect her, I wrote all my prices and main contract terms in longhand on the tender documents in the evenings after she had left the office and then posted the documents myself to the customer. But I admit to enjoying my own deviousness by dictating to her bogus prices and terms to type, which she would believe were to be sent to our customer, and which she would therefore copy to her spymasters. This whole performance, typical of the electronic industry at that time, was akin to working for a sleazy back-street car dealer, and I had become part of it. Nevertheless, it was a job and I had to get on with it.

Now that I was apparently settled to the new job at Plessey, which was near Kingston in Surrey, the time had come to sell our nice house in Bristol. I was too hard pressed to get involved with the sale while I struggled to cope with the awful job at Plessey. I would arrive at my office at 7 a.m. and rarely left it before 7 p.m. when I would go straight to a pub. I was largely on my own, desperately worried at my inadequacy with this unknown world of electronics and I drank as I had never done before, even in my worst periods of the war.

Habitually every evening I started by sinking four double gin and tonics: I couldn't get them down fast enough and I learned from that experience something of what it is like to be an alcoholic. Then every evening I had dinner and a bottle of wine by myself at the same expensive restaurant in Richmond and afterwards, helped by a double whisky, staggered along to the small hotel where I had a room to sleep. Up again at 6 a.m. to repeat the performance. It is little surprise that I was found collapsed one day at my desk with, as was recognised later, my first heart attack. I was aged about 45.

I longed for Saccie but I couldn't tell her the extent of my troubles nor about the minor heart attack. She had more than enough on her own plate as she set about selling the house at Dennyview Road outside Bristol, making arrangements for the storage of the furniture near Richmond and moving Aza to a new school. She completed all the jobs with her usual quiet competence, so that I didn't have to give any thought to those practical problems. While searching for a house, we lived, all four of us when Jeremy and Aza were on holiday from school, in three rooms at the Ivy Hotel near Richmond Bridge. It was not as expensive as might have been expected because the hotel was run-down and waiting to be sold. Although the rooms were rather shabby, Saccie somehow made them look and feel homely and pleasant with a few of our bits and pieces of photos and ornaments in our bedroom which, with its television, we all used as our main sitting-room. She had the great gift of making a home for us wherever we were. We came to know and like the fellow-guests at the hotel, most of whom, like us, appeared to be long-term and *en passant* between one stage of their life to another.

It took us about four weeks to find a house we liked and could afford because house prices were so very much higher in that suburban area of London. We had sold the house at Dennyview Road in Bristol for about £12,000 and, for that money, bought a very small bogus-Georgian modern house at East Sheen, very close to the gates of Richmond Park. Although the bedrooms were tiny, it was a pleasant home and we were happy there except, of course, for the basic problem for me of working at the much-loathed Plessey.

Never mind my misery at work, because lots of new things were happening to my family.

Aza had chosen to take up ice-skating at the famous Richmond rink, which was a relief since I had rather feared she might want to take up pony-riding at one of the many local stables. One saw so many young girls of her age in that Richmond area, bobbing about on their fat little bottoms astride ponies, and I was so thankful that such an activity didn't appeal to her. The first time I had taken Aza to the ice-rink, I had expected to show her how to skate, since I had at one time as a boy played ice-hockey. But quite the opposite happened: she started off with astonishing balance and high speed to bash into the barriers at each end of the rink, since she had no idea at first how to stop. And I was left to stagger along behind her. After several months of her startling progress under a young instructor, I approached Roy and Betty Calloway, who were regarded as the two top ice-dance coaches in the world and normally only coached upcoming champions. They were immensely snooty on my initial approach but, when I eventually persuaded them to watch Aza, they were impressed enough to take her on, initially as Roy's pupil, and then in due course for training by Betty, who was recognised worldwide as the supreme coach. It was she who in later years would be coach to Torvil and Dean, the world ice-dance champions.

Aza, at age fifteen then, was well launched into a career of ice-dancing which, in spite of the very considerable cost of having her coached by the Calloways, gave Saccie and me great pleasure, as with her astonishing ability there was potential for her to become a star. And it was a joy just to watch her skate at the various tournaments. Her competitors were girls who had been skating since they were seven or eight, so she had a lot of leeway to make up and moreover, since many more girls than boys took up ice-dancing, there was intense competition among them to find a boy suitably good as a partner. I was in danger of becoming known as 'the old queer of the Richmond rink' since, every time a new boy appeared at the rink with potential as a good dance partner, I tried to persuade him into partnership with Aza by offering him incentives of ice creams and cakes at the rinkside café! In due course, Aza formed a tournament partnership with a young man called Mick Baker, and they enjoyed travelling to different competitions and winning a few trophies here and there. Unfortunately, when the time came to 'change partners', there was, again, a lack of another partner of suitable standard for her.

Jeremy, who loathed his boarding school near Dublin probably as much as I detested my work at Plessey, went out on the town with two American boys from the school and they were caught in Dublin late at night. At our house in Richmond, I received a telephone call from the Headmaster, or Warden as he called himself, to tell me that he was expelling Jeremy. I advised him that, if he did so, I would sue his wretched little school for negligence and for failure to care properly for my son. I pointed out that Jeremy, during his three years there, had rarely been in any trouble before whereas the two American boys, who were only at the school to avoid the Vietnam war, had hardly ever been out of trouble. I recognised all too well, I said, that he feared to expel the other two boys, because of their very rich and influential father, without also expelling Jeremy. Much of my argument was pure bombast, of course, but I wasn't going to allow my Jeremy to have his future blighted by expulsion from school for just a schoolboy escapade. I was frightened and angry at the very thought of it and told the Headmaster to think again ... which he did. He consequently agreed merely to rusticate Jeremy for the last two weeks of this his final term and he mumbled something also about beating Jeremy severely. I told him to forget that idea too as, although I did not disagree in principle with use of the cane for boys when appropriate, Jeremy had caused absolutely no trouble or harm to anyone during his escapade and therefore did not merit that type of punishment. And anyway, he was too old for it.

Dear Jeremy came home to Richmond and I pretended to be very stern as I opened the front door to him, when everything inside me wanted to give him a hug and a truly loving welcome as did Saccie, his Mother. Oh why, why didn't I do so? Why could I not have realised that the silly threat of expulsion from school was in reality of no significance at all and, contrary to my fears at the time, would not have mattered a jot to his life in the future? I suppose that I thought it was the thing to do, to play the heavy father .... Stupid, stupid man that I was because it affected our relationship for long months after. Also, instead of his holiday and as a silly sort of punishment, I arranged for him to take an immediate clerking job with a firm of solicitors in London before going to university in Dublin. Although it was actually more in the hope that he might become interested in the law – which was a forlorn hope, as he hated it!

So Jeremy in due course that year returned to Dublin where he had managed to scrape into Trinity College. It's no good pretending otherwise, Jeremy hated the pressure of exams. What he really liked, and was so good at, was people. Also, as the result of his main pleasure in avidly and carefully reading good literature, he was capable of writing well. Neither of these characteristics, however, helped him to learn much at university and so at the end of his three years there, he had to scrape around again to obtain a not-very-good degree. As for our father-and-son relationship, I was gradually growing up and relaxing as I realised that things such as degrees were really not all that important to a young man who, although basically very under-confident as yet, was so happily at ease with his peers. He would do all right, I reckoned, and anyway I loved him and would be around to give whatever support he might need in the future.

Back to me at Plessey where, by working long hours, I was just about coping with my management job in this new electronic and radar industry, but it was clear that my basic ignorance of the product would prevent me from making any career progress in this particular business. Moreover, except for two good friends, Mike Peters, a brilliant member of the design team and Ronald, who was the senior clerk in my commercial department, I didn't much like the people with whom I had to work. Ron, as he was known, had started in the department as a sort of tea-boy clerk, but being highly intelligent, had learned and knew the commercial terms and procedures of the company down to the nearest dot. That young man quickly recognised my ignorance of our electronic and radar products but, for some kind reason, befriended me and gave me unstinted help in the details of my job, leaving me as the boss to deal at the higher level of customer negotiations. Ron's support was so unusual in large-scale industry where the norm would have been for him to undermine me, with intent to take my job, one which he was perfectly capable of holding down. What a super young man he was and I do so hope that Plessey eventually recognised his ability and gave him his due promotion.

CHAPTER TWELVE

Rolls-Royce

An advertisement appeared in the *Daily Telegraph* seeking a commercial manager for Rolls-Royce Aero Engines at their main factory in Bristol and, as I read it, the specification for the job bore an almost uncanny similarity to my particular experience in the aviation industry. At home that evening, I received a telephone call from, of all people, Hugh Conway under whom I had worked at Shorts and who was now Managing Director of the huge company of Rolls-Royce. I grovelled with delighted surprise on the phone as this immensely important man, actually not all that much older than me, spoke briefly to suggest that I respond to the advertisement. It appeared that he had me in mind for some particular position in the company. I formally applied for the job and, in due course, was invited for a two-day visit to Bristol, where the company had arranged for me to stay at the Grand Hotel. As far as I could see, I was the only applicant. It was arranged that I was to meet members of Conway's senior management team in their offices during each day and to talk with some of them more informally over dinner at the hotel each evening. I got on well with them and apparently they liked me and appreciated such knowledge of the aviation business as I had to offer. And so a week later I received the formal offer of the job as a Commercial Manager.

The procedure I have just described is known as 'headhunting' and inspires the purest joy into the heart of the hunted, especially if he is longing to relinquish his current job!

I was appointed first of all to Bristol where I settled into a pleasantly large office and, so to speak, awaited an expected onslaught of work. But in those first weeks, I spent most of the time attending meetings, mostly as a listener and learner of their administrative and commercial procedures, since I had not been given the authority of having a particular engine or project to manage commercially. However, the real plot of my appointment at Rolls-

Royce Engines unfolded at a meeting with my immediate boss, Mr Orford, the Commercial Director of Rolls-Royce. We never did get on well together, either then or in the years to come; maybe he was boot-faced with me at the outset because in effect, I suppose, I had been appointed by Conway over his head. I suspect it gave him some pleasure, therefore, to inform me that I was really required at the Bristol-Siddeley Works in Coventry where reorganisation of the commercial and estimating departments was needed and I was the man, apparently, who had been headhunted for the job. It was a blow because Saccie and I were looking forward to living in Bristol again, and we had already started house-hunting there. At the time we were still living in Richmond but had moved to Morley Road near to the ice-rink where Aza needed to skate in the very early mornings when the rink was clear of the general public, enabling Betty Calloway to teach selected pupils. In preparation for the move to Bristol, we had made rental arrangements for Aza to live in a small flat right next door to our house. She was by now working part-time at a small department store in Richmond to earn some money towards her skating, and had made several friends there among the staff as she helped out in the various different sections.

Meanwhile, I was exceedingly peeved that Orford had not told me at the outset that my job would be in Coventry, rather than in Bristol where I had naturally assumed it would be. Being newly appointed (and desperate for the job) however, I could not really afford to object and, anyway, this major task of reorganisation would be the opportunity to put myself about a bit and to make my name in the company. Moreover, the promise was made that I would return to work in the main offices in Bristol on completion of the task. So I had better just smile and get on with it, although it seemed sensible at that stage to keep our home in Richmond and for me to commute each week-end from Coventry.

I received a very good expense allowance and so I rented a rather ugly little modern furnished flat near the factory in Coventry and, at times during school terms, Saccie came to stay for a week with me there. But normally, every week-end after I had finished work at mid-day on Saturdays, I bombed down to Richmond in my MGB sports car, which I drove very fast. Then I would leave home at 7 a.m. on each Monday to arrive at my office in Coventry at 8.30 a.m.

In fact, that was a late start for me as, during the rest of the week, I usually arrived at my office at 6.30 in the morning while it was still dark and when the night-shift were coming off work from the factory floor. This was as ridiculous and as dotty a way of life as I had led at Plessey, but I was determined to complete my reorganisation task as soon as I could possibly do so and, as well as that task, there was so much other foreign travel and negotiating work to be done. On looking back now at the long hours I always worked in industry, I recognise that it was my lack of background learning and training that made such hours necessary: I was forever playing 'catch-up' with my competitive and professionally-trained colleagues. Moreover, the two hours of extra work in the early mornings put me, so to speak, ahead of the game for the day and gave me an advantage over the heads of other departments, as those early hours enabled me to prepare for the inevitable meetings with them each morning. There was so much aggro between the various administrative departments at Coventry, particularly between the production people and our commercial department; it was this general air of antipathy in the workplace which made my progress towards reorganisation of the commercial department so difficult. The general manager of the place was also the Production Director; a brute of an ill-mannered man from the shop floor with a one-track mind and no vision, a dinosaur.

My department, with a staff of some thirty-five clerks, was involved in dealing with orders from airline and government customers for spares and modifications relating to several aero engines, but my main project was the Viper engine. This was a jet engine particularly suitable for the small fighter cum ground attack aircraft, which developing countries around the world wanted for their airforces, and I led a negotiating team dealing with communist officials in Yugoslavia, Czechoslovakia and Hungary. This involved constant travel, which I loathed, but it was unavoidable. Dealing with these communist countries, I learned quickly to identify the commissar among the team of negotiators opposite to me at the long table. Not difficult because whenever I put an important proposition to them for decision, the eyes of the head man opposite to me, usually an army Colonel, and those of his team would swivel round to one man amongst them; usually a clerk at the end of the table and probably a man with no engineering experience at all. But there would be no progress until he had given the nod. A ploy I learned to use was to suggest that we split our negotiating teams into two or three sections, each dealing with different aspects of the contract, and so the wretched little commissar would be in a quandary deciding in which section he ought to be, and having isolated him, I was enabled to make progress on the contract with their commercial leader.

The negotiating practice followed by all these communist countries was always much the same and started early at about 7.30 a.m. with a small glass of slivovitz (local brandy), followed by a similar glass with a cup of black, thick coffee on the hour thereafter, until mid-day when we would return to our hotel. In the afternoons, I would discuss and work out with my team our ploy for the next morning, as indeed, I knew our opposition would be doing. By the way, there were no calculators in those days to use during the negotiations and one needed to be good at mental arithmetic, but I also had the engineer of my team next to me who, as a wizard with the slide rule, could work out a close estimate in double quick time for me. At first, I used to do my own drafting or redrafting of the contract on the hoof, but later I could take with me, as part of the team, my own tame solicitor.

Dealing with these communist people was a weird business. Our hotel rooms were always entirely bugged and I had to conduct our team discussions quietly in the middle of the public rooms downstairs. Whenever the negotiations became bogged down, I found the answer usually was to invite their whole team to an expensive dinner at the hotel or a restaurant. Lots of wine and slivovitz would have to flow and somehow we had to hold our drink capacity better than they did or lose their respect. This was ridiculous but fortunately one of my team was a wartime ex-submariner and he and I together, with our naval background of pink gins in the wardroom, could hold our own in alcoholic drinking with these people, and it was absurdly important that we were able to do so. But such ploys were effective as contract terms could be agreed over hangovers the next day. Another aspect of doing business in those countries was that their political masters in the background appeared anxious to compromise me, as the senior man, in some way or another. For example, the absurd approach by a truly beautiful young girl of about eighteen, firstly in the bar of the hotel, and then at my bedroom door, not as a prostitute but as a companion provided by the Agency, she said, was straight out of 1920s-style fiction.

Here is one more story to illustrate the childish nonsense of that period of communist control.

I was in Prague on the evening before my return home, having eventually completed reasonable contract terms, when there was a discreet knock on the door. I opened it to find a middle-aged man who said he was English and had urgent security business to discuss with me. So we toddled solemnly into the bathroom where we flushed the loo and ran the bath water while he told me that he was a British agent with vital information to pass to London but he was so closely watched that he dared not board the aircraft with it himself. Would I take it for him hidden amongst my own business papers, as a matter of urgent national importance? I gave it some thought and then gave him a firm 'no'. Why should I risk my family life while incarcerated in some communist prison for years, for something as nebulously important as this? I could be in very serious trouble, dependent on the substance of his papers, if I were to be searched before I boarded the aircraft for home. The chap was furious and said that he had risked his life for this information and that it must be passed urgently to an address in London. I told him that my life as a naval fighter pilot had been at almost constant daily risk for five years during the war and that was the limit of my contribution as far as taking dangerous risks for my country was concerned. He must learn to take his own risks, I told him. The chap left my room white with anger.

To be honest, I considered then as I do now that all the spy mania of that time was a lot of unnecessary and blithering nonsense, perpetrated by the manic mentality of the communists.

I had to travel to other countries, notably Italy where I had contracts with Macchi and Piaggio, both small but well-known aircraft manufacturers to whom we sold the Viper engine. Business visits to Rome for talks with Piaggio himself, a famous and magnificent-looking old man from prewar aviation, were quite fun as he was a good host, whereas talks with the Macchi company in Milan were rather more dour and businesslike, but more profitable, as their little fighter aircraft, with our Viper engine, was selling well. Brazil was another country where I completed negotiations for their manufacture of our Viper engine under licence. It was more interesting to travel there because I usually stayed several days in Rio. I remember that I once needed an extra £500 for my expenses and was unable to obtain the sum from the Brazilian bank using my Bristol-Siddeley business card. But the money was immediately forthcoming when I offered my Rolls-Royce card. 'Oh for Roll a Royce,' exclaimed the manager, 'that is a different matter.' And yet, of the two companies recently merged, Bristol-Siddeley was the more successful at the time. A business visit to Rio, which lasted over a week, was the only occasion when, in need of female company, I ever invited a girl to join me. She was a pretty girl, who worked at the bank, and we spent the day together swimming and dinner in the evening … no, nothing else. Nevertheless, I felt guilty thinking how much Saccie and I would have enjoyed the day together, and so I bought a huge blue precious stone to take back for her which, as I intended, she duly sold for a nice fat sum. Saccie was the very last sort of female to be interested in baubles.

Business travel, even to places like Brazil and Portugal, was a bore and chore since, whatever country I visited on business, it was in effect just another hotel and conference room. Plus there was the perpetual worry of whether I would be able to get a flight back home, either by company aircraft or commercial airline, in time for the weekend. I would have preferred a hundred times over to be in England at home with Saccie.

It became apparent that the Orful Orford, as I termed our Commercial Director, desired me to remain at the works in Coventry where an effective reorganisation of the commercial department had been completed and where I had put together a good negotiating team, which was bringing in a lot of new orders from abroad for the Viper engine.

Saccie and I had a discussion and decided that we might as well accept the situation and make the move to Coventry, since it appeared evident that Rolls-Royce now wanted to keep me working there. And so, having made the arrangements for Aza's accommodation in Richmond, we sold the house in Morley Road and moved to Humphrey Burton Road in Coventry. We found that Coventry was rather a dreary city in which to live, but the house itself, with quite a nice garden, was pleasant enough. The move was not popular with Jeremy or Aza, and Saccie and I were not happy there either, but at least we were all together during the holidays.

A year later there was yet another reorganisation (Orford again) and now the company wanted me back in Bristol, not as a manager with a commercial department to run, but this time purely as a contract negotiator, mainly with foreign governments and airline operators. I had ceased to care just so long as we returned to Bristol and that the company paid all my moving and other expenses, which of course they did. Moreover, I enjoyed negotiation which is a skill, almost an art form, whether it be with trade unions, HM or foreign Governments or airline operators. Success is rarely achieved by scoring clever points in a negotiating argument, and only causes the other party to nurse their resentment. The essence of the skill is to create a sense of mutual respect, which leads to trust and even to friendship between the two parties in a negotiation. Once that is established, an eventual contract, which satisfies both parties, becomes possible. (Sorry, end of lesson; but so many people imagine that being a clever dick is being a good negotiator.)

Rolls-Royce

But, having been sent to Coventry as the saying goes for two years, I found on return to Bristol that while I was in Coventry, I had been jockeyed out of position in the rat-race for promotion at Bristol where, of course, lay the hub and commercial centre of Rolls-Royce. It was probably largely my own fault; for I couldn't stand that man Orford who so reminded me of Rear-Admiral Vian, that arch poseur who, as Admiral in charge of the Carrier Fleets at Salerno, the Far East and in the Pacific, had made life so unnecessarily dangerous for us aircrews of the Fleet Air Arm. Although Orford, as our Commercial Director, was not of the same status obviously as the Admiral, they were both out of the same mould; bullies and arrogant poseurs. Orford's initials were O and O and I usually referred to him at meetings and discussions, although admittedly not in his presence, as 'OOO', being short for 'Orrible Orful Orford'. It was naughty of me because he came to be known as that in both Bristol and Coventry. Those two men in their different professions might have got away with their bombast and unpleasant manners, in my opinion if they had been more efficient in their jobs, but Vian had known little or nothing about naval aviation and Orford knew nothing of management skills and was entirely bereft of them.

It was now 1969 and I was approaching fifty. With the children nearly settled, I was beginning to wonder if I could possibly find a way out of this rat-race of large industry. I had in mind that I would very much like a new career in teaching but how could I break into such a new profession, and could I afford the very much lower salary? The answer, as Saccie gently pointed out, was a clear 'no' since Jeremy and Aza both needed my support, and so it seemed that I must continue to batter my way on at Rolls-Royce and, remembering my past of having to strive for work, I should be properly thankful for a job at all. Having been far too outspoken on a number of occasions, there was little prospect of my ever achieving Board level where life, I knew, was so much easier.

I really don't know how Saccie managed to be kind and sympathetic with me when I was restless in my job like this; she had suffered with worry as few other young wives had done as I had struggled for work after the war, then when I eventually came good at Shorts I had thrown it all away. I had struggled again after job redundancy at BAE, I had been miserable and useless at Plessey and now, at last, I was in a good well-paid and settled job at Rolls-Royce. Yet her daft and dotty husband was thinking now of seeking a new profession! Saccie's patience with me was almost beyond belief.

CHAPTER THIRTEEN

Clifton College and Preparatory School

THE FIRST YEAR, 1970

I had kept in mind the possibility of taking up the teaching profession, even at this late stage in my life, and discussed it again several times with Saccie of course, but I also mentioned it to some squash-playing friends of mine, who were schoolmasters at Clifton College Preparatory School, known as the Pre, and so referred to hereafter. They introduced me to Jim Hornby, the Headmaster of the Pre, who said most sensibly that I ought at least to try teaching before I thought seriously of taking it up. He offered me the opportunity to take some classes in French and current affairs with the eleven-year old boys on Saturday mornings. I jumped at the chance and just hoped that I would be able to get back on Saturday mornings from whatever negotiation I might be involved with abroad. I enjoyed enormously the experience of teaching a class of young boys, although I have to admit that I was not particularly good at it. Nevertheless, the boys were orderly and, for current affairs, seemed to enjoy my stories, some silly, some serious, based on reports taken from the daily newspapers, and also responded cheerfully to my attempted conduct of the whole period of a French class in French. In those days I was a heavy smoker and they loved it when, unthinkingly and totally involved in trying to teach, I absent-mindedly put a cigarette in my mouth. The boys watched expectant and entranced as I started to light it, would 'Sir' actually commit the heinous crime of smoking in class? Well, I stopped just in time but, for a moment, with all the faces of the boys looking up at me and giving me their rapt attention, I thought I must have within me a great gift for teaching. Until I realised that the cigarette was the attraction, of course, and certainly not my inspired words. But the pleasure I found

CLIFTON COLLEGE AND THE PRE   167

in the school environment, albeit for such brief periods, was not helping me to feel settled at Rolls-Royce.

Clifton College and its Pre, located next to the Downs at Clifton in Bristol, was well known as one of the top public schools (now known as Independent Schools) in the UK and at that time had six hundred boys, mostly boarders, in the Upper School and four hundred and fifty younger boys, half of them as boarders, in the Pre. Shortly after I had started teaching (in a manner of speaking) in the Pre on Saturday mornings, Jim Hornby asked me into his study to inform me that the College was actively seeking a new Bursar and that advertisements for the appointment had already been published in the national newspapers. He hoped that I would be interested and suggested most strongly that, with my desired association with school life added to my background as an experienced man of business, I should apply for the post without delay. Interested I most certainly was because the job appeared to be everything I wanted, including the expectation of a reasonable salary perhaps not much lower than my current one. I was so thankful that Saccie had realised how much I wanted this type of work at a school and responded to my enthusiasm by urging me to go for it. I did so immediately and posted a carefully drafted letter of application with my CV to the College.

I found out all I could about the possibilities of the job and learned that the College had changed Bursars three times in the last two years and was desperate to find the right man, but already there had been over four hundred applicants, which didn't look good for my chances. These applicants were being weeded out by an expensive firm of management consultants in London, aiming to produce a short list of six for the Council of the College to consider.

After a while, and it seemed a very long while to me, I received an invitation from the consultants to attend an interview with them at their offices in London. As the result of that interview, I was surprised to be informed two weeks later that I had been selected for the short list and would be required to go before a Committee of the College Council. All my enquiries about well-known, independent schools had shown that the Bursar was almost always an ex-member of the services and a senior officer such as a Brigadier, a Captain in the RN or even a Rear-Admiral or a non-flying Commodore from the RAF: nearly all of them were from the pay branch of their service, good chaps no doubt doing essential pay and logistic jobs, but people whom we aircrew during the war had tended to refer to under the generic term of 'pay wallahs'. Hence, as an ordinary businessman from commerce and industry, I was surprised as well as absolutely delighted to be short-listed.

Before meeting that Committee, I asked to see a copy of the Royal Charter of the College because I wanted to understand exactly how the College was constituted. After all, a Royal Charter was bound to be a different cup of tea, I thought, to the Memorandum and Articles of a company, with which I was familiar. (Actually, I found that there was not all that much difference.) There was quite a delay before I was invited to a small office at the College and shown a copy of the Charter in the form of a large and flimsy white document, looking rather like a huge old five-pound note, and done up in red ribbon. I gained the impression from the lady secretary who showed me the document that nobody had looked at it for years. I was glad to see from it that the Bursar was responsible directly to Council and not to the Headmaster, as it seemed obvious to me that these two top people in a school, each with different areas of responsibility, ought to work in tandem rather than one on top of the other.

I also noted that all the non-teaching staff came under the sole authority of the Bursar.

Came the dreaded day of the interview with the Committee. Dreaded because getting this job had become so very, almost desperately, important not only to me but to Saccie too. The interviews that day were well-organised and I never caught sight of the other five applicants who, I learned from the head porter as he escorted me to the council room, were all retired senior officers from the services. The interview took place in the grand council room with a long table along the centre at which sat five middle-aged men at one end, while I was to be seated facing them at the other. The Chairman of Council introduced himself and the others, who were the Treasurer, two other members of Council and the Headmaster. I knew none of them, but I noted that Jim Hornby, Headmaster of the Pre, was absent, which suggested hopefully to me that he had already supported my application, and therefore could not properly be a member of this selection committee.

But the interview went very badly, I thought. Despite my considerable experience at being interviewed, as well as interviewing others, I had overdone my questions to the committee, and I had probably been too bombastic in my answers to their questions. As, for example, after I had asked for the total number of pupils in the College and been given the answer, I then asked if this number was lower or higher than in earlier years. When the Chairman disclosed that the numbers had fallen, I had asked to what he attributed the fall. My question appeared to make him rather cross and short with me when he said, 'Well, Mr Adlam, if you were to be appointed Bursar, you would be expected to find the answer to that question for yourself and for us too.' Another question, and this from the Treasurer, was whether I would be able to adapt to the lower level of finances at the College, after dealing with many millions of sterling in the aircraft industry. To which I replied, much too airily, that I would just knock a few noughts off the end of the figures. Because, I went quickly on to say, the principles of good business management, which were the essence of both, were no different. The Treasurer gave a bleak smile to my answer.

I returned to our home in Beaufort Road in Clifton and told Saccie that I had blown this one job which we both by now desperately wanted, as I had been over-confident and even arrogant in my manner. It was about six o'clock in the evening; we were so despondent and depressed that we went out to a pub where none of our friends were likely to be and we drank a great deal of gin together; not our style normally, but we were so very sad and disappointed. We returned home quite drunk some two hours later and lay down side by side, stretched out on the floor of the sitting room, and cried together. The telephone rang and I stumbled off to answer it.

The caller was Stephen McWatters, the Headmaster, to ask on behalf of the Council if I would accept the appointment as Bursar.

For the first time in my working life, the twelve years with the College which followed from January 1970 gave me real and almost continuous pleasure, with few serious worries. In retrospect I realise that the hours, which included most week-ends, were long, and, my necessary supervision of the many building projects every year allowed Saccie and me very little time on holiday; indeed for two whole years, we took no holiday at all except for long week-ends. But for me, what a joy it all was, compared to life in industry!

However, I can find no answer even now to the question of how or why Saccie put up with me and my absurd enjoyment of the College. Her method of dealing with me and my over-enthusiastic attitude to being Bursar at Clifton was, I believe, on the basis of the well-known saying, 'If you can't beat them, join them.' Because, during those twelve years, Saccie undertook every task at the College for which she was needed, usually in an emergency when someone or other couldn't turn up. During those years, in various emergencies she worked several times as an assistant matron in a boarding house, she assisted the Matron in the Sanatorium, she served the boys their sweets and drinks in the 'Grubber,' she served the boys in the sports shop and, probably best of all, because she knew many of the boys in the Upper School and they knew her, she acted frequently as a kind of agony aunt to some of the boys. She had that gift, so rare now with modern women, of listening without interjecting and perhaps at the end quietly and wisely expressing a view. Saccie was the only wife of a Bursar at Clifton ever to take part in the daily life and activities of the College.

Before the school term began in mid-January, I studied the accounts, Council minutes, minutes of other meetings and much of the correspondence for the previous years, and concluded that there really was a hell of a lot to be done. My predecessor as Bursar had committed suicide after not much more than a year in the job, the man before him had had enough after a year and decided to leave to take up an appointment in hospital management and, before him, an ex-colonial administrator as Bursar had retired early. But I had an advantage in that the Chairman of Council and his main colleagues on it, after two years of weak Bursars, very low boy numbers and an apparently huge overdraft, were prepared to give me all the leeway I wanted in setting up new management structures and procedures. Early in January, I asked the Chairman, Jack Britton, for the opportunity of a private discussion with him on the affairs of the College generally and, in particular, I wanted to talk about its management procedures. He invited me to his house just outside Bristol at Pucklechurch, where we had lunch and a valuable discussion together.

The first consequence of it was that the many and various sub-committees of the Council, which had been formed and had proliferated during previous years, were disbanded. The number of meetings each year was reduced from twenty-eight to six, thus there would be one meeting each per school term of the Council and of its Finance Committee. That was the first essential step done, since it really is not possible to run any business properly by committees.

Looking at the financial affairs of the College, it seemed to me then and subsequently that it was no more than a moderately-sized business without any of the complexities of the large-scale aircraft industry to which I was accustomed, but which nevertheless needed to be operated in an entirely business-like manner. Not only did the futile sub-committees have to go, but the manner of conducting the essential Council and Finance meetings needed some changes too. For example, it was rare for anything other than a simple agenda, as agreed by the Chairman, to be circulated to members prior to a meeting. Bearing in mind that the majority of the twenty-two members of Council only visited the College now three times a year and, to be frank, had very little knowledge of its inner workings but yet were responsible for decisions on its management, I thought it was obvious that they required briefing papers dealing with items on the agenda. This is not to be derogatory about the members of Council, each of whom was paramount in his or her own field and many of whom had already earned their K. But, however many brief visits they might make, they would never become part of or understand the complex inner pressures, feelings and different viewpoints which comprised and drove the close community of the College.

Thus for my first meeting of Council, after consultation with my Chairman, I prepared briefing papers for each item of the agenda in which the various considerations were spelled out and a suitable conclusion suggested. This latter suggestion being of particular importance since, if presented with subtlety, it could manoeuvre the meeting towards the right resolution. I so arranged matters too that we had a basic management team consisting of the Chairman, the Treasurer, the Chairman of the Finance committee and myself, sometimes joined by the Headmaster. We met always three days before Council meetings to discuss the agenda I had prepared and to decide upon the resolutions we needed at the forthcoming meeting and the arguments we must employ to achieve them. All these various arrangements constituted from then on the pattern of all Council and Finance meetings during my time as Bursar, except for a period during the chairmanship of Norman Travis.

Before my first Council meeting, which took place a few weeks after my appointment, I checked the set-up of the council room with Charlie Whybrow, my head porter, and noticed a high oak desk and stool set about three feet behind and to the side of the Chairman's chair, and, of course, asked Charlie what it was for. 'It's the Bursar's desk,' he told me, 'from where you take the minutes, Sir.' I told him to take the whole archaic apparatus away and to place me, in the proper place for the Secretary of Council, on the immediate left of the Chairman to whom I could then pass information and papers during the meeting, as necessary. These meetings, which hitherto had continued all through the Saturday, were considerably shortened by the briefing papers since everyone now knew what they were talking about from reading them in advance and, in consequence, the meetings were always thereafter concluded before lunch. I made sure that members of Council had plenty of sherry before enjoying an exceedingly good lunch and wine, with time afterwards now to watch the school rugby or cricket matches or talk to teaching staff in the afternoon, before they departed for home with, I hoped, a comfortable feeling of achievement and full bellies. If they had enjoyed the day, they would remember it and tend to be that much more malleable at the next meeting! It was my good fortune that, during that first year and many more, I continued to have full support from my Chairman, the Treasurer and the other members of Council, particularly those who lived locally, and with whom Saccie and I were in due course to form firm friendships.

My all-important relationship with the Headmaster, Stephen McWatters, was never a problem. He was a charming man, very much more astute than his housemasters and teaching staff ever gave him credit for and, in his quiet way, very determined. After my first term, he and I found that there were a number of fundamental changes upon which we both agreed as priorities. Let me write about our first priority, the introduction of a cafeteria system in the dining hall of the Upper School, which was my first experience and a prime example of how extraordinarily difficult it was to introduce any form of change to teaching staff. Under the existing system, the dining hall appeared as a scene of bedlam overborne by an appalling cacophony as metal trolleys containing clattering cutlery and plates of cold food were wheeled about on the wooden floor. Above all that was the noise of housemasters, house tutors and boys having to talk and argue at the top of their voices to be heard at all, as they waited impatiently for the food trolleys to be wheeled from the kitchen to their tables.

You would think as I did, wouldn't you, that the teaching staff would jump at the opportunity of changing and improving all this? Not a chance of it. In the first place all the powerful housemasters were against a cafeteria because the existing tables, being arranged in houses, enabled them to keep contact with their boys and to give them messages, instructions or notice of events, and so on. Also, and this was a laugh in the face of such bedlam, to check the manners of the boys! The rest of the teaching staff were against it because, of course, they ate in a separate dining room whereas, under my proposed cafeteria, meals would be provided for everybody, all seated with whom and wherever they wished, at round tables to seat six boys and/or masters. That is, all of them able to enjoy a good meal like civilised people. As to the meals at that time, however, these were truly awful, being badly cooked, cold and without choice. And so, for Stephen and me, an essential part of our thinking and planning was first of all to appoint a much better catering manager, with improved kitchen equipment purchased and installed in due course as well.

Stephen had the task of bringing his teaching staff round to accepting these proposed catering arrangements and, in this, he had the benefit of his Senior Master, David Gibson, who was of high intelligence and rare among schoolmasters of having had experience of the world outside of school life. He had suffered what is often described as 'a good war' in the army, having risen in the intelligence service to Lt Colonel. David had considerable influence with his fellow teachers and quietly put before them the advantages of the proposed cafeteria.

My part in the cafeteria, may I say, was more difficult. I had to get rid of a bad catering manager together with several of his staff cronies in the department, and these could be described kindly and at best as 'unhygienic'. In fact, they looked and were filthy. But they had been employed for some time and provided with accommodation in College property. In consequence, the firing and ejecting of them without serious trouble had called for firmness and all my knowledge of employment law. The whole lengthy affair of converting to a cafeteria would have been even more difficult if, by the greatest of good fortune, at the first interviews for a new catering manager I had not found Peter Cole, the perfect man for the task. He was an ex-army caterer, a big man in every way who knew his job thoroughly and arrived in time, firstly to help me get rid of the bad staff, but principally to select the new kitchen and cafeteria equipment. I did not attempt to persuade Jim Hornby, Headmaster of the Pre, to adapt his separate dining hall to cafeteria because clearly it was not so suitable for his younger boys who needed supervision at house tables. But he agreed that my new catering manager should also take over responsibility for the kitchens, the staff and the quality of the meals in the Pre.

Having appointed Peter Cole as the new Catering Manager, I could to a large extent set aside the problems of dealing with the 52 members of catering staff needed for feeding the boys and teaching staff of both the Upper School and the Pre; although, as the total boy numbers in the Upper School and the Pre increased quite dramatically over the next ten years, from 1045 to a maximum of 1252 boys, so the number of meals per day, including those for teaching staff, rose to over 4000 meals per day. I was convinced that a high standard of school meals played a major part in the happiness of boys and staff at the College and I was sure too, that it was a factor in the huge improvement of boy numbers during the 1970s. Hence how damn lucky I was to have discovered and appointed such an able and competent man as Peter so early in my bursarship.

My only slight worry, when taking over as the new Bursar in January 1970, was the accounts of the College and to what extent I would have to take part in the management of them. I had assumed that the day-to-day accounting and annual accounts of the College would have been hived off to be done by a firm of chartered accountants. If that was the case I, as Bursar, would have to keep an eye on their work and, although in all my previous business affairs I had been involved in budgets and monetary control, I was no accountant. However, what I found to be the case astonished me, and do please remember in reading this about the College accounts, that £1 million in 1970 was a massive and huge sum regarded with awe rather as £1 billion is now. I found that the whole of the accounts department, which kept account of twelve boarding houses, upkeep and maintenance of school buildings and grounds at value than of about £9 million, salaries and wages of some 320 employees, fees and extras for three terms of over 1200 boys, costs of food, electricity, gas and the preparation of the annual accounts... I found that all of this was in the hands of one man, John Rogers, and his staff of three clerks! I found them upstairs at the top of our office building located in a couple of small rooms. Nowadays, although there is no basic difference in the size of the College or its function, the accounting of its finances apparently requires an expensive computer and an accounts staff of two qualified accountants and five clerks! John Rogers was quite a young man in his mid-thirties when I arrived in 1970 and he became the man on whom I most relied during all my time as Bursar and who, despite his heavy workload, would produce precise and totally reliable costings for me within a few hours on any aspect of College affairs I might want. Computers may produce a result a little faster, but rarely with such entirely reliable accuracy.

In that first year, there was so much to be done and indeed so much to learn about school life, that it was difficult to see where to begin. I had arrived during the operation of a major fundraising effort for which the College was employing a professional firm of fundraisers. They had been at it for the past year and only raised so far £140,000 of which £80,000 had been an astonishingly generous donation from Jack Britton, the Chairman. Such a sum came nowhere near that which would be required to pay for the architect's grandiose plan of rebuilding most of the boarding houses of the Upper School on the lower Close, that is, on the lower part of the famous playing field in front of the College. The members of Council and the teaching staff, particularly the housemasters, all thought it was a cracking good scheme but obviously, from the lack of response, neither the current parents nor the Society of Old Cliftonians (OCs) liked it. And these people were the main source from whom the money was expected to come. In the meantime, as one of my self-allotted tasks, I had completed a detailed tour of all the twelve boarding houses of both schools. As is sometimes easier for a newcomer to see, it was strikingly obvious that the funds so far raised (and there were unlikely to be any more) were desperately needed to modernise the existing tatty and old-fashioned boarding houses, particularly of the Upper School. When I quietly discussed this with the Headmaster, Stephen McWatters, he agreed with me that refurbishing first the boarding and then the day-boy houses were the priorities for the senior school. But he could hardly go public with this view since, as Headmaster, he was the main speaker at meetings with the parents to raise funds for the scheme of building on the Close.

So, for most of that year, meetings of housemasters with the architects were held every month to design the ideal boarding house for seventy boys, which would be the first to be built on the Close under the grandiose scheme. It was my function to conduct these meetings, if not to chair them because the schoolmasters cannot bear to see a Bursar actually in charge of events, and I deliberately allowed the architects full rein in their excited response to all the ideas and requirements the housemasters threw at them for an ideal boarding house. It was sad in a way to watch the enthusiasm of them all, particularly that of Ernest Polack, the housemaster of the projected boarding house, knowing as I did that the inevitable result would be an estimate of building costs from the architect which would be far, far beyond the limited cash available. The plans for the new boarding house inevitably would have to be rejected at the end of the exercise. But it was the only way to instil some sense of realism into the minds of Council members and teaching staff and, meantime, there was no harm in spending a full year before any actual building commenced. It would allow time possibly to raise some more funds and, more importantly, for Council and Headmasters to think again about what our sensible priorities with limited funds really were: modernisation of the existing boarding accommodation for a start, in my view.

As regards maintenance of all the existing buildings, I found that the policy for years past had been for College to employ its own team of maintenance tradesmen, i.e. masons, carpenters, decorators, plumbers, etc., with a foreman in charge of men and materials. The team had comprised some twenty-two men. Shortly before I arrived, however, a good decision had been made by George Palmer, the Treasurer, to appoint a Buildings Manager and they had selected Brian Parrott who, in his previous job, had been responsible for the maintenance of university buildings. When I came to examine the situation, I found from the earlier accounts that the usual annual expenditure on the maintenance of buildings was less than 2% of gross annual income, and most of this minimal expenditure was on the wages of the maintenance team. Little wonder that almost all the school buildings were in such a bad state. The concept of these twenty or so maintenance men bumbling around the College looking for jobs to be done seemed hopelessly uneconomic and ineffective. Consequently I set about reducing their number. Henceforth the Buildings Manager would recommend to me the priority of works to be done, select appropriate outside contractors and negotiate the right price and time factor for each job, while the College maintenance team was gradually reduced to four men. In due course, as the development programme for the construction of major new buildings got under way, I was able to negotiate a substantial percentage reduction in the architect's fees, by using Brian Parrott to take part in supervision of the contractor's work on site.

A small but interesting job to be tackled that first year was the revision of the Royal Charter and this was made necessary by the existing terms of that clause of the Charter dealing with Trust monies. In effect, we were very limited indeed by the clause in the type of investments we were allowed to make and so even George Palmer, the Treasurer, who was usually intensely cautious, had realised that the restrictions needed to be relaxed. Our College solicitor, Sir Denys Hicks, commenced the long-winded task of obtaining approval for the Charter to be altered and, while he was at it, I discussed with him one or two other necessary changes which affected the administration of the College. The most important of these, in my view, was to make clear that, while the Headmaster had sole power in the appointment and dismissal of teaching staff, as already provided for in the Charter, the Bursar must have sole authority in the selection and appointment of non-teaching staff. Sir Denys incorporated this provision in the amended Charter which was approved first by the Council and, in due course, by the Royal Authority.

In the small world of Clifton College, the Chairman of Council is in a supremely powerful position, and if he wants to stay on, it is difficult to remove him. Under the terms of the Charter, the Chairman is elected annually and, on such a basis, it is customary in any organisation for a Chairman to be nodded through, unless he indicates that he will not be standing for re-election. A Chairman should normally have the grace and sensitivity to realise, after three years in office, that people have had enough of him and, like any well-bred guest after a dinner party, he should know when it is time to go. How I was to regret some years later, therefore, that we had not taken the opportunity to alter the provision for the election of Chairman of Council to be fixed on a three-year basis, rather than an annual election.

There was a minimal office staff to run the affairs of the Headmaster of the Upper School and the Bursar and all of them were accommodated in a pleasant house opposite the main school buildings. Just four people, as I have written, to deal with the accounts, and a secretary each for the Headmaster and me, with a registrar and two more staff to run the reception on the ground floor. I had an Assistant Bursar, Peter Hill, who had trained as an accountant, had a clever brain and was a wiz with monetary figures, but evidently he had been disappointed when, over a short period, three men from outside the College had been appointed over his head as Bursar. He found it difficult to accept the reality that he did not have the business experience, background or personality for the top job. It is understandable perhaps that, although he was my assistant, he was not much help to me personally. Instead I gave him responsibility for several specific tasks, such as managing the funds of the Composition and Discounted fees. My secretary, Roma Butler, was a strikingly good-looking young woman, with rather charming old-fashioned manners and attitudes, whose young husband had sadly died before she took the job as Bursar's secretary. We worked together for the next twelve years and I guess it was rather like a marriage, in a platonic kind of way, as we had our occasional tiffs. But Roma was a good and loyal friend to me throughout all those years.

The main challenge for me in that first year was to adapt to school life and to reach an understanding with the teaching staff of both Upper School and the Pre. I had the feeling early on that schoolmasters had a kind of instinctive suspicion of and aversion to the Bursar who by tradition as it seemed was the bogey-man, the creepy crawlie in the woodpile, the cause of all their problems with his negative attitude to their ideas and aspirations. I may have picked up this feeling from reading the enormous amount of correspondence which had been written back and forth between my predecessors and the teaching staff of the Upper School. It was as if Bursar and teachers lived and worked in different organisations and needed to write long letters to each other. It was absurd and I had to put a stop to it, but how?

The teachers at the Pre, on the other hand, were absolutely no problem; they were relaxed with me, they all knew me anyway from my earlier attempts to teach in the classroom and I always got on well with them and their Headmaster, Jim Hornby. And so I pondered what to do about establishing a similar happy relationship with the teaching staff of the Upper School. It seemed that they were an altogether different type of people than the Pre teachers, tending to be edgy and suspicious of me. The obvious solution was for me to get to know them better and for them on their part, in naval speak, to give me a fair wind and a chance to show my goodwill. As a first step, I suggested to Stephen, the Headmaster, that I attend formal meetings, which he held early every term with all his sixty or so teaching staff, and which took place in our large lecture room. It was unprecedented for the Bursar to attend these meetings and Stephen looked doubtful at first, but agreed. I told him that I would like to say a few brief words but, after that, I was there only to listen and that I had no intention of speaking again unless anyone had a question to ask of me as Bursar. I spoke at the beginning of that meeting to tell them, simply, that I would make myself available at almost any time to discuss their individual problems, that the door of my office would be almost always open for them to come and talk to me, or that I would come to their houses for a discussion if anyone would so prefer. But – and I laid emphasis on this – I would probably disregard letters and memos written to me and I would not answer them in writing. There was much for me to do, and there were more important things for all of us to be doing, than writing inter-school memos to each other, when we could more easily and effectively be talking. Judging by their stony faces, this little speech went down like a lead balloon. It was effective though, because thereafter it was rare for me to receive an internal memo. And in time, my presence at these meetings became a useful opportunity, maybe to explain to the whole gathering of teachers why such-and-such a bursarial action had to be taken.

The second thing I did was a frightful black, although I didn't realise it at the time or until much later. I went to the Masters' Common Room in the Upper School for mid-morning coffee. By tradition, no-one ever enters their common room unless an invitation is given, and now here came this new Bursar bouncing in uninvited! But the common rooms are where informal discussions take place about every aspect of school life between masters and with the Headmaster, every morning of term time. They are the places wherein so many problems and difficulties are ironed out, and sometimes quite heated arguments between staff can be heard. If you want to get a feeling for how a school is going along, either well or badly, go to the common room, and listen to the conversations. It wasn't long before the people got used to me and I was accepted in the common room. Moreover, my presence there provided the opportunity for people to tackle me about whatever bursarial-type problems they might have. Frequently, I would arrange to meet afterwards either in my office or on the site of their problem.

The difference in style between the teachers of the Pre and Upper Schools constantly surprised me. In the Pre Jim Hornby set the tone with his relaxed manner. It so happened that he also had a passionate desire to economise everywhere in his school and so should have been a boon to any Bursar. But a function of the Bursar, as I saw it, is not merely to support the Headmaster but to help promote him as the front man of the business. It is not enough for a Headmaster to be good at his prime function of selecting and leading his teaching staff, he must also sell the school to parents and the world generally, and for this he needs all the trappings of his position, and his office and his house must be impressive with lots of sherry and that sort of thing on hand for his visitors. Contrary to all this, dear Jim, Headmaster of by far the largest private preparatory school in the UK, had a small office, grubby with age and with faded carpet and curtains. His house was a shambles, being half-filled with the more timid younger boarding boys of his school, who needed cosseting by Clare, his wife.

It should be apparent from all I have written that he was a brilliant Headmaster, but his appearance needed to be taken in hand and I was the Bursar to do it.

When the time came a year later to spend money on refurbishing the Pre, I waited until Jim and Clare were on holiday before completing the entire redecoration of his office, including a new carpet and furnishings. He put on a show of being quite cross at first on seeing his lovely new office but, in reality, I reckon he was jolly pleased.

The teachers at the Pre were much the same; they rarely grumbled in those early days about their poor accommodation or teaching arrangements. Their common room for some forty masters, for instance, had been no bigger than an ordinary-sized dining room, with a centre table and book-sized open wooden lockers fixed to one wall. I had some personal experience of how totally inadequate it was when trying to teach before I became Bursar. Without even consulting Jim therefore, as obviously I should have done, I converted the two biggest classrooms into one large and well-furnished common room with proper man-sized lockers, sufficient for each member of staff. I was able to do this having provided more classrooms in a house immediately adjacent to the main school, which was no longer needed as accommodation for my catering staff. No wonder my name smelled of roses to the teachers of the Pre. But it wasn't just the provision of a proper common room for them that made for our cosy relationship; the truth is that they were on the whole a happy group of people with whom it was a pleasure to work. It was a joy to enter their common room for coffee during a morning break to be greeted, sometimes from right across the crowded room, with cheerful calls of welcome. What caused the difference from the Upper School, I wondered, where all the teachers appeared so comparatively grim and earnest? Maybe, teaching younger boys was less demanding and more easily rewarding? And with Jim Hornby of course, they had the benefit of an astonishingly relaxed Headmaster of long experience. Indeed his formal meetings with teaching staff, which I usually attended as a matter of course, were a bit of a hoot with his working announcements often interspersed with cheerful discussion and banter from the floor.

Not fair of me to have described the Upper School teachers as grim and earnest; they were simply on the whole a more serious group of people, having most probably a more difficult job to do. Teenage boys are notoriously more difficult to teach because they have reached the age when some of them may be argumentative and generally difficult. But, above all, there is great pressure on teachers of this older age group to bring all their pupils, whatever their attitudes and abilities, to high examination standards for university entrance. This latter pressure was not made any easier at Clifton College by having such a large preparatory school which could produce sometimes excessive numbers of young boys, all of whom were expected by their parents automatically to be accepted into the Upper School, regardless of whether the boy was of sufficiently high standard academically. In some cases, it would have been better for Clifton (despite the loss of my school fees!), if boys who were less bright than their peers had been passed onto schools elsewhere.

Gradually over the following years I came to know the teachers of the Upper School well and found many good companions and made a number of close friends among them. With only a few exceptions I admired them, for they were without doubt, during my time in the seventies, teachers of the highest quality and many of them, especially in the arts, were quite brilliant. Never before in our lives had Saccie and I had such opportunities to enjoy such good theatre and music as was produced, seemingly as a matter of course, by the teaching staff at Clifton. In comparison with the intense and solemn peers of my previous life in industry, the schoolmasters from both the Pre and Upper Schools were interesting and amusing people to know, and it was a wonderful change for me to be working with people whose company I enjoyed. But, having written how genuinely I enjoyed their company, I have to declare my view that schoolteachers are different and not the same as those of us who have to work in the real world outside of school life. They are a little bit quirky and odd in many ways, but not at all unpleasantly so and I wonder if, perhaps, their quirkiness may stem from dealing for most of their time with young pupils and the practice of talking instructively down to them, rather than as if to equals. In fairness, I ought to explain that view and cite some examples of the whimsicality I found among schoolteachers.

The first thing is that schoolteachers cannot bear to be interrupted in whatever they may be doing or thinking at the time. Most of us ordinary folk expect to be interrupted at almost any time by our bosses and by colleagues in the workplace, or by those who work for us wanting to know this or that, and especially by our business customers to whom we must give instant attention. We accept it as all part of life to be interrupted in what we are doing and having to refocus our minds onto a new subject. But not so for schoolteachers; although they do sometimes try to hide their irritation at an interruption, they are quite unable to disguise it entirely. It is as if they are in full flow of their peroration on a subject in class, when some wretched boy puts his hand up to ask a silly question.

Another aspect, which I could never understand and which used to astonish me, would be the offhand manner in which a successful producer, actor, musician or whatever, would be greeted by his peers on arrival in the common room for coffee on the day following the successful production. Instead of congratulations from his colleagues, he would be fortunate indeed if he received so much as a grunt of general approval for his show from any of them. It wasn't that anybody was jealous of his success, it was apparently bad form to be enthusiastic. Whilst I, who had been waiting impatiently for coffee time, would come bounding into the common room and rush across the room to tell the chap how much I had enjoyed his production. My manner was obviously not at all *comme il faut* and the watching teaching staff would look on my behaviour with evident disapproval. In due course, the Headmaster would arrive to greet the producer and to give his customary and measured congratulations.

Being a teacher by profession appeared to give some teachers the confidence that they knew about so many aspects of life that they could pontificate on any one of them, not only to young pupils, but to all and sundry. And thus, most probably armed by reading the morning issue of the Guardian newspaper, a teacher might go forth for the day prepared to share his wisdom with all who might be in need of it. An example I remember was on a morning in the Upper School common room, when the launch of a new Aircraft Carrier had been announced in the newspapers. One of the teaching staff, a most brilliant science teacher and a delightful man whom I liked, spoke to me about the Carrier and explained carefully to me what a disastrous mistake it had been by the Government to build it, since no ship of that type could possibly be protected against a full-scale attack by aircraft. I listened to him as gravely as I could manage, while remembering so clearly, as he spoke, how in 1945 our four Aircraft Carriers of the British Pacific Fleet had withstood attacks from wave after wave of suicide Kamikaze bombers, day after day, without loss. A lot of chaps had been killed on our flight decks of course, but our own air operations had never ceased, enabling us to knock down most of the Kamikazes before they reached our Fleet. There was no point in telling him all this and to be angry at his insensitivity; the horrors of that time were entirely outside his experience and beyond his imagination. In fact, I never spoke of war to those who had not experienced it; it would be rather like trying to explain how to play cricket to a Frenchman.

None of those typical, what I call whimsical characteristics of schoolteachers, affected my pleasure in their company or my respect for them. My greatest respect was in response to the unselfish nature of the demands which they made on me in those early years of my bursarship at Clifton. Oh yes, of course they continually wanted this or that done or finance for something else, but it was immediately noticeable to me that, whatever they might want or need was for the ultimate benefit of their boy pupils. It might be some enlargement or improvement to their particular classroom, some special books or equipment or, for housemasters, nearly always such things as improvements to a dormitory, study accommodation or the changing room. I don't recall ever, in those early years, being asked by teaching staff of either the Pre or Upper School for something which would be of personal benefit to the man himself. I like to remember this because, by 1975, there was to be a significant change from this remarkable and genuinely unselfish attitude of the teachers.

As a profession, school teaching had been poorly paid for many years, long before my personal introduction at Clifton to the world of education. The salaries of those who taught in independent private schools, regardless of how famous and well-known such schools might be, were not all that much higher than for those teachers who worked in state schools. On the other hand, there were valuable perks available for those who taught in the private sector, such as free meals, good accommodation at peppercorn rentals and much-reduced school fees for their children. At the start of the 1970s, however, trade union pressure in the state sector was beginning to effect an improvement in teachers' pay throughout the whole educational system in the UK and, of course, the independent schools would have to follow suit by paying higher salaries.

Contrary to logical thought that more pay would bring greater satisfaction in their job to schoolteachers, higher pay seemed to have the opposite effect. This was certainly the case at Clifton where, from about 1975, teaching staff became ever more demanding in their personal requirements. In an appointment interview with the Headmaster, for example, it might not be enough for a young prospective member of teaching staff to be offered accommodation in a nice flat, he might also insist that it be newly and smartly redecorated for him. The Headmaster, if he wanted the young teacher for his team, would probably have to accede to this and do so in the hope that the Bursar subsequently would find the means of paying for it. But there was an inevitable domino effect to this sort of thing because then, of course, other teaching staff would want redecoration and alterations to their accommodation too, and so it would go on. The stage was reached towards the end of the decade, as new housemasters of boarding houses were taking over from those retiring, when the first thing they would demand would be that the whole of their private side of the house be refurbished. In some cases this even would include poaching an area of the boys' part of the house.

Perhaps the ultimate example of aggrandisement was the demand for a new and larger common room for the teaching staff of the Upper School. The scheme for this involved the conversion of three large and rather lovely old original classrooms and was very expensive. I really put my foot down on this one because it was so obviously an unnecessary nonsense. For one reason, their existing common room, on two floors, was suitably provided with lockers downstairs and comfortable chairs and tables upstairs and, altogether in actual area, it was three times that of the new common room for the Pre. The request for this bit of nonsense was presented to Council by the Headmaster almost every year until my retirement in 1983, but each time I had pre-empted any possibility of agreement to it by quietly convincing each of my successive Chairmen beforehand that there was no finance available for such a project. All this sort of thing was a far cry from my early years as Bursar, at the beginning of the decade, when the wholly laudable and first priority for all teaching staff had been consideration for their boy pupils. Put it down to human nature, I suppose, the more we have, the more we want, as the old saying goes.

It is also quite an interesting comment on the changing emphasis of education at Clifton College to note that, later on in the 1990s, the conversion of the three best classrooms in the West Cloister to the Upper School common room was eventually agreed, while the three other best and oldest classrooms in the East Cloister were converted to a study for the Headmaster and for his secretarial offices. One would have thought that six large classrooms, beautifully built for the purpose in the 1860s, would be more conducive to the education of the pupils than the provision of a smart common room and grand offices for teaching staff.

But I must go back in this narrative to the end of 1970 when there were so very many things still to be done at Clifton College. One of the most important was to attend to the non-teaching staff, particularly the more senior members, some of whom had been working for the College for many years. These were people such as bursarial assistants, accountants, secretaries, sports managers, senior porters, grounds men and maintenance men for whom no pension provision at all had been made, and the best that some of them could expect from the College on retirement would be a nice little 'thank-you' speech from the Bursar and maybe an appropriate cheque. The Treasurer, George Palmer, had been giving all this some thought before I arrived, but I was appalled to find that a famous College could be so lacking in care for its long-term employees that it had failed to provide any proper pension arrangements for them. To introduce a pension scheme, to be funded entirely by the College, capable of providing a reasonable pension to about thirty senior non-teaching staff some of whom had already served fifteen years, was going to be very expensive. And so it was, and in consequence took the best part of a year, well into 1971, before the scheme received unanimous approval from the Council. The pensions for teaching staff, on the other hand, had been provided under government legislation since 1948, and this was a compulsory contributory scheme, which provided excellent pensions for the teachers.

Everything was so joyful for me and Saccie because of my wonderful new job at Clifton College, and everything was going so well that first year of 1970 that sensibly, knowing our yo-yo type of luck, we ought to have had some sense of foreboding.

Saccie and I were guests at a House Supper at the end of that winter school term, just before Christmas 1970, and on our return late that evening noticed that Jeremy had taken Saccie's Triumph Vitesse car. Unusually for him, he had not asked us beforehand. An hour later, two policemen were at the front door to tell us that Jeremy was in the main Bristol hospital and badly injured.

We learned that, in the dark and the pouring rain, the car had crashed against a lamppost on the edge of the Clifton Downs on a bend in the road, just minutes away from the house. It had been there for over an hour while cars passed continually, until a young man and his wife had stopped to see if anyone was hurt inside the crashed car. During that time, Jeremy was unconscious but with his face, already lacerated by broken glass, resting on the jagged edges of the smashed windscreen. By the time the young couple had stopped to see if help was needed, both his eyes had been badly gouged by the jagged glass on which his face was lying.

Saccie came with me to the hospital but we were warned that Jeremy was in a critical condition and they were most anxious that he should not move his head. He was a ghastly sight as his head had to remain unbandaged and the skin of his face was in shreds with a nurse attending constantly to his wounds. He was conscious but he did not utter any sounds of distress and even tried to speak to us. He was about to be rushed to Frenchay Hospital where eye surgeons were waiting for him. We followed close behind and waited there for a desperate period while Jeremy and his eyes were operated on.

After an hour, the surgeon came out of the theatre to tell us that the left eye was gone completely and that it was very doubtful if any repair could be done to the right eye as there were so many pieces of glass embedded in it. Thus Jeremy would be entirely blind and his face would remain very scarred. Saccie, still holding herself steady despite the horror of the last few hours, begged the suregon to do everything he possibly could to repair the remaining eye, to give some slight sight to it at least. Some time much later, the surgeon returned to say that Jeremy was now in the recovery ward and that there was just a possibility that the right eye might be saved, but there was still some glass in it which could never be removed. It would be imperative, if the eye was to be saved, that Jeremy keep his head absolutely as still as he possibly could all day and night for the next two weeks.

Two days later, Jeremy was taken to a ward in the Bristol Eye Hospital where, of course, he had to lie completely still with his eyes firmly bandaged. When Saccie and I arrived there, we were horrified at the noise level and to find visiting children running about this large ward, while Jeremy lay in considerable pain and striving uncomplainingly, with all his endurance and courage, to be still and to ignore the noise around him. The consultant, after I had demanded to see him immediately, agreed that Jeremy must be moved to a quiet room on his own without delay. The bandages were removed two weeks later. It is difficult to describe the anxiety and fear as they were slowly unwound because nobody could know whether or not Jeremy would see anything at all, or whether everything might remain just blackness for him. I can remember now, as I write, the delight which came over Jeremy's battered face as slowly he was able to focus his eye on the room around him, and to smile at us. In due course, Jeremy came out of hospital and was fitted with a glass eye on his left while, gradually and miraculously, good sight returned to his right eye. Only Saccie and I and Aza knew of the tiny pieces of glass remaining in his one eye and feared that at some time in the future they would blind him. We never told him and he never knew of the awful possibility.

CHAPTER FOURTEEN

At Clifton: Years 1971 – 74

As the year 1971 started, Saccie and I experienced the warmth of being part of the community life of a college like Clifton and its Pre for, although we had only been working for a year there, so many of its people including some of the boys went out of their way to express their sympathy for the dreadful accident which had occurred to our son. How different it was from life in industry where nobody would have known about it anyway.

Yes, the boys too were beginning to know us and this was because, unlike any of the Bursars either before me or after me, I became very much involved in school life and Saccie, as I have written, did the same. It would have been totally daft, as I saw it, to spend all my time in an office, as if I was working in Industry still, when out there was a whole wonderful new life going on, to be enjoyed. Moreover, I reckoned that the more I knew about life in the College, the better as a Bursar I would be. The most joyful thing for me was to play Rackets again and, with enormous encouragement from the professional, Terry Whatley, I was able to develop my game from when Father had curtailed it at aged sixteen in my second year at Harrow. Indeed, as I had hoped to do all those years ago at Harrow, I was able to reach the standard of the second school pair. Just as much fun too was coaching the boys at all levels at Squash since, at this game, I had kept up a high standard even at my age, by then of nearly fifty. In the summer terms, I also played a lot of Lawn Tennis with the boys, at a standard good enough to play with their top team.

But there were many activities, other than sports, in which to take part. I had a go at the debating society, and was absolutely hopeless at it compared with the boys. I tried acting but was again hopelessly bad and was relegated to funny, speechless parts since I could never remember my lines when on stage. I attended madly erudite evening lectures to the boys on art but was banned from further attendance for disagreeing with the lecturer. In the winter evenings, I sometimes undertook to play Bridge with the boys but their house rules were 5p per hundred and, as they cleaned my pockets out, I couldn't afford to play against them too often. Both Saccie and I made a bit of a return to churchgoing as we found the services in Chapel, with the beautiful organ music and the singing of the choirs, moving and irresistible.

There were always plays put on by the Upper School in the comparatively new theatre to watch, although we sometimes wished that they weren't quite so lengthy and serious. But their productions such as *Oliver* and the comic sketches were superbly good. The shows produced on the Pre stage were more knock-about type of comedy and the unsophisticated Bursar and his wife found them hugely enjoyable. I always attended all the art exhibitions of each school every year and, to tell just one more quirky schoolmaster story, I remember being rebuked by both the Second Master and the Art Master together, for criticizing one of the boy's paintings. 'What on earth, as a Bursar, do you know about art?' they demanded. Evidently I had ventured out of my proper place as Bursar and they considered that, in foolishly attempting to enter their own rarefied world of academic art, I deserved to be put down. I doubt that the awful arrogance of their remark occurred to either of them, but there was no answer to it at the time. They would never know that, later on in my retirement years, my marine and aviation paintings were sold to the value of over £50,000!

I must get back to the work because there was much to be done in 1971. The Manager of our Westminster Bank in Bristol had been putting the frights on our Treasurer and the Council in the recent years because our overdraft at the end of each financial year had been, on the face of it, frighteningly high. Perhaps it was just a matter of presenting the accounts to the bank in a better light? Our expenditure was bound to be at its height at the end of a financial year, before the fees for the following term had arrived to be banked. Accordingly, I asked my guardian angel upstairs, John Rogers, to set out for me an assessment of the average overdraft or credit for each month over the period of the coming year. The result didn't look too bad; most months in overdraft of course, but not all that high and the occasional credit month did appear too. Armed with this, I arranged an appointment with Mr Jannaway, the Area and Bristol Manager who became most friendly, after I had hosted a nice lunch with him to talk about the school and its prospects. He agreed a slightly lower rate of interest on our overdraft and even extended the amount of the facility for the future.

AT CLIFTON: YEARS 1971 – 74

About the only perk for a Bursar at Clifton was to attend the annual conference of bursars from all the Headmasters' and Headmistresses' Conference schools, i.e. independent schools, which usually took place in Cambridge during the Easter school holidays. I had been far too busy even to contemplate attending the conference in my first year at Clifton but now, in my second year, perhaps I might go along to see what it was all about. I would take Saccie because we had only taken a week of holiday in the previous summer and she deserved a break too. On the Thursday afternoon, we booked into a good modern hotel just a mile outside the city, and settled in for the long week-end. I had been invited for drinks in the early evening to meet the Committee who arranged the conference. On arrival at the drinks party, I was greeted warmly as a new boy by the chairman and the five members of his committee, who explained the programme for the week-end and then asked me, rather anxiously I thought, how I was getting on at Clifton.

I told him that it was fine, a bit busy with lots to do but I was happy in the job. I had the feeling that he did not quite believe my reply. He seemed to think that I was putting a brave face on the well-known difficulties of a Bursar's life at Clifton College. He confirmed this view when he then disclosed that Clifton College was always known in the bursarial community as 'the Bursar's graveyard'. My immediate predecessor at Clifton, who you may remember had committed suicide there, had been well known to them since, before Clifton, he had been Bursar at Roedean. His awful death, plus the early departures of previous Bursars, had resulted in this 'graveyard' reputation for Clifton College. All their well-meaning but rather dismal sympathy did not quite accord with the actual cheerful life Saccie and I were leading at Clifton, but obviously they were not going to believe me, so I left it at that.

To be frank the conference itself was a bore, consisting of dry lectures during all of Friday and Saturday about how to overcome bursarial problems but, since I didn't have any, I cut all the lectures after the first morning and took Saccie out to Cambridge for shopping and that sort of thing. However, I did meet many of the Bursars at the bar in the evenings where I could have sensible discussions about school finance with those who wanted or indeed needed such discussions. I don't mean to appear snooty but bear in mind that so many of these chaps, mainly from government or the military services, had little or no background of business experience. Bursars from the large and more famous independent schools were well clued up (to use service jargon) in the management of their schools, while the great majority of Bursars on the other hand are dealing merely with quite small businesses. On the Saturday evening, there was a drinks party followed by a formal dinner. (Saccie joined up with a party of about four other wives who had accompanied their husbands.) The Bursars' dinner was well organised but I wouldn't describe it as a particularly jolly affair since the Bursars sitting near me were rather a lugubrious lot and spent most of the time exchanging moans about the difficulties of their jobs. When I disclosed that I found my job at Clifton so far to be rather fun, they promised that by next year I would have a very different story to tell. But I only attended the conference once or twice more, and in much later years.

I had planned that 1971 would be a fallow year for new building projects and Stephen, the Headmaster, knew this and agreed with it and so, while the housemasters were happy designing a new boarding house on the Close which would never materialise, we set about getting rid of the professional fundraisers who, judging from the poor results, had been an expensive waste of time. I found it a little difficult at first because they had a long-term contract, but soon I was able to bid farewell to the nice-but-useless, old boy who had been allocated to us as the fundraiser. By this time only about a net £145,000 been raised, but a large part of it had come from Jack Britton, our Chairman. Make a mental note, I told myself, next time we would do our own fundraising.

The next meeting of Council in this summer term of 1971 would be vitally important. There were four main items which I personally was desperately anxious to see resolved:

The first was for Council to formally discard the plan of building boarding houses on the Close. The Old Cliftonian Society loathed the project, as did many parents.

The second would be to agree in principle the priority of allocating the existing funds towards improving the existing boy accommodation in both boarding and day-boy houses, plus improvements to the classrooms of the Pre. Both Headmasters were in favour, although Stephen would have to overcome the customary grumbles over this or that from some of his teaching staff, who always had different ideas.

The third would be to agree a proposal to bring in a direct debit system for payment of the school fees. How the parents would respond would be a gamble, because no other school had thought of the idea as yet and so there was nothing to go on. But direct debiting was beginning to become adopted by major suppliers in the UK, and there seemed no reason why we shouldn't use it at Clifton to collect our fees at specified dates three times a year. The certainty of receiving the fees at fixed dates before the school terms began would be an advantage in itself, but the scheme could also provide extra interest on the total sum collected in advance. I had been advised on this by Roger Newman, who was an OC and a director of Hill Samuel, the merchant bankers. He had explained to me how credit sums in our Westminster bank could be transferred quickly and at any time to Hill Samuel, who would be able to place the funds, at very short term, with the advantage of interest on them. Hence there would be value to us of a system of direct debit, if the parents would accept it.

In the event, the Council approved the direct debit system although it was not until the following year that we introduced it. I confess that I never actually mentioned in Council the matter of the transfer of funds, from time to time, to a merchant bank. Once formally organised in writing, it was so simple; I merely had to effect the transfer of the credit sum, if only for a day or two, by telephone to our bank. Of course, my Treasurer, now Charles Cooper, knew of the arrangement as did Bernard Waley-Cohen, also a director of a merchant bank, who approved the procedure. In due course, it became a matter of routine for our bank to transfer credit sums to Hill Samuel.

The fourth resolution I wanted at the forthcoming Council meeting was approval of my budget for next year with my proposed further increase in fees. The high increase of the previous year had been swallowed by the parents with remarkably few grumbles from them, and indeed the forecast of boy numbers by the Headmasters for the next year indicated an increase in the number of boys in both schools. With the Deputy Chairman, Roderick Collar, strongly advocating higher fees, the majority of Council members were now in favour too. So, hey presto, up went the fees with the aim at last of a sensible 5% surplus of income over expenditure for the year. This compared with a net loss in the years prior to 1970. Also, as one example of detail, I was now budgeting for a 7% rise in expenditure on building maintenance, in place of the 2% per annum in previous years. I was also adding, within my overall budget, a 10% contingency sum on most of the departmental budgets prepared by the teaching staff. I didn't tell them this, of course, because the total of their contingency factors gave me a fund to use for more major projects, which any one of them might need during the year. People used to wonder, sometimes, how I could suddenly manage to find the money for a project they wanted; well that's where it came from.

The impetus behind my financial machinations was that of my accountant and guardian angel upstairs, John Rogers, who fed me with the accurate figures and forecasts I needed. But perhaps his ability as an accountant was best shown in the competence with which he dealt with the auditors each year, ensuring that they received all the information they needed but, at the same time, negotiating with them on the best presentation of our accounts. I would have been at a complete loss at that sort of thing without him.

By the end of 1971, the stage had been reached when the scheme of relocating all the Upper School boarding houses on the Close had been recognised by everybody as financially impractical, and the project of building just the one such boarding house (Polacks) on the Close was now accepted as vastly too expensive. At last, therefore, I could get cracking with the architects with the agreement of most people to use the development fund for the refurbishment of all the boarding and day-boy houses, and the Pre main building. Most of the boarding houses of the Upper School had three big dormitories with beds for twenty boys or more in each. Few of the houses had any lavatories at all upstairs, so that the situation for a boy at Clifton was the same as mine had been at Harrow thirty-five years earlier, when the only lavatories had been four flights downstairs. (Mind you, I wasn't at all sure that this appalling situation had changed at Harrow either!). The basic plan was to transpose the large dormitories into study-bedrooms, some of them with upper bunks, sufficient to accommodate the same total number of boys, while lavatories were to be provided on each floor. The time schedule to refurbish the twelve boarding houses of both schools, probably four at a time, would be during the many weeks of the school holidays throughout 1972 and 1973.

At the same time, this refurbishment was the opportunity to provide proper and safe escape routes for the boys in event of fire. The poor standard of fire safety precautions in the boarding houses had worried me considerably ever since I arrived at Clifton and the provision of outside fire escapes, and of a safe route along the corridors to them, would be at my insistence an essential factor of the refurbishment, albeit a very expensive one. However, I had the benefit of an experienced Buildings Manager in Brian Parrott, who negotiated well with the Fire Officer to establish escape routes which fully met all the requirements of the Fire Precautions Act at the lowest cost to the College.

These two years of refurbishing the houses were interesting and a pleasure for me because I came to know the layout of all the rooms and studies in every one of the twelve houses but also, rather more importantly, I developed a good relationship with the housemasters since they and I had to work closely together with the architect in formulating the new layout of the study-bedrooms. Before we started refurbishing a house, it was essential too that I had agreement with each housemaster on a strict specification for the work, so that I could fix a firm unchangeable price for the work with the builder. Not easy for them to stick to a specification as all sorts of improvements would come to their minds as work progressed.

This was the era too when the paramount interest of the housemasters was to produce the best result for the boys, and never mind their private, family side of the boarding house. As we worked together, I much admired their zeal for the boys' side of the house and for setting aside much of their own personal interest. However, that was the old guard of housemasters, so to speak, and attitudes changed over the following years as new housemasters were freshly appointed, some of whom had more expensive demands for their private side of the house than for the boys' side.

Not only were total boy numbers increasing but the ratio of day-boys to boarders was tending also to increase, so that major alterations were needed to cater for this situation by enlarging the two existing day houses in the Upper School while a new and third day house, East Town, was built into an available space under the common room. At the Pre too, the boy numbers were increasing quite rapidly and, while we were at it so to speak, this was the time not just to refurbish the main Pre building, but to enlarge it with new classrooms, a science block and music rooms. The finances for all this were getting a bit tricky as the fund from the Appeal was nowhere near enough. Moreover, to meet the extra expenditure on all these new plans, we could not just rely on our improving boy numbers or the surplus from our increased fees, improved finance arrangements with the bank and strict budget control. But we did have a Composition Fee Fund.

The Composition Fee Fund was formed from a scheme for the advance payment of school fees with a capital sum, payable by the parent at any time before his boy entered the school, to cover an agreed number of school terms in the future. At that time, nearly all the major independent schools operated such a scheme, which would be managed on their behalf by a broker, but Clifton was one of the very few such schools, if not the only one, which invested and managed its own Fund, without paying a percentage to a broker Hitherto this Fund had always been regarded as sanctified and never to be touched in case to do so would jeopardise our liability to cover future fees. But I had my eye on it.

The Fund had been well invested by George Palmer in those earlier years and had grown considerably to be worth £360,000, which was some 34% more than the liability to the payment of future fees, in other words there was about £120,000 lurking in the Fund ready for me to raid if only the Council would let me get my hands on it. In due course, after approval from the Chairman and the Treasurer, the Council eventually conceded that a small percentage of the Composition Fee Fund might be sold and the proceeds applied towards the development work.

Another very good little earner for the College was the Health Insurance scheme, which we offered to parents. Under the scheme, for a charge on the parents of about £8 per term, the College undertook to pay back the fees for that term if their son was ill and missed his schooling for a period of more than four weeks, and most parents, particularly of boarders, entered into this arrangement. There was nothing unusual about the basic scheme as most of the larger independent schools offered it but they did so via their insurance broker who, as you would expect, took both the risk and the profit. But we decided to take the risk to obtain the profit ourselves, because why, after all, should we let the broker have it? The main risk was the possibility of an epidemic of illness throughout the College but now, with advances in preventive medicine, such epidemics were becoming a rarity in schools. Furthermore, we could insure against the risk of epidemic for a very small annual premium. Thus we were the only independent school at the time to operate our own Health Insurance scheme and indeed it did well and was little trouble to operate.

In 1973 I had some luck while playing Bridge with a retired judge at the Clifton Club (a well-run local social club for businessmen) who told me of his intention to sell his house - which, as he told me about it, I realised was right opposite the main building of our Pre. To cut the story short and, following an urgent consultation with my Chairman, he agreed to sell it directly to the College at a most modest price. It was a big house and just what we wanted for the Pre, as we were able to convert the top two floors into a science school and the ground floor and basement into a new day-boy house.

The conversion of the top floors to two science classrooms, complete with work benches fitted with gas and electricity connections along them, was designed by our Buildings Manager. As regards our other two requirements for a music and an art school, these were met by utilising a house immediately behind the Pre, which hitherto had provided accommodation for catering staff. The work of converting the house during the winter was done by our remaining maintenance team in conjunction with our ground staff. One way and another, therefore, we had enlarged the Pre in the most economical manner.

Jim Hornby had enough to do as Headmaster of the largest Pre in the UK and was content for me to get on with these new buildings and rarely concerned himself with either design or money matters. In fact, so little was he concerned with money affairs that he had failed to sign on for the Government pension scheme and had to rely on a pension from his earlier Headmastership. This was folly on a grand scale. It was my job to persuade the Council that the College needed to buy back the past years of unpaid pension for him on the government scheme. It would cost £15,000 for the College to do this but, in the event, it proved easier for the Council to agree this sum than it was to persuade Jim to accept a vastly-improved pension arrangement!

It was a busy-enough life during every term of those years but, with so much building work going on during the school holidays, it was difficult for Saccie and me to get away from the College for our annual holiday. Indeed there were two whole years when we had no holiday at all except for an occasional long week-end, when we would bale out to a country hotel somewhere for a break. Having no holiday was my own fault in a way because, in drafting my own major contracts with architects and builders, I made a point of including and emphasizing a clause which prevented anyone other than me, e.g. Headmasters, housemasters, etc., from altering the fixed specification on each contract without my authority. If any alteration to the specification really needed to be made, as the work progressed, then I would be able to negotiate a price for it. It was the only way of keeping firm control of the building costs. My insistence on drafting my own contracts with the builders had meant refusing to accept the standard form of contract, devised by the building federation, which was complicated and designed to enable the builder to drive a horse and cart through any of those clauses which would have been of benefit to the customer. All my many contracts with builders, then and thereafter, were fixed price for fixed specifications and typed usually on no more than a couple of A4-size pages.

I have written this far about some of the working part of life as a Bursar at Clifton, all of which was pleasant enough indeed, but there was also the fun and enjoyment of the facilities of the place and the companionship of the boys as well as the teaching staff. Saturday was usually my best day, except when there was a Council meeting or some such thing, and I would spend the morning going the rounds to listen and talk to people, starting with the porters and groundsmen. Then most probably on to the Pre for a second chat with Jim Hornby (we also met on Wednesday mornings) and coffee in the common room with the teaching staff. Probably I would have arranged next to meet Peter Cole with his catering staff in the kitchens and dining room of the Pre. Time by then to talk with the kitchen staff in Big School, that is, the dining hall of the Upper School, and then to join the cafeteria queue for first lunch, where I would join the boys at any convenient table. Most of them would know me well enough to moan about the meals or anything else, if they felt like it. Which reminds me how, during the early days of my Bursarship, a fair-haired boy, Beresford, once approached me in the Quad to complain about the loo paper and invited me to come with him to inspect a sample in the main lavatories. He was quite right; it looked and felt more like brown cardboard than paper, and I discovered that the head porters had been ordering the same stuff for the past fifty years or more!

Still on Saturday, and at 1.45 p.m. down to the courts changed and ready to coach Squash, either for the school team or for junior players, until 3.30 p.m. when there would be time to watch the second half of the rugby match on the Close, before going on to the Rackets court to play against the boys. At 6.30 p.m., time to change at home and to collect Saccie, who would have been working in some part of the College, and off to the pub where we would meet Terry Whatley, the rackets professional, and other good friends from the teaching staff. What a lovely day ... and I was being paid for it as well! If at all possible, Saccie and I kept Sunday to ourselves as a family day, except maybe for Chapel in the morning.

On some Saturdays, I would join the professional in taking either the Rackets or Squash teams to an away match against another school. Terry would take about nine boys in one of the school vans and I might have another five crammed into my car and really, win or lose, it was always a happy day, especially for me as I usually could get a game against the games master of the other school. On the way back and if we had won, we made it a practice to stop at a pub for a glass of beer all round or, to be honest, we stopped anyway if we had 'nearly' won. I remember one boy in particular whom I always took with me in my car. He hardly stopped talking all the way and, on the way back in the car, he would entertain us by describing in exciting and meticulous detail every aspect of every match that had been played that afternoon. His name was John Inverdale and now he is doing exactly the same brilliant expositions on games for TV and radio and, no doubt, being paid a bomb for it! He must surely have had 'sports commentator' written across his belly-button at birth.

These journeys to Away matches were an eye opener for me into the school lives of the boys for, with the excitement of the game they had recently played and maybe with the added boost of a glass of beer, they seemed to become totally unaware of my existence as I drove the car back to Clifton. They would talk animatedly about life at Clifton and, among many other aspects of school life, I learned their views and opinions on the abilities of their teachers and it surprised me how sensible and mature so many of these boys were at their ages of between fifteen and seventeen. However, I regarded whatever I learned as for my ears only and I just locked it securely away into my memory. Sometime during the mid-seventies, a Junior Common Room was formed, using some rooms alongside the Close, which was rather a grand name as a club for the senior boys over sixteen which they ran themselves, although there was a master in overall charge, and where they were allowed to drink beer and soft drinks. When it was first formed, I was very chuffed indeed to be voted by the committee of boys to be an honorary member, the only adult to be so honoured, I believe. Perhaps the fact that, as Bursar, I had contrived to make available the club premises and a small annual allowance, might have had something to do with it? Anyway, it was a great pleasure during the summer terms to sit outside the club premises, on the grass with a glass of beer, watching a cricket game or nets on the Close with the boys. But only for an hour or so; the thing is for older people never to impose themselves on the young for too long.

CHAPTER FIFTEEN

The Norman Years, 1973 – 78

Jack Britton retired and Norman Travis was elected as the new Chairman of the Council in 1973. Norman was on the Board of both Rio Tinto and Borax, of which he was Chairman, and, since these two companies together formed probably the biggest mining organisation in the world, you could rightly say that he was one of the very biggest of the big wheels in British industry. It was extraordinary that he hadn't got his Knighthood already. I never entirely understood why on earth he decided to take on the chairmanship of Clifton College, which was a comparatively insignificant task. Admittedly, at one time half the Council members had their K from their real activities, but surely Norman could not think he might get his K from being Chairman at Clifton, could he? But he certainly went flat out at the task. Far too intensely for my liking, because he and I never got on well together and I believe that the essence of our difficult working relationship was that Norman, so typical of all the very top men in industry, was accustomed to and expected almost immediate acquiescence to his views and decisions. Working with him, therefore, I was thrown back again into the ghastly world of large-scale industry, of which I already had so much experience.

But Clifton College and its people was entirely unknown territory to Norman and, although the College needed to be run in a businesslike manner, it was not quite the same as a normal commercial or industrial enterprise. There were other considerations involved of which he was unaware and, in consequence, some of his proposals regarding the management of the College were manifestly wrong. As Bursar, I regarded it as my responsibility to tell him so. It is not surprising then, that there followed difficult years for me under his leadership. I recognised, of course, that Norman had a brilliant background of achievement with a fine, incisive mind able to go quickly to the crux of a problem and I believe that he, on his part, recognised my knowledge of the College and my influence in it. Thus we sought to reach a *modus vivendi* in our working relationship.

Much of our business was conducted by Norman on the telephone from his office in London or from his home or even from America, and I could expect to hear his voice grinding on at me at various times every week, and most frequently in the late evenings and week-ends, regardless of whatever I might be doing at the time. From my experience in industry, I was well accustomed to this autocratic attitude that one should always be available at any time to talk business, and so I didn't resent it as much as others might have done, but I hadn't expected to suffer it in the sheltered and academic world of a school!

Sometimes our telephone discussion might be so unsatisfactory that I would take the train to his London office, where it was easier for us to reach an understanding and agreement. Usually, I waited for him in a comfortable conference room next to his office and I was amazed and really rather amused to see senior executives waiting in the hall to see him, looking quite white and shaky at the prospect.

On one momentous evening, a Friday evening when I was unavailable, Norman had left an instruction for me not to proceed with an urgent matter which I had in hand at the time. To avoid yet another of Norman's long grinding arguments on the telephone, I set off by car on the following morning at 6 a.m., accompanied by my dear long-suffering Saccie, to arrive at Norman's home in Essex in time for breakfast. To say that he was startled is putting it mildly, but he certainly realised the value I put on the matter, and an hour later we reached agreement for me to proceed as I had intended. Meantime, Saccie's embarrassment at arriving unexpectedly for breakfast was put at ease by the gentle charm of Betty Travis. Those two wives were very much alike in looks and character, and they got on well together. I guess that both of them might have been equally long-suffering with their respective husbands!

Like all top people, especially Captains of industry, one of the first things they do when they take on the new job is to sack the chaps down the line below them. This is mainly to show everybody that they are going to be a new broom. Norman was no different and typically let it be known within a few weeks of his chairmanship that Stephen McWatters, the Headmaster, was to 'retire'. And so Stephen, who had been a quiet, effective and excellent Headmaster for the past nine years, was bundled out of Clifton. Fortunately, he had the sense to accept a pleasant headmastership of a well-known preparatory school in Winchester and was happy. I suspect that Norman would have preferred to get rid of me but realised that he would need to use my knowledge of the school management and anyway, with all my support in Council, I would be no pushover.

I remember Saccie and me meeting the new Headmaster Stuart Andrews and his wife Marie at their welcoming party in Auburn House in December 1973. It was absolutely vital for each of us personally and for the College that he and I should get on well together and so, unusually for me, I wasn't sure how to handle this first meeting with him. I didn't want to appear to rush up effusively as if I wanted to ingratiate myself with him but, on the other hand, I didn't want him to feel that I was keeping my distance. In the event, his manners were so much better than mine because he it was who first came up with his charming wife to greet Saccie and me. A tall, good-looking chap, very young too, so that I felt positively fatherly towards him as we talked, and I mentally vowed to help him in his difficult job as best I could and with all my influence. And so I did during the next nine years until ill health forced me to retire.

Despite the spats between Norman and me, some good building work was completed during his chairmanship and, notably on the initiative of the new Headmaster, the possibility was considered of rebuilding two large houses in College Road to form a new teaching block. It would contain not only new classrooms, but a Computer Room and a Technical Activities Centre. I was pleased to have obtained a promise, through my contacts with Rolls-Royce, of some lathes and drills for the Technical Centre, as a gift. The College now was in a much better position financially to undertake new building works such as this because, since early in 1973, the Council had agreed to establish a Reserve Fund out of the surplus income which we were generating each year. Our fees remained as high as I could get away with, on presentation of my annual budgets to Council. Complaints from the parents about the high level of fees were rare and this was largely because, in my opinion, they were glad to see the amount of new building and refurbishing going on at the College and, more particularly, I reckoned, because in that period of hyper-inflation under the Wilson Labour government (26% at one point.), the unfortunate and hard-working parents barely knew half the time, whether they were on their backsides or their elbows financially. But it was interesting that, during Norman's regime, he and I never disagreed about keeping the fees at a high level.

The Norman Years, 1973 – 78

The arrival of Stuart Andrews as Headmaster was a good time to promote a new Appeal for a College Development Fund, because Stuart, who had experience as a successful fundraiser in his previous school, could bring his much-needed expertise to the task. Moreover, as we were to discover, he was a first-class speaker at fundraising meetings. The most important thing would be to select the right objectives this time: those which were needed by the College and which also would be supported by the Old Cliftonians and parents. Thus, the replacement of the old and tatty outdoor swimming pool with a new indoor one, plus the provision of a sports hall, were announced as the main objectives, together with the inevitable bursaries which, as I had learned, were always regarded by school people as a right and proper objective and must be included.

This time too, with the benefit of Stuart's knowledge, we would make our own fundraising arrangements and do our own promotion work, using our usual public relations agents. Stuart selected an excellent secretary, experienced in fundraising work, to deal with the correspondence and she was a great success. Not so was my own selection of the man whom I appointed to act as our main fundraiser, with the task of visiting OCs and parents. He was a charming Old Boy of the College, knew lots of people and spoke well but, as I had failed to recognise when I interviewed him, he hadn't got that essential determination, thick hide and toughness required of a true salesman. I, of all people, should have known better as I had employed a number of salesmen in my time. It was also the cause of another row with Norman, who telephoned to tell me immediately after I had made the appointment, to say that I had no authority to appoint such people. To which I had replied by referring Norman to the terms of the Royal Charter, which gave me responsibility and authority to make all appointments at the College, other than of teaching staff. It was particularly galling, therefore, when it became apparent that I had made a bad appointment. Nevertheless, over the following years, the Appeal went moderately well and raised enough to allow us to start thinking seriously of building at least a new swimming pool.

One of my main concerns during the years of the Norman regime was the determined attempt by the trade unions to infiltrate this 'posh' private school, as they regarded it, and take control of my non-teaching staff, with particular emphasis on the catering staff. I remember well an interview which took place in my office, at my invitation, with the cocky representative of the TGWU, who reckoned he was onto an easy winner here, being about to deal with an inexperienced and retired ex-services officer. He wanted me to sign the customary union agreement under which a company, or in this case the College, formally acknowledges the presence and strength of the union among its labour force and agrees to observe union procedures and privileges. He didn't seem to realise, bless his heart, that I had pre-empted his visit by talking with my people, with whom I had a very good relationship, and explaining to them why any higher wage rates would not be possible and warning them therefore that, if they joined a union, they would be paying union dues every week for nothing. I reminded them too of the particular benefits working at the College gave them, such as payment during the long school holidays and free meals during term time.

And so it was that when the man from the union presented his document, I asked Roma to get him a nice cup of tea while I told him that his percentage of union members among my staff was nowhere near high enough to justify any such agreement between the College and the union. There would be no point in further discussions, I told him, unless he could obtain at least a 30% union membership among my staff. (I knew that this was the recognised minimum percentage required for such an agreement.) I never reported to Council on the pressure from unions to infiltrate the College until eighteen months later, when I could be sure that the threat was overcome. I feared that Norman, with his big industrial boots (figuratively speaking), would have ruined my more delicate approach to the problem. In fact, it was rather less than a year before such staff as had joined the union realised that they had received no benefit from doing so and allowed their union dues to lapse.

There are always people in every workforce who are loud in their support of a trade union, however benign their working conditions. I had two at Clifton, one of whom was the head of a group of four Portuguese boys who worked hard and well in my Upper School kitchens. His name was Tony, an intelligent young man of about thirty, and he had learned to speak excellent English. I was aware that he had been vociferously urging all the catering staff to join the union. His Achilles' heel was that he and his three compatriots were thought to be almost certainly homosexual, which made all three of them vulnerable to dismissal. Indeed, I had sent for Tony, once I had been informed of their proclivities, and told him that I could understand and accept their homosexuality (which he admitted in the privacy of my office) but there would be no preliminary warnings if any one of them made contact or flirted with the boys, because I would dismiss them instantly, regardless of employment law. Therefore, when he began agitating my catering staff to join the union, I reminded him again of his vulnerability, and he shut up.

The other one was a well-educated young man who worked particularly well and intelligently as a groundsman on our more distant sports fields. He was bursting with socialist ideology, hence his choice of job perhaps, and liked to articulate his beliefs. But I didn't regard that as any problem because I had already decided that he was just the man to become head groundsman when the current elderly head retired, and had made arrangements for it. I had learned from earlier experience that, if you give managerial responsibility to an ardent socialist, his socialism will evaporate just as fast as the amount of responsibility you give him. And thus it happened in due course.

As the time approached for another annual election, it became evident that Norman had every intention of staying on as Chairman for his sixth year, and probably on and on after that. To stay on as Chairman for so long shows a high degree of self-satisfaction and arrogance, but he was even mooting the possibility of creating a new permanent position and title for himself as 'Warden' of the College. Aside from my own personal difficulties in working with Norman, I thought that his continued chairmanship over any longer period would be disastrous for Clifton College, and I found that I was by no means alone in such thinking. But, in the comparatively small world of the College, the Chairman of Council is inevitably in a supremely powerful position and, if he wants to stay on, it is difficult to remove him. One reason being that the other members of Council, especially those who are suitable for the job, are too busy in their own field of activity and don't want it.

Other than by a majority vote of the members of Council, therefore, the President of the College is the only person with authority to ask an overlong-serving Chairman to stand down. Jack Britton was then the President and, unless he did took this step, it seemed to me that the pattern would be set and we could be stuck with Norman for years to come.

One evening at home, at the end of yet another grating telephone call from Norman, I talked to Saccie about a recent advertisement from the Bristol City Council offering a new appointment of a Leisure Director. The job appeared to be the financial and administrative management of all the leisure activities, such as the museums, art galleries, historic buildings, sports facilities, etc. of the city, all of which involved quite a large labour force. I said that it might be interesting to apply just to see what came of it.

Saccie, with a monumental sigh in despair of me, expressed the hope vehemently that I was not seriously intending to leave Clifton College where I had an absolute peach of a job with a reasonable salary which I enjoyed enormously and which included a beautiful free house for us and our family. Was I, she asked, quite dotty? I reassured her that I had no intention whatsoever of resigning from the College merely because of the difficulties and irritations of working with the 'dreaded Norman', as Saccie and I always called him. But I believed it would be worthwhile, I told her, to put the strength of my position *vis-à-vis* Norman to the test, not just because his continued chairmanship caused unnecessary aggravation to me, but very much also to the Headmaster of the Pre and lately, to some other members of Council. The reality was that the man was already well past his sell-by date as Chairman and I intended to see if I could do something about it.

And so I applied to the City Council for the job as the Leisure Director, citing Admiral Sir John Bush, His Honour Judge Sir Ian Lewis and Jack Britton, the current President of the College, as my referees. Having so to speak 'dropped the names' of these rather imposing people into the arena, I relaxed and awaited events. As I had hoped and indeed expected would happen, I received a telephone call from one of the three referees to ask, off the record, my reasons for seeking another job. I replied that, although I would regard Norman Travis as a valuable member of Council, I had found him very difficult indeed to work with as my Chairman, and I made no more comment than that.

There followed a most interesting new experience of interview procedures because, only a short time after sending my application, I received first of all a formal single invitation, without Saccie, to an evening social party at the City Art Gallery. This turned out to be an unusual and sensible way to enable members of the City Council to meet and talk, over drinks and a social atmosphere, with the five people who had been short-listed for the job of Leisure Director, and thus for them to make their own assessment of each candidate. The evening was fun and I thoroughly enjoyed meeting and talking to these people, all with such different backgrounds, and learned from them that the main worry was labour difficulties with strong trade unions at the leisure centres. I was quietly happy because, earlier that same evening, I had received a tip-off on the telephone from one of my three referees that the problem, which had been discussed between us earlier, was about to be resolved before the Council meeting next week, and I was advised not to make any impetuous decisions.

The next morning the formal interviews took place at the main City Council chambers and, to start with, we five candidates were put into a large room together (very bad form incidentally) to await our interviews. The telephone call on the previous evening had confirmed my intention not to leave Clifton in any case but, now that I was here for interview, I might as well see it through and enjoy the experience. I was the first to be asked into the Council chamber where I was shown to a solitary chair facing a whole mass of people, ranged in tiers upwards and in a big semi-circle, while directly in front of me, at a slightly higher level, sat the Chairman on a sort of throne. It might have been quite a daunting sight to anyone anxious to get the job. I answered questions put to me from people all round the chamber and, at the end, the Chairman asked me if I would be prepared to accept the appointment, if offered. After all that, it seemed rude to give a blunt 'no' to the question so I replied, sensibly enough as I would have said it anyway, that I would wish to see a detailed picture of the management structure and responsibilities of the people who would be working for me. Very shortly after I had returned to the room where the other four were waiting, I was given a large paper showing the pyramid of senior staff and their authority and, bang at the top, was the Leisure Director but linked equally with the Art Director. I would never have accepted a shared authority like that under any circumstances. And so I was able on reasonable grounds to withdraw my application for the job, without appearing rude or casual.

The following week was Commemoration Day or Commem (other schools call it Speech Day) with the Council meeting in the morning and, unusually, there was to be a dinner and dancing in the huge marquee in the evening. What a day, I shall never forget it. For one thing, it poured with rain all through the previous night and the day, so that the Close and the marquee were a sea of mud where some five hundred people were tramping all over the grass. Despite that awful weather and the mud, however, it was one of my best-ever days at Clifton College because, at the Council meeting that morning, Norman Travis had announced his decision not to stand again as Chairman for the coming year. In fact, it had not been his decision but that of the President. The matter had been discussed with the

President, he said, who had subsequently asked Sir John Bush if he would be willing to undertake the task of Chairman, if the Council now voted in favour. And so, after the usual murmured plaudits from the Council members to Norman for his past work as Chairman, we had Admiral Sir John Bush, KCB, DSC **, a war hero if ever there was one and the Vice-Admiral of the United Kingdom, voted in as our new Chairman! It was all very sudden and exciting. But for Saccie and me, it was also as if we had lost 'the Old Man of Hoy' from around our necks. For the dinner and dance that evening, we shared a table with, among others, Norman and Betty Travis, which was extremely awkward under the circumstances of the abrupt termination of his chairmanship as Norman was obviously well aware of the part I had played in it.

It occurs to me that some further explanation should be given of my antipathy to Norman and his manner of management, and the following story is typical.

I had learned that the Church authorities in Bristol wanted to dispose of the church immediately alongside the College, on the boundary of the Close. It was a handsome church, built at much the same time as the College of similar stonework and it even looked as if it were part of the College. I was delighted with the thought that it could be made into a superb Art Centre and would be big enough to serve both the Pre and Upper Schools. In the Upper School, it would replace the then top floor art studio, which in turn, could be used as extra classroom and library accommodation for the English department. Accordingly, I made contact with the secretary of the Dean with whom, in due course, I discussed the possibility that the College might purchase the Church. In fact, the Dean and the Bishop of Bristol were entirely pleased with the idea because they wanted the church to be used for some good purpose such as public welfare or education, rather than be sold to property developers. After another meeting, we reached agreement in principle on a moderate price in the order of £20,000.

The stage had been reached for me to report to my Chairman and, if he supported the project, it would be put on the agenda for the next meeting of council. After receiving my report, Norman telephoned to tell me that he fully supported the project but, from then on, to leave the negotiations to him as he knew the Chairman of the Church Commissioners in London well and could clinch the purchase, probably at a lower price. Meantime, the project was discussed at a meeting of the Finance committee, which also welcomed the proposal.

The only dissenting voice in the College, strangely enough, came from the art master at the time, who had an objection which he seemed unable adequately to explain. In any case, it would not be right for an art master at any one time to jeopardise the art facilities for future generations of pupils. The bombshell came later when the Dean let it be known that there had been a change of mind and the church would probably, after all, be sold to developers. Unofficially it was also made known that there was some resentment in the Bristol diocese to interference from London. In his desire to be at the head of the project, Norman had killed the golden goose.

CHAPTER SIXTEEN

Clifton College, June 1978 – 82

The next three years with Admiral Sir John Bush as Chairman were particularly happy, as far as Saccie and I were concerned, but they were also good constructive years for the College, with increasing boy numbers every year. The first bonus was that Sir John, unlike old Norman, was a gifted speaker whose carefully crafted and timed speeches at Commem each year and on other occasions always made amusing and interesting listening to the captive audience of parents, Old Cliftonians and teaching staff. John and his vivacious wife Ruth lived at some distance away in Hampshire but they visited Clifton at least every month and he kept in close touch with the Headmasters and me by telephone, but during normal working hours. They usually stayed with Saccie and me on their visits to Clifton and Saccie and I would stay at their house whenever he needed me to come and talk College business. Yes, it was business during those visits but they also included highly competitive croquet matches, walks in the countryside and delicious meals cooked by Ruth.

Those years at Clifton College were constructive, despite all the appalling difficulties perpetrated on the country by Wilson's Labour government including, of course, the very high inflation. Many of the difficulties for the College were caused by the continuous strike actions, year after year, relating to power supplies and civil services. However, we had the means at the College to combat some of these difficulties. For example, the huge mass of accumulated school rubbish during service strikes was collected and disposed each week by using our own buses and vans with the willing labour of our porters and cleaners. The Easter term was always the worst each year with seemingly inevitable power strikes by either the gas or electricity unions, or sometimes by both of them. As our kitchen equipment was gas-operated, there was the constant worry of cooking some 4000 meals every day during a strike, when the gas supply would be severely limited. To cope with this situation, I was lucky enough to find and purchase loads of large 6-ft gas cylinders to augment the gas supply to the kitchens whenever it was low. We stored these cylinders at the back of the Chapel and I was amused to see four of them still there when I visited the College as a Governor many years later.

Heating the water for boys' showers in the boarding houses of the Upper School was another problem and I decided, with Council approval of course, to bite the financial bullet of using some of our Reserve Fund from the annual surplus to install modern heating systems. And so, in place of the old 600 gallon hot water boilers which so soon drained away when the boys used the showers after games, I contracted with a firm of engineers called Multi-Heat Ltd for the installation of new systems which were designed to provide immediate hot water whenever it was needed. Needless to say, it was a while before the new systems worked properly and I got some stick from the boys, notably from those at School House where I was invited, albeit courteously, to change and use the cold water showers there after playing Squash. My good friend Tom Gover, the housemaster of School House, which he ruled seemingly from behind a mountain of books and files in his study, was a considerable character much loved by his boys. Tom invited me one evening for light supper and wine, before I was to join him and the boys at evening prayers in their main hall. A heartfelt prayer was sent up that the Bursar and his engineers, known as Multi-Cold, might one day be successful in producing hot water for School House. I took the strong hint and, no doubt with help from above, bullied the engineers into successfully concluding their work.

Charles Cooper, who had been Treasurer of the College and had given me so much quiet support during my time as Bursar, retired in 1977 and was replaced by Tony Eve. Tony was young, about forty probably, yet despite his youth he was the senior partner in the Bristol office of an internationally-known firm of accountants. I found very quickly that he was the possessor of a mind as keen and sharp as a razor blade and, even at our first meeting, I realised that I would be up against formidable opposition, if it should happen that we disagreed on any aspect of the College operation. However, I remember that, during all our six years of working together for the College, no such disagreement ever occurred. Tony's quick mind complemented my own rather ponderously slow brain, which had always required such tediously long hours of work, usually in the early mornings, if it was to achieve what I needed it to do. As it turned out, Tony gave me the type of backing with his quick mind which I had come to need, because there had been new appointments to the Council and it had become more difficult at times, under the chairmanship of Norman Travis, to obtain approval for projects which, as it seemed to me and the Headmasters, were necessary for the College. Tony Eve's support gave that extra edge and bite to our arguments and discussions in Council. It wasn't all dry as dust; Tony and I had some amusing visits on investment business to London where Bernard Waley-Cohen, a member of Council and a famous merchant banker, would chair the meeting with our stockbroker and fall asleep as he did so. Investment business was new to me and I found it interesting, exciting and not all that difficult to be successful when having a reasonable cushion of large margins.

The government had commissioned a report on teachers' pay from a professor called Houghton during that period of the late 1970s and he had recommended huge increases, which were implemented immediately in the state sector and so, of course, the independent schools would have to follow as best they could. It didn't surprise me as I had long realised that, despite benefits such as four months' holiday each year, teachers generally had been poorly paid. But it proved difficult to persuade our new Chairman, Sir John Bush, that the teaching salaries at Clifton must be equally raised, since he believed that the particular perks offered at Clifton of free meals, cheap accommodation and reduced fees for boy children of teaching staff more than compensated for lower pay. However, the force of argument from the Headmasters, Bursar and Treasurer eventually prevailed in Council and the teachers at Clifton received the high salary increases. My view was that the parents would not squawk too loudly at the inevitable fee increase to follow, regarding it as just another part of the high rate of inflation. And anyway, I thought that the salary increases, although in reality too big a jump at one go to be reasonable, were appropriate in the longer term and would be unavoidable.

Life as the Bursar of Clifton College was not always the bed of roses I have tended to describe in these pages, and it seemed to become more difficult as teaching staff at Clifton began to flourish and blossom with their higher pay. Some of the new housemasters, as I have written, wanted the private side of their house refurbished with new kitchen and bathroom furnishings and all that kind of thing. I always recognised that the job of a housemaster was an onerous one, with a twenty-four hour responsibility for the boys in their care during term time, and if I could possibly find the funds for their extra niceties in the private side of their house, I would do so. On the other hand, I tended to be unresponsive when those in school accommodation, at almost peppercorn rentals, wanted their premises to be redecorated. In my view, they should pay for such embellishments themselves, as people have to do in real life outside school but, if I had put my foot down too hard on this sort of thing, it would not have helped the Headmasters obtain the quality of staff they wanted.

Some of the teaching staff even became ambitious to take part in managing the College. A senior member of the science department in the Upper School, as one example, decided that the main building of the Pre needed total rewiring. Well of course it did; it was just one of a dozen such maintenance problems which, after an earlier and proper professional examination, had been rated not to be an immediate safety risk and had been put in its appropriate place on my priority list. The science master, in writing to the Chairman about the wiring, was as a child wanting to be noticed, but it indicated too that he had idle hands and not enough of his own work to do. Another example of idle hands was a maths master who wanted to examine all the accounts of the College, unaware that mathematics have little relationship to the accounts and management of a business. From this request, Tony had the good idea of giving a lecture on the College accounts to all the teaching staff of the Upper School. He did this so concisely and well that they all appeared to be gob-smacked and had barely more than a question or two at the end of it. All such matters were irritations rather than problems, but were indicative of how much the attitudes of teaching staff had changed from those of my early years as Bursar.

From time to time during the early 1970s through to the 1980s, the subject of bringing girls as pupils into this famous College for boys would be raised and I was always entirely opposed to it. My point of view probably stemmed from the experience of my daughter, Aza, who had wanted to attend Methody College, a co-education school in Belfast, where her standard of academic work had deteriorated and had never recovered. It seemed clear to me that neither boys nor girls benefited from co-education, especially at a boarding school. At that time, it was easy for me to clobber such co-educational ideas on the grounds that the number of boys at Clifton was increasing so that there was no financial benefit from the fees to be gained from having girls whereas, as I constantly emphasized, girls were costly creatures needing particularly smart and expensive boarding accommodation.

On the other hand, I could see an advantage in sharing some facilities with Clifton High School, a high-quality day school for girls, which was located only a few hundred yards from the College. They had many good facilities such as an indoor swimming pool, which I coveted, while we at Clifton could offer extra teaching subjects to their girls. And so during the later '70s, I thoroughly enjoyed plotting with Ann Cotton, a Bursar of long experience at Clifton High School, towards the merging of the facilities of the two schools to a limited but useful extent. We got as far as putting their Chairman of Governors onto our Council, but then there were so many other matters to deal with that we eventually let the whole idea lapse. And anyway, by then, I knew without doubt that I was going to build our own new swimming pool and probably a sports hall too.

Much later in the 1980s, after I had left the College, the issue of girl pupils at Clifton was raised again rather more vehemently, when the boy numbers had fallen and the College overdraft was thriving splendidly under, at that time, a spendthrift Council. The poor financial situation was bad management but, whatever the cause, finance should not be a reason for bringing in co-education, merely to raise the fees from pupil numbers. The only new factor which might make the intake of girls worth consideration was that most of the preparatory schools had started co-education, mainly as an economic necessity in their cases to keep their pupil numbers up. Thus, many of the famous independent schools thought it necessary to follow suit and to go co-educational also. But it is interesting that Harrow, located on the edge of a city as is Clifton, firmly rejected any idea of co-education and has been thriving as never before and now is even building more boarding houses for boys. Whatever criticism I have written about Harrow as it was in my day as a boy there, I have no doubt that at this present time in the 21st century, it is the best independent school for boys in the UK.

In 1979, I became aware that a number of independent boarding schools were starting to operate their own school laundries and claiming to save money by doing so. I decided, therefore, to go walkabout around these schools, as I had done before when installing the cafeteria system, to see for myself how well or otherwise they operated their own laundries. I found that on the whole and compared to the normal cost of using a professional laundry, they were making some savings, but the Bursar and his staff were suffering a lot of hassle in learning and trying to operate a school laundry of their own.

Since lack of management expertise was apparently the problem, it seemed sensible to ask the owner and manager of our professional laundry if he would contract to undertake the management of a College laundry, on the basis that the College would provide the equipment and pay the labour costs. Surprisingly, he was keen on the idea and, under his guidance, electrical laundry equipment was purchased and installed in three empty basement rooms, and no more than four semi-skilled staff were selected by him and employed by the College. The whole of this small enterprise was an astonishing success. It took a couple of terms to sort out the wrinkles but, after that, the school laundry actually doubled the amount of laundry provided for all the boarders, simply by being able to concentrate the operation all day and every day on our own requirements, and it would do so with a 35% saving on the previous professional annual costs. However, such is life as a Bursar that when I announced this doubled output and reduced costs at a meeting of housemasters and wives with their house matrons, all I received were grumpy requests for boys' jeans to be included in the wash as well as extra pants. As for expressing any appreciation, no, not a word! The laundry manager went on to contract with other boarding schools to operate their laundry, so evidently he too had benefited from our arrangement.

In 1979, it was suggested by Stuart, the Headmaster, that I should create a new appointment of a Domestic Bursar, who would be able to spend more time helping, for example, with any problems the housemasters might have, particularly with their domestic staff. Swallowing my slightly hurt pride at the implication that I was no longer able adequately to cover such problems as well as my other workload, I appointed Michael Roope as Domestic Bursar. And how pleased I became that I had done so because Michael, a retired RN Commander, was excellent at dealing with all the non-teaching staff and in establishing good relations with them while negotiating their pay and conditions. Thus he took a substantial load off me. Nevertheless, I was glad to have overcome earlier before he arrived the malevolent threat of the trade union involvement with the College.

One of the most significant and effective financial actions we took at this time was to introduce what we called the Discount Scheme. We already operated the Composition Fee Fund, which was the advance payment of school fees over the long term. This new Discount Scheme, on the other hand, was for the shorter term, whereby the parent could choose to pay up to five terms in advance at a discounted rate of fees. It was a winner straight away, especially during a period of high inflation, but also because it was the equivalent for the parent of investing without paying tax on the interest. The parents responded to the scheme with an enthusiasm which increased every year. The Scheme enabled the College, rather like a bank, either to invest the advance payment of fees or to use them to the best advantage. I wanted it for building purposes and therefore put much of it, including the interest, into our Reserve Fund in the meantime. Although I have to tell that the Council took a lot of persuading from Tony and me before agreeing to all this, but the procedure is quite safe provided that there is little or no overdraft and a good annual surplus is being made. Subsequently many of the other major independent schools have adopted this Discount Scheme, but it is good that Clifton was again in the financial forefront.

During the three years of Sir John's chairmanship of the Council, the Appeal fund began to grow under Stuart's leadership and with the benefit of his and Sir John's ability to speak forcefully and well at meetings with potential donors. The Appeal was renamed 'The New Objectives Development Fund' and financial support from industry as well as from the usual sources was coming in. In 1979 the new mathematics and technical centre, called the Coulson Centre, was completed and, incidentally, at no more than a mere £300 above my initially-negotiated price. The boy numbers were now at 700 in the Upper School, compared with 598 in December 1969, and 540 in the Pre. All this was indicative of high-class teaching, because parents don't send their boys to an expensive College unless the academic results are good. The new objectives of both the new swimming pool and a sports hall were now firmly in our sights, although at the time only sufficient funds for the swimming pool seemed certain. Nevertheless, I remember making a personal promise at that time to Peter Knight, the head of PE, that a sports hall would be built.

I liked to think that the considerable improvements that had been made to both the Upper School and the Pre, such as those to all the boarding and town houses, the much-improved catering and the provision of new teaching facilities, had all been a factor in the remarkable increase in boy numbers. And so they may have been, but a more important factor was the high standard of teaching at that time, because parents don't send their boys to an expensive school unless the educational results are good. Such good results during that period of the seventies reflected the quality of the Headmasters, Stuart Andrews and Jim Hornby, who were responsible for the selection and leadership of their teaching staff. The main factor in the success of an independent College and Pre such as Clifton, however, lies in the overall influence of the Headmaster of the College in his dealings with the parents and the general public. He may not like the thought of being a super salesman but that is what he has to be, with a presence and manner which will impress parents and convince them that the prestige of Clifton College and the high standard of education it provides for their sons, are well worth the cost of the high fees. It is a heavy responsibility to the College and a difficult task for which his success is not always recognised at the time or until he has retired and gone. Moreover, none of the poor blighters who are appointed to the headmastership of a large independent school have any training whatsoever for the complex task and few of them have previous experience for it, other than maybe as a housemaster, and housemastership no more than touches upon the wide range of knowledge and expertise which the job of Headmaster requires. The general difficulty which a Headmaster has at such schools as Clifton College is that his tribe of teachers has no Indians in it and only Chiefs, most of whom reckon they could make a better job of it than he does. As the result, reaching agreement with his staff on any matter can be unduly difficult for a Headmaster.

So everything was going merrily along at the College and, now that the Coulson Centre had been completed and no other major building projects were yet in hand, Saccie and I were able to take some holidays abroad for two weeks with Jeremy and Aza during the summer breaks. At games, my particular interests were Rackets and Squash at which the College was doing particularly well in those years under the coaching of Terry Whatley. For the first time ever, Clifton was challenging Harrow, Eton and Marlborough to be the top school at these games, and this gave me a lot of pleasure.

It was not to be all sports and games for me to enjoy because the head of the English department, Brian Worthington, overheard me in the common room speaking disparagingly about a chap called Chuckorf, one of whose plays I had seen and disliked on television. With a wit which I could not help but like, he reproved me publicly for my ignorance and told me I must attend his 6th form class on Chekov during that school term. I forgot all about it until, two mornings later, I was approached by the College Marshall (responsible for the discipline of the boys) and told sternly that I was late for class. I thought, to hell with the office where Roma was waiting for me to dictate letters and minutes, and hurried off to the classroom to be rebuked by the Master for being so late. What fun it all was and, indeed, I attended and enjoyed that class every week. At the end of the term, I was given my reports for the term written by Brian and by each boy in the class and including a housemaster's report (Tom Gover) with the Headmaster's report. The reports were not good, I have to write because, truth to tell, I never did get to grips with Mr Chekov and his famous plays.

In September 1981, Sir John Bush had completed three successful years as Chairman and, as a man well accustomed to power at the top of the tree, knew it was the right time to retire and did so, but was prevailed upon to accept the less onerous Presidency of the College from Jack Britton. His place as Chairman of the Council was taken by His Honour Judge Sir Ian Lewis, who had only recently retired as a judge in the Colonies and now lived in Bristol. Again the College was fortunate to have such a man to lead it and I too was happy to work under his direction. In all my time in business, I have never known a better chairman of a meeting, and to chair a meeting when there are twenty members almost all of whom are at the top of their own professions is not easy. He would start with a description of the agenda item with a lucid outline of the considerations involved, then invite the Headmaster, or whoever had promoted the project, to speak on it. Never the Bursar to speak at this stage, incidentally, since as Secretary I would have made my points already in my explanatory paper on the agenda item, already circulated to Council. Thereafter, he would ask each member to express a view, then give the Headmaster or whomever, including the Bursar, the right to reply, before summing up precisely and clearly to put a resolution to the vote. Textbook procedure, but how effective and quick such procedure is when done properly, particularly by an experienced judge.

The following year passed normally, with boy numbers and development funds still on the increase. Such a rare quiet period was an opportunity to get something else done and I turned my attention to our main sports fields of about 90 acres at Beggars Bush, about two miles from the College across the famous Suspension Bridge. Every day during the term, except Sunday, some 600 boys had to be transported to and from these fields and, for this purpose, elderly single-decker buses, purchased cheaply, were used and maintained by a full-time mechanic at Beggars Bush, where four members of ground staff also worked on the sports fields. There was a demand from business organisations in Bristol for such sports grounds as these, and it seemed such a waste of College assets that these grounds should lie fallow when not in use by the boys. My ear to the ground for information such as this was always the Clifton Club, quite near the College, where I met friends and lunched with some of the business people of Bristol during the school holidays.

At one such lunch, I met a local director of a major UK insurance company who disclosed his need for a sports ground and social facilities for his clerical staff of some three hundred people. This was just what I wanted to hear because I had in mind the development of our furthest field of about thirty acres at Beggars Bush, which was rather a barren area and insufficiently used. For instance, it was so cold and windswept that it had never been possible to create a decent cricket pitch on it. The field had a separate entrance from the main road, also rarely used, which had a potholed little roadway leading to it. In the previous year, at a cost subsidised almost entirely by the City Council, I had caused to be planted some five hundred fast-growing trees, which in due course would form a wind barrier across the windward boundary of this area.

The insurance chap was just the man I wanted, a sort of gift just when needed, and he was happy to negotiate for his company the basis of an agreement with me, which gave excellent terms for the College. In effect the insurance company would have use of the field after six p.m. every day, throughout each year. In consideration of this, they would build a pavilion with changing facilities and showers for the boys to use during the day, and a lounge with a bar, which would be locked and not available to the boys. They would also undertake to build and maintain a proper road to the pavilion and a car-park area adjacent to it. The proposed agreement would terminate after fourteen years when the insurance company would leave and the new pavilion and roadway would remain the property of the College.

I was pleased with the terms of this proposed contract and regarded the whole arrangement as a pilot scheme which, if it worked well, could form the basis of other and more extensive development of the whole area of our sports grounds at Beggars Bush. The next stage was to discuss the proposal with my Chairman and I hoped, with his approval, to put the terms of the agreement on the table at the next meeting of the Council for the members to authorise. Sir Ian considered the project carefully, made contact with the directors of the insurance company and then agreed that I should put it to the Council for approval. I was keen that the scheme should not become generally known about in the College unless and until it was approved. The teaching staff always had an extraordinary propensity to find some fault or difficulty with any new scheme, and this contract might be lost, if we were to waste time just talking about it. As it happened, after the agreement was approved by Council, an immediate start was made by the insurance people on building the pavilion. It was formally opened with a cricket match against a Gloucester team and then used by the boys that same summer. In a school environment, speed is of the essence to avoid unnecessary argument in completing a small project such as this.

Funds from the Appeal were building up, thanks almost entirely to Stuart Andrews, who was masterminding the various brochures about our objectives which were sent to local industry, as well as speaking at meetings to our usual sources, members of the OC Society and the parents. Moreover, on my part of ship, our other financial resources, such as the Reserve Fund, the Composition Fee Fund and bank deposits from the Discount Scheme, were all coming along nicely and I could see no reason now not to plan for a sports hall and new changing rooms, as well as the new swimming pool. Members of Council, who tended to be overcautious when considering large expenditure, might be a bit of a problem. They were all whizz-kids at their own different professions but, with so much new building planned for the near future, it would be an advantage for the College (and for me) to have a good architect on the Council also. I knew of one such architect well, John Collins, who was about to retire as one of the foremost architects in the west country and I contrived, with full backing from the Chairman, to have him bundled through a governorship and straight onto the Council. As I had hoped, he became a welcome help in encouraging his fellow members of Council to think positively about building the sports hall as well as the swimming pool.

It had occurred to me that another possibility of extra funds for these two major projects was the National Sports Council, promoted by the Government, whose purpose was to give financial support to physical education. The local area headquarters of this organisation was near Taunton and I visited there several times to make a case for Clifton College to receive some state aid towards funding the Sports Hall and Pool. This was a bit tricky since the limited funds available to them were intended for state schools and public organisations. I pointed out that Clifton College already offered some of its sports facilities to the general public and the intention was to set aside appropriate hours for the proposed new facilities to be similarly used by the public. There was no flannel about my argument, because I had in mind to set about hiring our facilities on a much larger scale, once the new hall and pool were in place. Anyway, it worked as eventually we received a grant of £30,000 which covered the eventual cost of equipping the new sports buildings.

As we came to the beginning of the year 1981 it was time for all the talking about finance to stop and for decisions to be made. At the meeting in March the Council was finally persuaded that sufficient funds could be made available and the decision was made, therefore, to contract for the building of both the sports hall and the new swimming pool. Tony Eve and his lively mind had been an absolute boon in persuading Council to this decision, as had been a good number of the recently-appointed members of Council, who could see the point of getting on with it while we had the opportunity of the fees from the highest-ever boy numbers, now standing at 712 in the Upper School and 545 in the Pre. Another small factor not to be dismissed, which helped towards a decision by members of Council to go ahead with this major building project, was the dinner parties given by Saccie on the Friday evenings prior to Council meetings. The Chairman and probably three other members of Council would be invited with their wives while, during dinner and afterwards with a glass in hand, the main subject of discussion would inevitably be the College and, of course, its development projects. How Saccie detested those dinner parties. But she regarded the preparation of them as a chore to be undertaken for my sake and, much as she would have preferred a quiet evening with the family, she was a good hostess and her parties encouraged conversation and interest in the affairs of the College. My function, of course, was to ensure that their interest leaned towards making a start on the development projects without delay.

On the valuable advice of John Collins, my architect chum on the Council, I decided to use a Design and Build company to avoid all the time consuming and expensive normal procedure of consulting architects, selection of design, using quantity surveyors, putting the design out to tender to builders, negotiation with the selected builder and finally the contract negotiation. All of this could take up to four months so that, in a period of high inflation, the eventual price negotiated might be twenty percent higher than it need be. Inflation was still high in 1981, although Maggie Thatcher was in charge now and commencing her fight on behalf of the country against the blundering power of the trade unions.

I was introduced to a Design and Build firm and was greatly impressed by their architect, who would also be the site and contract manager throughout the construction work. Within a month we had agreed upon the design of the combined building of the sports hall and the pool, which I was determined must include a range of new changing rooms below the hall and, since there was space, would also include a weight-training room, a fencing salon and an office for the PE staff. This major project of a huge new building was to be located right in the centre of the school and therefore special provision had to be made in the contract for major demolition and construction works to take place in school holidays, and other work to be kept quiet during school classes in the term time. The work was contracted to begin in July of that year and to complete in July 1982 and, sure enough according to schedule, a large and enormously high crane appeared on the scene in July, ready for work to begin.

I had negotiated a price for all this work at £460,000, but it was not entirely to a fixed specification because there were still areas of uncertainty for which an allowance had been made in the price. I was not sure about the heating and cleaning plant for the swimming pool, for example, and how efficient it needed to be for our purposes which would be for maximum usage all day from 6 a.m. to 10 p.m. both for the boys and for the general public. In the end I relied on the contractual guarantee that the plant would be capable of cleaning the water for a thousand bodies per day. Neither did I as yet know exactly what the PE and games teaching staff would want in the sports hall, but ultimately all their requirements were contained close to the original price. That price, of then nearly half a million pounds for the biggest building project the College had undertaken since the main hall of Big School, would be the equivalent now in 2009 of probably £6-7 million. A small enough price indeed for such a project, but the funds still had to be found and, on the next page, is a copy of my account submitted to the Council in May 1982, to show how the project would be funded.

Opposite is a copy of my paper dated May 7th, 1982.

C L I F T O N   C O L L E G E

INVESTMENT COMMITTEE - 7th MAY 1982

FUNDS APPLIED, AS APPROVED BY COUNCIL, TOWARDS PAYMENTS ON THE SPORTS CENTRE

1. **GENERAL FUND** i.e. Composition Fee Fund Investments capitalised :-
   *Encashment
   - (a) I.M.I. - October 1980   12,550
   - (b) Sales - April 1981   60,609
   - (c) 10½% Exchequer 1995 - March 1982   99,885   *173,044   173,044

2. **RESERVE FUND** Investments capitalised :
   - (a) 9¼% Exchequer Sept.1980   30,096
   - (b) B.A.T. - April 1981   12,804
   - (c) 8¼% Treasury - February 1982   47,984   * 90,884   90,884

3. **DEVELOPMENT FUNDS** (since June 1980)
   Donations, Gifts and Covenants (total £220,000)
   Cash received: *159,000   159,000

4. **DEPOSIT INTEREST**
   All liquid funds deposited with Hill Samuel & Co.   19,065
   Reserve Fund Investment Interest   ..   8,541   * 27,606   27,606

5. **COMPOSITION FEE FUND**
   Investments at Market Value at 5.4.82   245,576
   Less:
   Long term liability to Parents   ..   208,140

   Balance available for capitalisation   37.436

6. **SALE OF PROPERTY**
   Expected sale of flats at 7 Miles Road, Clifton (say)   75,000

7. **GRANT FROM SPORTS COUNCIL** (expected May 1982)   30,000

                         FUNDS available 1981/82   592,970
                         COVENANTS DUE 1982/86   61,000

   RATE OF PAYMENTS   TOTAL FUNDS: £653,970

                    August 1981   72,480 (paid)
                    September   71,088 (paid)
                    October   62,544 (paid)
                    November   54,704 (paid)
                    December   60,878 (paid)
                    January 1982   31,289 (paid)
                    February   29,427 (paid)
                    March   23,247 (paid)
                    April   22,928 (paid)   £428,585 ✓   £450,534
                    May   30,000 *

                              Total Buildings Costs: £ 461,000

                              Equipment & Furnishing of
                                     Changing Rooms: 22,000

                                              TOTAL: £ 483,000

CHAPTER SEVENTEEN

Clifton College, the Final Year, 1982

The Pre of Clifton College, with 545 young boys, was by far the largest independent preparatory school in the UK and yet its demands on me during my twelve years as its Bursar had been minimal in comparison with the Upper School. No-one could doubt my personal interest in the Pre because, during that period and on my own initiative and manipulation of funds, a new music school, a new science school, a new common room, a new art school and a new day-boy house had been provided for the Pre and, using the Appeal funds, all the boarding houses had also been refurbished. However, I had the nasty realisation that I had spent much less time worrying about the Pre and talking with staff in the common room there than I had done with the Upper School. There had been a couple of new young housemasters in the Pre in recent years who had been unnecessarily difficult to please but, aside from that, to work with the Headmaster of the Pre and his teaching staff had been a pleasure. I was determined in future to put myself about a bit more at the Pre.

It had become the practice every year for Gwyl Isaac, the Choirmaster and music teacher at the Pre, to take a group of boys on a cruise in the SS *Uganda* during the Easter holidays. These cruises were organised once a year in conjunction with the Preparatory Schools Association and many such schools would send groups of about twenty boys or girls, aged between ten and thirteen, on this cruise with the cost of it paid by the parents. The one or two teachers in charge of each school group would get a free cruise but, oh how hard they worked for it, as I found out. As part of my determination to become more involved at the Pre, I asked Gwyl if I might join his cruise with the intention of assisting him in looking after the boys. He made me very welcome and accordingly we set off with twenty-two boys on April 2nd 1982 to join the SS *Uganda*. I had hoped that Saccie could come but, in the event, the only accommodation available was for those teachers who were on board to look after the children. In any case, as I found, it was a full-time job all day and evening looking after the kids and being involved in the organisation of very competitive inter-school games. It was great fun and I enjoyed it all enormously, but how tiring it was with no chance of a rest until the boys had been chased off to their dormitory for bed.

It was a Mediterranean cruise intended also to be educational and so the ship came into port at various places. An early stop was to visit Venice where the youngest of our boys, Ben, twisted his ankle and was unable to walk. It was an intensely hot day and this stupid, vain old Bursar of over sixty at the time took the boy on his shoulders and tramped two miles back to the ship with him. For some reason at the time and place, we couldn't find a boat, taxi or whatever to take him back. It exhausted me.

Later, we visited Greek islands where I tried desperately hard to hide my laughter as young Munro imitated to ludicrous perfection the strange accent and manners of our foreign guide. Evidenced by my laughter, I had the same mind and humour as a thirteen-year-old boy. On to Egypt and by long bus-ride from Alexandria to the museum at Cairo where there was the anxiety of keeping twenty-two young boys in a group together, with the fear of losing any one of them if they strayed, while they were surrounded by ogling young Egyptian men. There was the same type of problem at the Pyramids. At the end of a long, long day, we arrived back to the ship to learn that the cruise was curtailed with immediate effect and we were headed back to Naples from where we would fly home.

Maggie Thatcher had insisted on going to war to retrieve the Falklands and our cruise ship would revert to its original role as a Hospital ship and was therefore required to join the Fleet on its way to the Falklands immediately. The Falklands; what a waste of the lives of so many courageous young men it was for so comparatively paltry an objective. But you can't stop politicians, who have never experienced war and have no knowledge of it, from revelling in the supreme ego trip of taking their country to war. A worse totally unnecessary waste of thousands of lives was to come a decade later, when the bounder Blair took the UK to war in Iraq and then, with even more fatuous futility, into Afghanistan. However, and all that being an aside, we drove back with the boys from Stansted airport in a large bus to be greeted outside the school by their waiting parents, one of whom was Ben's father in a silly tizzy because he felt that proper care had not been taken of his son. Remembering how exhausted I had been when carrying his boy all through Venice, I could have throttled the little man!

I really ought not to have gone on that cruise because there was a mass of work piled up for me on my return and, moreover, I felt damnably tired. The construction of the combined sports hall, swimming pool, changing rooms, weight-training, fencing salon and sports shop was on the point of completion and decisions on a mass of final details had to be made. But, in amongst all the excitement of completing this huge project, was the other rather disappointing situation that much of the work which had been done ten years earlier, such as the provision of study-bedrooms in the Upper School boarding houses and the refurbishing of the day-boy houses, now needed attention yet again for the second and in some cases the third time. As I knew well by now, it doesn't take long for sixty boys in their early teens to make havoc of newly-decorated rooms and studies, and much depended on the housemaster to keep good order. The day-house South Town in the Upper School, for example, had been an untidy shambles and the despair of the cleaning staff soon after it had been renovated ten years earlier, whereas the newly-built East Town, with a different style of housemaster, was in almost new condition still.

In addition to those matters, I had to prepare for critical meetings at which, with Tony's help, I would have to allay the fears of some members of Council who were still not entirely convinced that we had sufficient funds to pay for the big development project. There was no need for them to be worried but, to be sure of sufficient finance, they wanted to sell a small house property in Miles Road, which was temporarily empty. In addition to all the main college buildings and the boarding houses, there were fifteen house properties owned by the College, which provided fifty-two flats for staff accommodation on the campus, and I was strongly opposed in principle to the sale of any of these houses. These lovely and mostly Edwardian properties were not only a valuable and sound financial foundation for the College, but were a huge asset in the operation of the school. They enabled the Headmasters to provide attractive accommodation to help in retaining their existing teaching staff and as an inducement to prospective new teachers whom they might particularly want for their team. Moreover, these valuable properties helped to promote a social and community life for teaching staff around the campus of the College, as the alternative to their living away from the College in flats scattered around the city. For all these reasons, I regarded it as my responsibility to discourage Chairmen and members of Council from regarding these properties as an easy means of raising capital. However, I was overborne in that Council discussion and in due course the house at Miles Road was sold for £75,000. (Only five years later, it came to be worth £250,000.) Unhappily, I learned many years after my retirement that nearly all these houses of the College had been sold (during a period of low market prices incidentally), presumably to pay off a heavy overdraft or for some other purpose. There must have been an extraordinary financial circumstance at the time to justify selling the family silver.

High on my agenda of that previous Council meeting had been the promotion of a separate company for the hire of College facilities to the general public. For several years past we had been hiring out the theatre sufficiently well to cover its maintenance expenditure, but other facilities such as the bookshop and sports shop operated at a loss. Now I wanted to use the superb facilities of the new sports complex as a basis for launching a much larger business enterprise which would involve offering, not only organised coaching of all the sports, but educational courses in all subjects including music. Happily the Council approved the concept and in 1982 'Clifton College Services Ltd' was formed as a company with these objectives. It had a small Board of five directors, which I chaired, consisting of two members of Council and two teaching staff.

After a bit of an argument, because the teaching staff had thought that one of them should have been selected for the post, I appointed Terry Whatley as the Sales Manager. He had been the Rackets, Tennis and Squash professional of the College for several years and, in that capacity, had brought the boys to the highest competitive level against other schools. Although he had no business training, I had seen that he was an excellent organiser and, moreover, I had recognised him to be the natural-born forceful salesman, full of ideas and enthusiasm that I wanted. He proved to be the right choice. By the time the summer term started, swimming clubs were vying for the hire of the new pool and were hiring it every morning from 6.30 a.m. until 9.30 a.m., at which time the boys started to use it for the day, until 6.30 in the evenings, when the clubs took over again. It was much the same with the sports hall; cricket, soccer and badminton clubs were hiring the hall whenever it was not in use by the boys. The teaching staff, after a bit of an hesitant start, began to like the idea of extra income from giving tutorials to the public during the school holidays, and courses in all sorts of subjects were offered to the public, particularly in music and art.

From then on, all the other College facilities suitable for hiring, such as the theatre, operated under the umbrella of the C.C.S. Company Ltd. Terry Whatley left the company for another job a few years later and management of it was put in the hands of Mike Innes who has developed my company well, enabling it to undertake all sorts of enterprises using the College facilities. (I think of the C.C.S. Ltd as 'my' company since it was my brainchild and I promoted it.) Indeed, he must have observed the benefits from my original pilot scheme of using the capital provided by an insurance company for their shared use of College ground at Beggars Bush, and has developed the idea on a very much larger scale to provide magnificent sporting facilities for the public and the school at Beggars Bush.

During that summer term of 1982 and, once all the fuss and blather of the formal opening of the sports complex was over, I set about examining the condition of the accommodation in the boarding houses to prepare a schedule of maintenance work for the forthcoming holiday period. I had felt strangely unwell all that term and, while going the rounds of the studies in School House with Tom Gover and the Buildings Manager, Brian, I partially collapsed in a kind of faint. They helped me to return to my house close by, where the school doctor came to examine me. Apparently I had suffered a minor heart attack and, although I returned to work after a few days, I continued to feel tired and unwell. Eventually I was advised by the College doctor, who was also my personal doctor, to take two months away from all work and I did so but felt no better at the end of it. In October and still feeling no better, the doctor gave me an appallingly ominous and frightening warning that I would be jeopardising my life if I continued working. He told me that I must have a long sustained rest, i.e. retirement. I was not yet sixty-one years old, but the man frightened me to such an extent that I explained my illness and the problem of it to Ian Lewis, my Chairman, and gave him a letter from the doctor confirming his advice that I should retire. With it, I tendered my formal resignation as Bursar. It appears as I sit here writing these memoirs twenty-five years later and at age eighty-seven, that the doctor was dreadfully wrong. But who can say what might have happened had I continued to work?

The interest in schools and colleges such as Clifton College and the Pre is always concentrated, and naturally so, on life in the school, with stories about well-remembered Headmasters, masters and pupils. Mention is very rarely made of life behind the scholastic scene or of the people who administer the school and without whom the school could not exist. An excellent book about Clifton College, written by Derek Winterbottom in my time, was typical of this lack. But it is a pity that he neglected the background scene and the finances of Clifton, particularly at that time, because the College then was leading the field of famous public schools with innovative financial schemes, and he could have written of this. However and instead, I do hope that this part of my story, when I was Bursar of Clifton College, will show that life in the background of a boys' public school was full of interest, and also a lot of fun.

CHAPTER EIGHTEEN

Early Retirement

Having submitted my resignation as Bursar on grounds of ill-health in October 1982, I stayed on working at half-throttle until early January of the next year, while the College advertised in the national press for my replacement. I took part with Tony Eve in reading our way through all the many applications for the job and we weeded out all but four of them for a formal interview with a sub-committee of five members of Council. Tony was one of that sub-committee, which was a bit naughty because the man eventually chosen was apparently a personal friend of his. However, the new Bursar had a good background of business experience at director-level and so he ought to have been a success. I stayed on until the first few days of the next school term in January to see him installed.

Before I left the College, Ian Lewis as Chairman had sounded me out to see if, in recognition of my service to the College, I would accept nomination as a Governor and, of course, I told him how very honoured indeed I would be for that to happen. Moreover, I was to be given a leaving present of £15,000 in recognition of my twelve years of work for the College. I believe that Tony had more than a little to do with the generosity of that particular gift. I also much appreciated that the Old Cliftonian Society kindly made me an honorary member.

All this was rather spoilt temporarily when Saccie and I were invited as special guests of the College for lunch with the members of Council, after their next usual meeting. I had been given to understand, entirely unofficially of course by Ian, that my nomination as a Governor would be an item on their agenda for formal agreement, and so the lunch would be a cheerful occasion at which my Governorship would be announced. Oh dear; it didn't happen like that at all. Saccie and I sat all through that lunch like a couple of prunes while making increasingly awkward conversation, as the expected announcement failed to materialise. I learned, again entirely

Early Retirement

unofficially later on, that old Norman had achieved due retribution on me by opposing the nomination on grounds such as setting a precedent, etc. It was 'fair dos' I suppose, since I had been shamefully nasty to him when I had contrived, some four years earlier, to lever him out of the Chairmanship of Council. I was furious on the drive back to Hereford at the time, although it didn't really matter as the nomination was passed at a later meeting. But Norman had certainly spoilt the lunch party for us!

It was the finish of twelve very happy years for Saccie and me at Clifton and during that time our children, Jeremy and Aza, had developed their own lives as adults. Jeremy's car accident in late 1970 had happened just after he had completed his university degree and was deciding what to do next: it was to take up a teacher training course in Edinburgh, during which he met and shortly after married Liz, a girl from Markinch, Fife. Jeremy obtained a post at a huge comprehensive school with some eighteen hundred pupils at Sidmouth, but he was unhappy in the job of teaching large classes of very difficult and rowdy children, at the type of school where he only met the Headmaster twice in the two years after his initial interview. They lived in small rented accommodation, which Liz kept in a perpetual state of squalor, as Saccie and I found whenever we visited them. Next they moved to Eastleigh where Jeremy obtained a better job teaching at the Polytechnic College, but he and Liz never seemed able to settle down happily, and some years later they were divorced.

When I became ill, at about that same time in 1982, and because of the uncertainty implied by the doctor of my continued life ahead, I put down sufficient capital to buy a terrace house in Eastleigh for Jeremy, leaving a balance which was within his capability to pay by mortgage. I made the same arrangement for Aza by putting down sufficient capital for a similar little house in Bristol leaving her too to cover the balance with a mortgage. Both Saccie and I thought it better for each of them to have and enjoy what little money I could spare after making the best provision I could for Saccie who, much as I loved them all, was my priority. Moreover, this way, I would have the pleasure of watching them enjoy their own homes, being uncertain whether I would be granted the same pleasure from above if I were to die early as the doctor had warned. This scheme was much the same as I had offered, with Council agreement, to the teaching staff of the Upper School, when a large property in the road opposite the College was developed into flats.

After his divorce, Jeremy had become fed up with teaching at the polytechnic in Eastleigh. I don't know why, because his pupils, whom I had met when visiting him, had praised his ability as a teacher. He decided to leave, sold the house and took a job in Kiribati, a Republic in a group of islands in the Pacific, where he taught local young men and boys in a school funded by the UK government. He loved his life there. So much so that, despite my dire warnings that it would be a total disaster, he married Atauea, a local girl who, a year or so later, produced a beautiful daughter, called Alice. They later adopted another little girl, and made a happy life for themselves, with Jeremy entering into all sorts of ventures with the many friends he made out there. So much for a know-all Father.

In fact, he gave up most of his teaching eight years later, and led an exciting life working in partnership with a very good and close European friend of his, Derek, trading in all manner of ways with the villages which surround the internal lagoons of the islands. As well as trading in such articles as bicycles, footballs, building tools and materials, etc., their main activity was to encourage the villagers to catch all the variety of exotic fish and shrimp-like creatures which abounded in the lagoons. These would be retained in pools ready for Jeremy to have them transported across the lagoon and out to a cargo boat waiting offshore. In due course, these weird and exotic fish would be sold, still alive, to restaurants in Hong Kong and Japan. Another nice little earner, apparently, was to import neat alcohol free of duty from New Zealand, mix it with coconut and local fruit juices, bottle it and sell it among the villages as a very popular and drunk-making drink. Some of these activities could be very exciting and indeed dangerous at times, as I would learn from Jeremy's many letters.

Such correspondence between us never faltered and, because of it, we his parents were in some ways closer than if he lived in the next town. As a young man his self-confidence had been fragile, perhaps as the result of his fearful car-accident which had so disfigured his face, but out there in Kiribati he was popular with both the Europeans and the local people. In Atauea's village, for example, they had built him one of their outrigger sailing canoes to show their regard. In Kiribati, he became well-known and a person of substance.

Aza, with her vivacious and attractive personality, seemed several times to be on the brink of settling down into a potentially pleasant and happy marriage with various chaps, at least two of whom we as parents thought were super, but in the end she always preferred to retain her independence. And it takes a lot of determination and indeed courage from a girl to opt out of marrying despite many opportunities to do so. As she admits herself, however, she also had a penchant for male bounders and Saccie and I made the mistake with the first of these by showing him up as such. For doing so and regardless of the deep unhappiness it caused us, we were sent to Coventry for six months by our nineteen-year old daughter to teach us not to interfere. This became especially difficult when later on another one turned up anxious for Aza to move to Hong Kong with him. Sticking out of the back of his head, there was a placard which Saccie and I could easily and clearly read on first meeting the man, which said 'I am a vile bounder, already married and totally untrustworthy.' Whether the placard was visible to Aza or not, she went to Hong Kong anyway and stayed there for four years.

In the end, it was no bad thing that Aza went to Hong Kong for such a period of time. Having got rid of the bounder fairly quickly and, being a competent and intelligent young woman, she obtained a very good job with the Hong Kong Government. Moreover, she met a whole lot of interesting people in the process of working and living there. Hong Kong (Honkers as I always call it) was probably as good a place as any at her age to learn a little about life and how very harsh it can be. On her return to England, Aza worked for a while in Bristol for a university professor and then as a secretary to a senior partner in a firm of solicitors, before setting up her own very successful business with a framing shop in Bristol. In a sense, the framing business might have been too successful because it did not allow time for Aza, who is exceptionally gifted with artistic ability, to develop any of her various art forms. Her painting of miniatures is paramount and whenever she had time to send exhibits to the Royal Society of Miniaturists in London or to the Hilliard Society, they were given top plaudits and invariably sold well. Aza has relinquished the framing business and currently teaches miniature painting, ceramic restoration, stained glass construction and framing. With huge artistic talent, and now only aged fifty-eight, she has much yet to do, including writing.

In preparation for my normal retirement in due course, I had purchased in 1981, two years earlier, a maisonette at number 14 College Road, which was just fifty yards away from my Bursar's house and similarly overlooked the College Close. Now however, on my enforced early retirement, I found that I simply could not bear to remain so near the College and watch while the administrative structure I had set up would disintegrate under the new Bursar. And so, idiot man that I was, I sold the maisonette for a mere £56,000 to pay for the two small houses for the children and to leave enough for the purchase of an abode, somewhere or other, for Saccie and me. Of course, typical of my personal affairs, I had made an enormous boo-boo in selling the property in that year because very few years later, being in that prestigious location, it rocketed up to a value of at least £400,000. Completion date of the sale in the month ahead would leave us in the situation of nowhere to live and no clear idea of where to go, since I had the feeling only that I must get clear of Bristol, if I was to recover from the heart problems. In the meantime, we decided to take a break and stay at our favourite hotel in Thurleston in Devon while we thought about it.

At the table next to us in the restaurant of the hotel were a married pair, about our age, with whom we made friends. They were Teddy and Toni Sainsbury, farming people from Herefordshire who, when we told them about our minor troubles of finding a place to live, declared that they had an empty cottage on their land and invited us to come and stay with them to see if we liked their Herefordshire countryside. If we did so, then maybe we might like to rent the cottage while looking for a suitable house in the area.

We accepted their invitation and how pleased we were that we had done so because Saccie loved the cottage, which was small, having a living room with a wood-burning stove, a kitchen, bathroom with real loo and two bedrooms. The cottage was old, lovely to look at and set in two fields of about thirty acres which were surrounded by woodlands. It was on quite a steep hillside and above it was the large modern house and gardens where the Sainsburys lived. The only apparent snag was that the area in front of the cottage had become a dumping ground for all sorts of rubbish including old refrigerators and kitchen sinks. But, if we were to rent the cottage, Teddy undertook to clear it all up and to have the ground sculptured into a garden area. The whole prospect was irresistible, especially to Saccie who longed to create a garden out of the ugly shambles at the front of the cottage. We moved in using a small local moving firm of two brothers, Malcolm and Gordon Harper, whom we came to know well over the next eighteen years. I had already sold our large furniture when we left the Bursar's house in Clifton so that all our remaining bits and pieces just about fitted into the cottage comfortably, once they had been transported across the adjoining fields in the Harpers' van, which listed dangerously despite their careful loading of it.

Early Retirement

The place was idyllic. True to his word, Teddy had the ground in front of the cottage sculptured with a hired excavator, while taking Saccie's advice on how to shape the ground and what trees to leave in place, so that there remained the possibility of a lovely garden area. And how hard Saccie worked on that garden, almost all day, every day. I can see her now, either digging like mad or, with her little bum in the air, bent over and planting this and that in the fresh ground. Saccie always had the gymnastic ability, even at the age of eighty, to place her hands flat on the ground while keeping her legs straight. But she was lousy at ball games; if I chucked a ball at her, she would inevitably muff the catch and she passed this muffiness on to our son, Jeremy. Aza, on the other hand, is a naturally good athlete, which I like to think she gets from her Father. Anyway, back to the cottage and its garden, from where we could go for walks in the countryside of Coppet Hill and along the banks of the river Wye, which ran just a mile below us. I spent most of my time collecting and chopping wood for the stove and cooking, while Saccie created the garden. I began to feel much less ill, and Saccie positively bloomed.

There was a cow barn at the bottom of the field below us where Teddy kept a few 'Moolies' as I called them. But he had a whole fleet of the animals in about a hundred acres of fields on the other side of his house and at times Saccie and I and Toni would join him in herding them on a Moolie Run, for some reason, from field to field. Teddy's old herding dog was now obviously deaf and would fail to hear his whistled instruction to cease herding the beasts along faster, with the result that they ended up in a cowboy-style stampede along the country roads. A nerve-racking experience for me as I was never quite sure whether they might turn and mow me down because, after all, they were not milk animals but bulls. I gathered that all these acres of land were really regarded by the Sainsburys as a sort of toy farm for Teddy's retirement and pleasure, as they had sold their real-sized farm, which Teddy had inherited many years earlier. He was recognised in that famous farming county of Herefordshire as a top of the range farmer.

During all this time, I had assumed that as sitting tenants, so to speak, we would be able to buy the cottage and, without actually discussing the purchase, there had been an understanding between us that we would buy it. It wasn't until we had been living in the cottage for nearly two years that I thought to establish with the Sainsburys a date and agreed price for the purchase. Earlier, when fixing the rent at £180 per month, they had spoken in general terms of a value around

£35,000 for the cottage, which then I could have easily afforded. But I was realising belatedly that house prices were rising so fast that I needed to buy as soon as possible. Saccie and Toni met each other as friends almost every day to have coffee or to go shopping together in the town of Ross-on-Wye, but we arranged a formal little meeting in their kitchen to talk about buying the cottage. We were absolutely astonished when the Sainsburys told us that they had no intention of selling the cottage, which they were keeping as a present for their son Jeremy, aged twenty at the time, whenever he should marry and want to settle down. Moreover, as they pointed out, the cottage was now worth £55,000 which they understood to be beyond our range. I realised that they were probably right about the price because the cottage, set as it now was in Saccie's lovely garden, looked worth all of that sum, taking into account the escalation in house prices. However, I reckoned that, with a mortgage, I could still buy it, but they were adamant that they wanted to keep it. Unlike me, these farmers were no fools and had realised that every year the value of the cottage was going up by about £10,000. In fact, they did better than that because, only a year after we had left it, they sold it at auction for £88,500. It was bought by a private junior school, which poured concrete all over Saccie's erstwhile garden to make playgrounds, from whence the shouts and shrieks of the children all day nearly drove the Sainsburys dotty, as they told us later. So the Sainsburys had shrieking children as close neighbours, instead of quiet friendly neighbours like Saccie and me. Money ain't everything, is it?

Meanwhile, damn fool that I was, there was nothing else we could do but get out of the cottage just as fast and as soon as we could find another property within our price range, and before the prices escalated much higher. How, I ask myself now, as I have been asking all my life, did I ever come to be so almighty stupid over my own personal finances, compared with my proven astute business sense at my place of work? I think it must be that I have always had a vague idea at the back of my mind that friends would always be 'nice' about money. It stemmed, I suppose, from my own attitude of personal lack of interest in the stuff, so long as I had some. But there are some people who, however firm their friendship may be with you, kind of change slightly as soon as any money is involved. After acknowledging my stupidity and expressing my deep regret to Saccie and giving her a big cuddle, because I realised how she so hated having to leave the cottage and the lovely garden she had made, we now had to move fast to find another home. We weren't even sure what sort of home we wanted except that we liked this area in and around Ross-on-Wye.

Armed, therefore, with masses of paperwork from the various estate agents, we eventually found ourselves outside a small modern terrace house on a new but quite pleasant housing estate on the edge of the town. Saccie thought it was all so obviously unpleasant that she stayed outside while I went in to meet the owner, as already arranged. The owner turned out to be a young widow who was about to marry again, as I learned while going round the house with her, and live abroad with her new chap who, I gathered, was rather wealthy. In consequence, she was anxious to sell as quickly as possible. The house was a bit pokey but really quite pleasant inside, I thought, and the price she was asking of £22,500 was very low indeed. So now it was my turn to be nasty about money (I was having to learn) and I offered her there and then £20,000 for an immediate sale, in other words as soon as her solicitor could effect it.

The young widow accepted and, although only verbal, I would have to stick to the contract because there is a limit to how nasty a man can get. Somehow I would have to tell Saccie, who was still outside, waiting impatiently to view other and more acceptable-looking houses.

It was hard explaining afterwards to a justifiably upset and angry Saccie that my objective had been to get back onto the property market and to recover some of the capital value we had lost while renting the cottage. We found, after Malcolm and Gordon had moved us, that our furniture fitted very well into the little house which, with Saccie's flair for arrangement and decoration and Aza's hard work, was transformed into a comfortable and quite a handsome-looking home. Our furniture, which was mostly antique and good quality, always made a lot of difference to the appearance of our various houses. Hence, when I put the house on the market again for sale a year later, I was reasonably confident of finding a buyer at £32,000 which would give me a very good profit indeed. It enabled us to keep our eyes open for the sort of property in Ross-on-Wye where we would really like to live. I had a bit of fun during all that year in fighting the Herefordshire Council, which was prepared to allow a property developer to build another twenty-six houses on the estate. I argued on the basis that it was only possible to build one road through the centre of the estate, and the traffic generated to serve so many houses would constitute a danger to the children and elderly people living either side of it. It was a winning argument and the number of new houses to be allowed on the estate was reduced to six. It was my first brush with local councils and I rather enjoyed the experience.

But our time in that house was marred by the death of Cobbie, our short wire-haired little Dachshund dog whom we had bought as a six-week old puppy fourteen years earlier. We both loved him dearly, yes I too, in spite of my general dislike of dogs, for he had been a good-natured and loving little companion to us in all those years. I admired his courage too, because I had seen him fight back when attacked by larger dogs and also I think at times, although he never whinged, he was in pain from a slight fracture in his back. He became very ill and I asked the vet to come to the house to put him to sleep, so that he was relaxed among us in his home. I held him in my arms and wept as he died quietly after the injection. In reality, what better way is there to go when you are as ill and old as that, but it is denied to us humans. I never wanted to see or own another dog ever again but, three years later, Saccie wanted to replace Cobbie with a similar breed puppy, and we did so.

Saccie found the house she wanted at No. 7 New Street among a terrace of old houses, dated about 1850, almost in the middle of Ross-on-Wye. We didn't waste any time before buying it and moving in, with our usual help from Malcolm and Gordon Harper, who were getting to know us and our belongings quite well.

The house appeared deceptively small from the pavement immediately outside, but it had three floors with four small bedrooms and bathroom upstairs and a pleasant sitting room, dining room and kitchen on the ground floor. Its main feature was a long thin garden at the back with a huge wooden greenhouse. A previous owner had been well-known in the town for the vegetables and fruit he grew and sold from the front door. To be honest, the house was a bit tatty and decrepit in parts but the price of £38,000 I had paid left me sufficient cash to carry out repairs as they became necessary during the next three years, while we lived there very happily. Next door was a charming and quietly-run old pub, the Horse and Jockey, which we were surprised to discover was owned by the parents of the two brothers, by now our friends, the Harpers!

These were good times; Saccie was blooming again tending to a nice garden, where we could enjoy our morning sherries or evening gins together in the 'sherry shed' at the end of the garden. I started tentatively to play tennis again. There was a thriving tennis club on the edge of the town and I found a good partner and companion in Robert Milward, a retired Wing Commander who had survived a hectic war as a fighter pilot in the RAF, as his DFC indicated. Although he and I shared much the same wartime flying experiences, we rarely referred to them and got on with the main business of playing tennis. He was very competitive and loved to win whereas I was not so intense about winning but absolutely hated to lose, so we found it less stressful to play together as partners rather than against each other. As partners with a combined age of nearly 140, we played in matches for the club against other clubs and usually won. By this time we had made a number of friends in the area and our grotty little old house in the middle of the town was a good place for Saccie's chums to look in to have coffee with her after their shopping.

All very well playing tennis for three mornings each week, often mixed doubles with my partner Doreen, but I needed something more in life than that. I was asked by the local parish council to chair a sports committee, with the aim of funding, developing and promoting the main sports field for the town. I did so for a year but it was infuriating as the members of the committee never seemed able to start, let alone complete, any of the tasks which they had agreed to undertake. I couldn't fire them, as in managing a company, so I acknowledged myself a failure and resigned. But, at that same period of time, I had started to paint again and converted one of the top floor bedrooms into a studio and was 'daubin'', as I called it, nearly full time every day. My paintings began to sell at various small exhibitions but mainly at some art galleries in Wales and in the west of England.

So there we were during that first year at No. 7 New Street; Saccie in the garden gardening and I upstairs daubin' when not playing hard at lawn tennis. Too hard, as I should have realised, because now and then on the court I felt unwell, dizzy and short of breath. It was a clear warning and I should have recognised it and stopped … but I didn't. Came an evening when I felt suddenly extremely ill and Saccie called my doctor, who came immediately (they did in those days, do you remember?) and, after sticking something in my arm, called the ambulance. It was fifteen miles to the main hospital in Hereford and Saccie drove the car to follow me there in the ambulance. I recall so strongly my memories as I lay in the ambulance during that journey. I was very frightened believing that I was about to die and I kept telling myself to do so quietly and with dignity and to try not to show my fear. Such thinking was extraordinarily effective in calming me down so that on arrival at the emergency ward of the Hospital, I was almost as if asleep, until I remember the relief of Saccie coming to me and holding my hand as she sat next to my bed. The next unbelievable thing, a few minutes later as it seemed, was seeing Aza, with her anxious little face, coming down the ward. She lived in Bristol, so how had she got here so miraculously quickly? She had driven like the clappers, of course, on receiving the telephone call from Saccie and here she was only little more than an hour later. All that fear and anxiety and yet, only five days later, I was back at home after the heart attack. I didn't play tennis ever again … not likely!

All my life until then I had regarded the game of golf as intended and suitable only for old men to play. It seemed absurd to me (and it still does actually) that young men should play it seriously and some of them indeed even earn a lot of money from it. At their young age, they should be playing rugby, cricket, squash, even football, like real chaps. Golf is so perfect and good for old men; a nice long walk, a difficult skill to achieve in hitting the ball, good companionship and chat on the way plus some gentle competition and a glass of something nice to drink together at the end of the game. Well, I was certainly an old man now after the heart attack, and so I took up the game of golf. And, oh the gentle joy of it. Of course, I had played 'at' the game once or twice a year in earlier times and had tended to sneer at the game as I did so for being such a sissy activity. But now was different. I started to work at playing the game properly and, in time after a few years, achieved an authentic but unrealistic handicap of sixteen.

Another gloriously happy aspect of the game is that it is possible for old men to play it just as well as young men. For instance, in my youth, my bête noir on the squash and tennis courts had been young Martin Davies Jones whom, to start with, I could thrash off the court at both games. But as I grew older and he more skilful, so I lost every time at those games although, regrettably I have to admit, without his cheerful ability to lose gracefully. Now I was able to challenge Martin at golf and, such is the kind nature of the game, could derive the pleasure of winning once again. Usually, however, I trundled each week round the lovely Ross golf course with the same dear old men, endlessly and happily all of us repeating our same old jokes and golfing stories. What about the 'Ladies', you may ask, don't they also play golf? They do, but it seems that so many of them appear to prefer debating the rules of the game and whether there has been any transgression, rather than just getting on and enjoying the playing of it. (My apologies for digressing onto golf; but it was such fun in those years.)

For the Christmas of 1998, Jeremy used his last remaining capital from the sale of his house in Eastleigh to visit us with Atauea, his second wife. I had sold it for him at quite a good profitable price after he left England to live in Kiribati, but he had gone through the money like a dose of salts ever since and barely had enough now with which to make this first visit to us. It would be a very costly visit for him, a return airfare for one from Kiribati to England via New Zealand being I believe about £2,000 at the time. And so the visit had to be a considerable occasion for us all, but to be honest it really was not a great success. For a start, Atauea neither spoke nor understood English and it was difficult for either Saccie or me to establish a good contact with her. Jeremy, who amazed us by evidently speaking astonishingly fluent Gilbertese, would try to translate between us at meals and during the day, but it was hard work all round, particularly because it was such a strange-sounding language to our ears, seemingly being full of guttural grunts.

Atauea's main pleasure was to walk round the shops of the town just buying things, mostly clothes, but anything at all that took her fancy. I could see why Jeremy had gone almost broke already, as he didn't seem able to deny her. There didn't appear to be much point in her buying lots of things to wear because, while the features of Atauea's face were truly beautiful, her bodywork could frankly only be described as short and fat and it wouldn't really matter whatever garments were draped over it. Nevertheless, it was evident that Jeremy loved her and, for that reason alone, it was certainly not for us to comment on her childish extravagance. In fact, I must be fair to her, she was absolutely frozen, having never left her idyllic Pacific Island before, so it must have been quite hard getting used to English winter weather.

It really was a white Christmas that year, with lots of snow and ice everywhere, and we had to keep extra electric fires going all day and night for Atauea to feel even slightly warm. Jeremy and I enjoyed several visits to local pubs together, leaving poor Saccie to boil in front of the electric fires while trying to converse with Atauea.

To be truthful and, although it had all been worthwhile just to be with our son again, it was something of a relief all round when the time came for their departure. They were due to spend a couple of days with Aza in Bristol before flying back, no doubt gratefully, to the heat of their home in Kiribati. But, before driving them over the icy roads to the nearest railway station for Bristol, I had slipped a cheque for £400 into Jeremy's pocket. After all, I had made about that amount of shared profit under our mortgage agreement, when I had sold his house in Eastleigh for him. Moreover, having witnessed Atauea at full stretch in the shops, I reckoned he was going to need it.

Apart from the repair work constantly needed at No. 7, a brick coming out here or rain coming in there, the only snag to living in the house was the outlook from the single window of the sitting-room directly onto the pavement outside. Or, to put it more precisely, there was the necessity of keeping lace curtains up in daytime and curtains fully drawn in the late afternoons and evenings, to prevent people passing by from goofing in on us. Pedestrians outside were so close that they might as well be having a glass of gin with us in the room.

All of this is a preamble to describe and excuse the next major financial blunder I was about to make.

We visited some friends for a drinks party in their house, which was located in a quiet road behind the grounds of the Chase Hotel in Ross. I don't know if there was something in the drinks, but both Saccie and I fell in love with the house, which was called 'Fern Lea'.

It was a small Edwardian period detached house, with a pretty little garden in the front overlooked by an attractive coloured glass front porch and, at the back, a reasonably large garden with a well-established pond and a number of small trees. There was a big garage for two cars at the back of the garden, reached by a side lane. Inside, just three bedrooms but with a large kitchen-diner and a long heated conservatory leading through to the back garden. Perhaps best of all, from my point of view, was the basement, which had been entirely covered in wooden panelling and was well-lighted with fluorescent tubes. It was a ready-made perfect studio and I coveted it because, by that time, I was beginning to earn real money from the sale of my paintings.

We learned that these friends were leaving Ross and were about to put the house on the market and immediately, of course, I wanted it and so did Saccie. Although my finances had recovered as the result of our last exchange of houses, the reality was that the escalation in house prices had taken Fern Lea well beyond my reach at £95,000, whereas my slightly grotty No. 7 house was now worth less than half that amount. To purchase Fern Lea would mean borrowing a great deal of money with a mortgage, if I could get it. Of course I could get it. This was 1988 and the building societies and banks were shelling out loans to anyone and everyone who asked for one as if there was no to-morrow, and all on the basis that the price of houses was bound to go on escalating for ever and ever. It was considered, therefore, that a house could always be sold at a profit big enough to pay back any loan on it. Without any hesitation, therefore, I joined the army of other heavy borrowers in the UK, so that I could buy Fern Lea. The price was agreed and I was fortunate to have two months in which to sell No. 7 before the completion date for payment.

Again luck was with me, because a delightful young couple in their late thirties turned up within a week after the advertisement, with their offer to buy. I had vaguely warned them that, being an old property, little bits of repairs might become necessary from time to time, but nothing had prepared them or me for the disaster, shortly after they moved in, when part of the floor of the bathroom collapsed into the dining room underneath! They didn't make any complaint but, when we heard about it, Saccie said that I simply must go round to show some regret and see if I could help. And she was quite right, of course, we couldn't just ignore their plight. To hell with *caveat emptor* and all that and, although of course they should have used a building surveyor before buying, I felt that they had relied on me and inevitably they would regard me now as a suave old shark who had taken them for a ride. We need not have worried, the husband was astonishingly relaxed about it, explained that he was a DIY building freak, and had intended to put in an entirely new bathroom anyway. I breathed with relief because, feeling that I had been guilty of some breach of trust with these young people, I had come prepared if necessary to offer some sort of *ex gratia* contribution to the cost of the rebuilding. However, they managed to convince me without too much difficulty that they could cope with the problem on their own.

CHAPTER NINETEEN

Pensionable Retirement

I am not going to pretend that I regret borrowing money beyond my means to buy Fern Lea, in spite of the financial crash it caused me eventually, because Saccie and I enjoyed five such very happy years together in that house. There was a bit of a bonus to start with as I was now receiving my state pension, about £3,500 a year in those days, I seem to remember. On the other hand, 'they' had stopped the pension Saccie had been receiving for the past five years, since she became sixty, and now regarded my pension as providing for both of us; so I had to give half of mine back to Saccie anyway. I forbear to comment on what a penny-pinching, niggardly and parsimonious crew 'they' were to treat Saccie in such a manner! But I got our own back, as they say, when by chance I came across some old files in which was a Certificate of War Wounds awarded to Saccie when, as a young girl of twenty in the Wrens, she had suffered a serious accident while under training. She had fractured her back and been unable to move out of a hospital bed for six months and, moreover, had suffered periodic pain without complaint ever since. It took time and a lot of letter writing, but eventually I was able to wrench a decent annual 'wound allowance' of £1,500 in future from the appropriate Ministry for Saccie. They wouldn't consider any pay for previous years.

I had given up lawn tennis, of course, but played golf twice a week and made a number of very good friends at the golf club. No money problems either as, in addition to my three small pensions, I was earning more than a few bob from selling my paintings at various art shops and minor exhibitions, albeit at low prices. Saccie enjoyed her new garden immensely and occasionally would meet her friends in the town for shopping. She made acquaintance with people easily enough, but her inclination was to have just a few close friends whose friendship she would retain for life. One of these in particular was Ellie Cosker, wife of a successful farmer with a farm just outside Ross, and they established a strong and warm friendship together, which lasted throughout their lives.

It may be due to the up-and-down life I had led or maybe it is in my nature, but when life is as pleasant as it was then, I feel that it can't last and some doom-laden event would inevitably catch up with me to undermine it. And so I look for something I must do, some activity I don't like, which I must undertake to ward off the advent of the dreaded doom. So this time I volunteered to work for the Citizens' Advice Bureau, which had a small office in the middle of Ross. I had in mind that the work would be rather like the Samaritans, for whom I had worked many years earlier in Belfast. It would be a similar organisation for helping people in trouble, so I thought. The work probably would be unpleasant and eminently suitable therefore for warding off any thrust from a Damoclean sword. First of all I had to pass a rather intense sort of oral examination to see what I knew about the workings of the welfare state, which was absolutely nothing, but the chap passed me anyway. I could see the point of the exam later on, because eighty per cent of the work was delving through piles of welfare leaflets and pamphlets to see whether 'sub-section so-and-so of section this in paragraph that' was relevant to the young mother sitting in front of me who was in need of welfare money. I was relegated to dealing mostly with those cases concerning marital or family problems, which often were troubles of a more serious nature akin to those I had dealt with as a Samaritan. I worked at the CAB only for two mornings per week, which I reckoned was more than enough to ward off any doom coming my way.

I hope that by now, as I write this, the huge mass of welfare directions and instructions has all been fed into a computer, enabling a volunteer merely to press a mouse to find the information he needs for his troubled client.

The other activity I undertook was to deal with the tax returns and correspondence each year for two widows of ex-golfing friends. But that was a labour of friendship.

In our third year at Fern Lea, Jeremy and Atauea came to visit us again, this time bringing their little three-year old daughter, Alice, to meet us. The little girl was well-mannered and a delightful vivacious little thing, very pretty indeed and could already speak English quite well. Saccie loved having her in the house and so did I.

But Jeremy was in trouble. His six-year contract with the Aid Administration Ministry of our HM Government, which paid for such schools where Jeremy taught in the Republic of Kiribati, was due to finish in less than a year's time and, so he told me, the Ministry were reluctant to renew it. Their reason was twofold: first of all in principle they very rarely contracted any teacher for more than the six year period and had always been at pains to make this clear when offering a contract. Jeremy must have been aware of this when he insisted on marrying a local girl despite the advice from his Father, who had foreseen this very problem. In a short time he would be in the appalling situation of having a family to keep, in the foreign environment of an as yet undeveloped country, and no possibility of any other job for him there. The Ministry were also reluctant to renew Jeremy's contract because, now he told me, he had been ill with a form of hepatitis for a period of weeks.

Obviously this was the opportunity, now that he was back in the UK, to do something about the situation and one of the reasons why he had come back to us. Jeremy had proved himself many times in the past to be a young man of great courage and endurance, but he needed to see clearly what he was up against and what he would have to endure. He was absolutely hopeless, at that stage of his life, in the face of authority and could become speechless with helpless rage when faced with the barrier of bureaucracy. Later in his life, when he had gained more confidence, he largely overcame this inadequacy. But right then, he needed his Dad.

We had a long discussion about his work at the school. I wanted to find out about its administration and particularly about his Headmaster who, he told me, was an English teacher like himself but fifteen years older and had been appointed at the start of the school under a different long-term contract. Jeremy assured me that they worked well together. As for the pupils, local boys and young men, he got on very well with them apparently, because already he spoke their Gilbertese language with fluency and they knew he had married a local girl. Jeremy confirmed to me that he could rely on a good report from his Headmaster. I was still a member of BUPA at that time and so the first thing to do was to pack Jeremy off to the BUPA hospital in Hereford where, for the mind-boggling sum of £360, they would give him their thorough medical examination and subsequent formal report on his medical condition. I drafted a formal letter on his behalf to the Ministry to apply for a renewed contract with the request that consideration be given to four relevant aspects of his work at the school in Kiribati. Firstly reports from the Headmaster on his teaching results, secondly ability to speak the language fluently, thirdly his marriage in Kiribati and fourthly his enclosed full medical fitness report. To cut the story short, the Ministry remained reluctant to agree another six-year contract but offered another four years, which Jeremy seized eagerly. Before Jeremy returned to Kiribati with his lovely little daughter, I could only remind him that he was unlikely to get away with another extension of the contract and, since Atauea would not leave the area of the Pacific, he absolutely must apply himself to seeking other work for the longer-term future, maybe in Fiji.

After Jeremy and his little family had returned to Kiribati, life bumbled very happily along for Saccie and me. We took short two-day holidays from time to time in mid-Wales, usually staying in small country hotels, from where I could find wild Welsh countryside and mountains for my landscape paintings. I don't like 'pretty' paintings and all mine were of bare hills, rocky landscapes and exciting dark clouds, sometimes with a pair of Red Kites flying vaguely around. It was surprising really that I sold them. Aza had made a good start with her framing business in Bristol and was doing well, but it didn't leave her much time for more than an occasional visit. But the old clouds of doom were beginning to loom up again and this time in the form of urinary trouble which, according to the doctor, at my age of sixty-nine was to be expected. But at Christmas in 1990 the trouble became serious and, on Boxing Day, I had to telephone the consultant in Hereford, Mr Sole, who arranged for me to go straight to the BUPA hospital. He operated the next day and I had been so fortunate to have such a super surgeon because I ceased to have any more of that particular problem afterwards and, thankfully, he could also confirm that there was no cancer remaining.

But those doom-laden clouds were building up higher and higher on the horizon. The bubble of people living on borrowed money, as in my typical case, was about to burst. Banks and building societies, who had been lending without checking or caring for the security of their loans, now took fright and refused to lend any more to anybody, or so it seemed. Unemployment was rising fast as small firms and companies, unable to borrow more money to continue their businesses, went bust. House prices, which had been overvalued throughout the country, were falling and fast. Fern Lea, which in 1989 had been valued as high as £115,000, was already in 1991 well down below that, and my mortgage on it was £40,000. Moreover, at the time, it appeared certain that house prices would continue to fall much further and impossible to believe that they could ever rise back again to anything like their previous level. Thus, unless I could get out and sell quickly, my mortgage might become higher than the value on the house and I would be left without any capital with which to purchase another cheaper property. 'Don't panic, don't panic,' as that dear old boy on Dad's Army often used to say on the television. But I was seventy years old and panic I did! It was then 1992, and I considered that I was very lucky to find a buyer for Fern Lea at £90,000, which left me with about £50,000 capital. What a twit I was; why on earth did I not stay put and gamble that the prices would rise again, as indeed they did astronomically after a few years. For Saccie, life with Hank was one damn catastrophe after another but she seemed to take them all calmly in her stride without fussing or moaning about them. What luck for me to have such a wonderful wife, because there was plenty more doom to come!

With only just about £45,000 in my bank after selling Fern Lea, Saccie and I were looking around Ross for some sort of house in which to live. There was not a lot around at that sort of money, and there was no possibility of getting a mortgage now, but eventually we found 'Rose Cottage', which was in fact a very small old terrace house, in much the same style as No.7 New Street had been, only a lot smaller.

It was bang in the middle of the town in a sort of lane with similar little houses on either side and a small pub at the end of it. At the back was a tiny garden but with space to park a car and the whole of the rear area behind the house comprised in effect the back yards for all the surrounding houses. The house had a basement which was entirely decrepit but which, with some money, could be made into a nice kitchen with its existing steps leading up onto the little garden. But I hadn't any money. As it was, the kitchen was no more than part of a passageway at the rear of the house leading to the bathroom and loo. However, being old the house had a certain charm about it and Saccie seemed to reckon it was acceptable, particularly because of its location in the middle of the town. So I bought Rose Cottage and our two friendly moving men bunged our furniture into it. There were only two small single bedrooms upstairs separated by the rickety stairway between them, but there was also a comparatively large attic which we filled with all our gash furniture.

Immediately adjacent to the rear of the house was a barn-like building, recently made empty, which had been used as a meeting hall for a Methodist religious group. The first happening was an application to the Herefordshire Council, made by an ambitious young man already a member of the town parish council, to convert the Methodist hall alongside us, which he had purchased, into a cinema. Everybody in the town of Ross-on-Wye seemed to think that this was a brilliant idea, except the Adlams who would have to live with the blaring noise of a cinema on the other side of their party wall. Much of my time during the next two years was spent in writing letters to members of the Herefordshire Council formally objecting to the cinema proposal, lobbying them to visit the site, attending public meetings, writing letters to the local newspapers setting out my reason for objecting to the cinema, replying to hate mail which howled for the need of a cinema in Ross. Letters too had to be written to the editor of the local paper, who had nominated me as the number one NIMBY (not in my back yard) of the county and who continued gleefully to support the cinema project.

Most effectively, I invited the Chief Fire Officer of the county, who hitherto had not objected to the cinema, to see for himself that the so-called emergency fire exit led straight into a brick wall, allowing only one person at a time to squeeze past to safety, and that there was insufficiently wide an access to the site for a fire engine. (In the end, these were the winning arguments.)

Earlier in the conflict, I had caught the young man of the cinema, so very sure of himself was he, in the act of installing expensive cinema seating into the hall with the aid of two of his chaps. I waited until the end of the day when the installation was completed before reminding him that, now the hall was no longer empty, he would be liable for maximum rates on the building for the full year. Moreover, that I would make sure the rating office knew of the seating installation. One of his young thugs menaced me with his clenched fist and I thought he was surely going to hit me, but the cinema man pulled him away in time. The assault would no doubt have been physically painful, but would have given me the publicity I needed. At seventy years old, I still felt young in spite of the heart problems of recent years, but having to fight this unpleasant and pushy young man, so determined to operate his wretched little cinema in the midst of a residential area, was now beginning to affect my health, and the chest pains and breathless feelings were recurring.

As if the damn cinema was not enough, the next happening was to receive notification of a change to a higher rate band. This was ridiculous since Rose Cottage as a habitation was as bereft of facilities as a house can be, and reasonably could only merit the very lowest rating. Maybe the cinema man or a cinema fan had sent a suggestion to the rating authority, which had immediately acted upon it without proper investigation? Anyway, there it was, and the authority was insistent upon the higher rating in spite of my letters in opposition to it. I demanded to put the case before a Tribunal but, when I appeared before it some weeks later, I realised that I was on a certain loser. The greasy little clerk who represented the rating authority hob-nobbed on the friendliest terms with the members of the Tribunal, who all evidently knew him well, and even had their lunch-break with him while he could discuss his case against me with them separately. I objected, of course, but could make no impact on the Tribunal members. I lost my case, as I now expected, but I determined that I would object again next year before a Tribunal, when I would know better how to present my case and how to deal with the greasy clerk.

With all this going on, I had very little time for painting which was just as well because there was virtually nowhere in Rose Cottage to do it apart from a small area of damp basement. Which was unfortunate because I could have done with the cash from the sale of a few paintings at that time.

Another situation, which I found disconcerting, was that the house opposite to us in the lane was a thriving brothel and a location in Ross for the distribution of illegal drugs. Our front door of the house, which was part of the small front living-room, opened straight out onto the entrance pathway. Several times we answered the door to men who were seeking either sex or drugs and had come to our door instead of the house opposite. It was understandable because the blonde young woman who ran the business opposite and who, incidentally, had a nice little ten-year old son, was called Rosie and our house was Rose Cottage. Saccie regarded the whole situation as hilariously funny, or so she said, and from her bedroom window upstairs, often watched the arrivals opposite in the late evenings. My sense of humour could no longer stretch that far. Why did I not report the whole business to the police, you may well ask? And the answer is that we had to live there and I already had enough aggro on my plate from the cinema and the rates tribunal.

The final straw for me was that some of the houses around us, which overlooked the back yards and little bits of garden, were taken over by the local Council and converted into Housing Association accommodation mainly for single young men. I was quite happy with that in principle, but when these young men, evidently drunk, began shouting and being sick out of their windows, that was the end of Rose Cottage for me. 'Enough is enough and this time it is too much!' I had no right to make decisions without asking Saccie, but I had enough of fighting all the problems of living at Rose Cottage, and I just made the decision that we must move again. Living there was not as it had been in our youth at Gulson Road, where we had been in similarly poor circumstances, but in those days we had been fighting our way upwards in life. This time we were in our seventies and, as far as I was concerned, this was no way for either of us to end our lives. I was determined that we must get out of that awful little house, which had caused me so much stress and worry, and I believe that Saccie understood that.

We had a number of friends in Monmouth, an attractive and famous old town on the edge of Wales, only sixteen miles from Ross. Our particular friends were Ken and Irene Brown who lived there and he and I had put on a couple of painting exhibitions together at a gallery in the town, both of which had been successful. Ken was a much better artist than I being both naturally gifted and trained whereas, as I have always been well aware, I was merely a hard working dauber and I have never kidded myself as being anything else. If I sold more paintings than Ken, it was only because I set out to do so since I needed the money. Anyway and regardless of the wretched need for cash, painting was always an absorbing interest and joy in my life. And so, having a number of golfing friends as well as the Browns in Monmouth, I suggested to Saccie that we bale out of Ross and look there for our next house. If she heaved a great sigh of despair at moving again, she hid it well as usual and off we went house-hunting in Monmouth.

I was on the brink of selling Rose Cottage to a builder who reckoned that, during his spare time over the next year or more, he could reconstruct the interior of the house and so eventually make it into an attractive home for himself and his wife. He had agreed a price of £48,000 but did not want to complete until two months ahead. Meantime, on the edge of Monmouth, we had found a small property in my price range which we both quite liked. It was a minuscule modern sort of terrace house located on a side road and, at the back, its tiny garden was up against the very old fortification wall of the town. Hence the name 'Burgage', which I learned was the name given to the area immediately outside the fortress where the serfs could live. How appropriate. Other than that, it had three single bedrooms, a well-equipped kitchen, a pleasant living room and a garage which in due course we converted into a studio-cum-conservatory. But everything was in miniature.

I wanted to buy it without delay, before another buyer offered more for it, but none of the money-lenders (now generally known as banks and building societies) were prepared to arrange a bridging loan for me. These people who had happily almost thrown their loans at me (to my undoing) a few years before now would not even lend me a pound note. There was only one thing for it: I invited my old friend Martin, more usually known to me as young Midas because every business project he touched always turned to gold, for a game of golf and lunch with me at the Ross Club where I gracefully permitted him to win. Then, much as I hated to do it, I asked him if he could provide the bridging loan for me. Which he did and, indeed, would have done anyway, of course, even had I won our game of golf.

And so I bought the Burgage. Subsequently, back at Ross, that creep of a man with his cinema had finally been refused planning permission for it, and so I learned that I had won my two-year battle after all. Dear Rosie with all her brothel girls had been moved on by the police. And the Housing Association flats, containing the young drunks, had been converted to a quiet family residence. Thus, had I only known that all these things would happen, there would have been no need for us to move again. Such is typical of my life.

Our move into the Burgage in1995 was completed yet again by our usual moving men who, by this time, knew every item of our furniture and could even suggest where to arrange them to the best advantage in the new abode. In fact, much of the furniture had to be crammed one piece on top of another in one of the three tiny bedrooms. Never mind, it was a comfortable, clean little modern house and for me at that time it was a place of placid peace compared with the fighting cockpit of Rose Cottage.

However, instead of Rosie and her girls opposite to us, we now had a huge comprehensive school and its playground, which sounds horrific but in fact only once did we have any trouble when a group of the younger boys were rude to Saccie. I caught them making their rude remarks and laced into them verbally at which, as boys of that age would do, they laughed. Without hesitation therefore, I marched into the main building of the school and demanded to see the Headmaster and would not leave his secretary's office until he was called out of a classroom (which surprised me) to meet me. He was a tall man, quite young, who appeared to listen carefully to my description of the boys and said he would deal with them. My expectation was that nothing would come of it, as there were some eighteen hundred pupils of ages from twelve to seventeen in the school, and he could hardly be expected to know one from the other.

At mid-day the next morning, however, there was a knock on our front door and there stood a master with the five boys, whom I recognised as those who had been rude to Saccie. Each boy came forward one by one to apologise to Saccie and to hand a scrap of exercise book to her on which their apology had been carefully written also. I was flabbergasted firstly that the Headmaster had been able to track down the boys from my description and secondly at the evidence of such good school discipline. I met the Headmaster on some occasions later and, after thanking him, asked how on earth did he achieve such discipline; did he still use the cane, for instance. No, he said that he was fortunate to have good staff, able to identify the culprits from my description, and secondly good relations with the parents who supported him. There was never any more trouble with the schoolboys after that, and I had learned greater respect for the comprehensive state system.

One of the best aspects of living at the Burgage turned out to be the excellent doctors' surgery just at the top of our road and, shortly after we had moved in, a kidney stone which had been causing me some pain was diagnosed by the doctor. My first such stone in 1975 had necessitated major surgery and two months to recover, but now the method of dealing with the stone was to zap it from outside the body with a laser beam until the thing disintegrated. Saccie had driven me to and from the hospital to have it done and we were back home at the Burgage only three hours later. Fortunately, this zapping was done for free by the NHS because I had cancelled my BUPA membership as too expensive. Saccie, thank heavens, was well but I was particularly thankful to have such good doctors close at hand because my queer turns were occurring from time to time and, as usual` without any apparent reason or warning.

A rather worse turn than usual occurred while we were in Hereford on a shopping expedition and Saccie, who rarely drove but was always good in an emergency, loaded me into our little Polo VW car and threaded her way driving through the Hereford traffic to the hospital. Here they put me through a whole range of 'ticker' tests lasting almost a week and at the end the consultant, whom I respected as first-class at his job, told me that these recent attacks were in fact diagnosed and known as 'panic attacks'. I resented the word panic and still do. I resent it very much because, had I been the type of character prone to panic, I would never have survived five years of combat operations as a fighter pilot flying from Aircraft Carriers. Had

I been prone to panic, moreover, I would almost certainly have killed those who flew with me and under my leadership.

Why do the medics have to give these attacks the name of panic attacks, a name which implies that the sufferer is a craven wimp? The symptoms are frightening admittedly. A feeling of intense fragility and of being outside one's body, out of breath and about to faint. These feelings are akin to those I used to feel years ago, sometimes when walking across the flight deck ready to climb into my aircraft cockpit, but in those days they were called the twitch and were triggered by real and justified fear before a combat operation.

But at that time in my retirement and now, as I write, I recognise from experience that these similar feelings and symptoms are in reality very minor heart attacks which may occur at any time and without any apparent reason other than, perhaps, physical tiredness. They need not be at all dangerous, provided that the proper action is taken immediately, i.e. to sit down and rest (usually about twenty minutes) while breathing slowly and deeply into cupped hands and essentially to take a 300mg aspirin with a good strong slug of whisky. Hence, as I still have these attacks twenty years later, I never go anywhere without the aspirins and a whisky flask. I do realise the physical danger of these attacks, which can develop into a full heart attack. But panic is not what I do.

Saccie and I were reasonably happy in our tiny little pad in Monmouth. We had nice neighbours on either side, which was just as well since we lived almost on top of one another. But we had found a wonderful holiday location at Tenby, a fishing port and sandy beach holiday resort on the Welsh coast. The set-up was that we rented a large modern flat in an ugly-looking but large apartment block overlooking the north sands of the resort. This may sound to be rather awful but indeed it was not, because the large living room and the main of the three bedrooms was all one window from floor to roof and looked down onto the sandy beach and scattered rocks below, where many children played. Under the agreed procedure with the agents, once we had booked the flat we could continue to book it every year ahead for the same two weeks. Thus it was exactly the same as having a time-share property but without having to pay capital for the privilege. For the next six years, we booked the flat on this basis twice every year. Saccie, Aza and I all loved going there.

We were coming up to the fiftieth anniversary of our wedding on July 17th of 1998, Saccie and I, but we had been unable to book the flat in Tenby for that week and so planned rather vaguely to meet Aza somewhere for lunch at a nice pub. We didn't really want any of our friends for the occasion, just Aza, our only family in England. Not very enterprising of us, but there you go, what else was there to do since Jeremy, our son, was stuck out on some island on the far side of the world in the Pacific? On the morning of the 16th, Saccie answered a knock on the front door and nearly fell over with shock. Standing there on the threshold, grinning all over his face, was Jeremy! And hiding behind him was Aza, laughing delightedly at our shock. Aza, bless her heart, had been planning this occasion with Jeremy for many weeks past and, wildly generous character that she is, had paid most of his fare. (Jeremy's fishing business had suffered a financial set-back when one type of the exotic fish he sold to Hong Kong had apparently poisoned many of the restaurants clientele there!)

There was no room at our Inn, so to speak, so our good neighbours found room for Jeremy to stay for the visit, while Aza went to and fro from Bristol for the duration of his stay. And so, thanks in the main to Aza, whose whole nature is to delight in giving wonderful presents, we enjoyed a most happy anniversary. Aza wasn't finished there, because she had also made a beautiful photo album for us as a gift, which she had filled with all the best of our many family photos.

I should have been content, living with Saccie in our nice little rabbit-hutch in Monmouth and with nice friendly neighbours. But I was not content. We were living there as the result of my own crass and stupid financial mistakes; the first mistake being of impetuously selling my maisonette in College Road, Clifton which was now worth quite literally ten times the price of £56,000 at which I had sold it. And secondly for not having the gumption or the good judgement to risk staying on at Fern Lea, to wait for the high prices of houses to return. But I began to feel more and more strongly that, stupid as I had been, neither Saccie nor I deserved to be punished so severely by fate as this.

My past life had been one of hard, and for the most part, successful endeavour. I had fought for five years for my country, I had worked for it and had negotiated successfully for contracts worth many millions against competition from the USA, France, Germany, etc., and, in semi-retirement, I had been the major influence in bringing Clifton College out of the financial doldrums. Saccie had been a part of me in all of that and we did not deserve to be denied some gracious living at the end of it all. Well, that's what I thought and what I felt.

My thinking was to realise belatedly that, while house ownership was regarded as a necessity according to my upbringing, why should it be necessarily so, especially in my situation now? Our little abode, the Burgage, was worth very little capital but, on the other hand, my three small pensions together provided me with quite a good income. So what was so wrong with renting a home? Nothing at all; it was only traditional in England and in our upbringing to buy one's own home. In consequence, I started to keep a look-out among the estate agents for the sort of property I had in mind and which would be on offer at a rental. It was difficult to get Saccie interested, and who could blame her, she had taken more than enough of following me from one wretched little house to another. But this time I knew that I was right and I continued quietly on my own to look at one or two properties to rent. Not to hurry this time, I must make absolutely sure that it would be a home in which Saccie would be happy, as well as I.

And at last I found it! A house called 'The Chantry' located on the large Perrystone Estate of some 3500 acres some three miles from Ross-on-Wye. This huge estate was owned by Henry Clive, in whose family it had been for some time, and it has to be written that he managed the whole estate and farmland immaculately. Every field, every tree and hedge and every house or cottage on it was beautifully maintained. And in the middle of all this beauty was the Chantry, which I guess had been the dower house and was about a quarter of a mile walk, through an avenue of sixty high and fully grown elm trees, to the main Manor house. The Chantry was a handsome building of the Georgian period with its own gardens and greenhouses and surrounded by miles and miles of beautifully kept farming countryside. It contained three floors of pleasantly large-sized rooms and there were four garages beside the building. Next to the gardens at the back of the house was a farmhouse of the same period with its byre and milking shed nearby.

The first floor provided two good-sized bedrooms, kitchen and bathroom with a big living-room of typical Georgian proportions, and all having wonderful views over the countryside from similar-style windows. The top floor was more or less identical although with slightly less height to the rooms. This, to be frank, was the gracious place to live for which I yearned and I proposed to rent the two top floors, with garden and two garages. The rent, in my opinion, was ludicrously low for such a property at £750 per month and, what's more, I could afford it. All that remained was to show the house to Saccie and beg her to move just one more time. I had found the Chantry just in time while Jeremy was on our anniversary visit and so the whole family came with me to view what I suspect they all three regarded as 'Dad's latest folly'. I knew that Saccie would never refuse me anything that I really wanted so badly but, although the house appeared so beautiful, she was cautious about it and I think suspected that it might be a lonely place to live. As for Jeremy and Aza, they appeared to be merely bewildered that I should want to move from the Burgage at all. But then this is the general truth about family life, isn't it, that while the parents constantly think about their children and how they are developing, the children rarely give thought to the background of their parents and how they come to be as they are. They either love or dislike their parents (sometimes both at the same time) and, either way, just accept them. So, maybe it was difficult for them to understand why their Father needed to bale out of the Burgage.

Having received the dubious approval of my family, my only worry now was to secure the tenancy on a long-term basis of at least five years with an ongoing option to renew thereafter. But this too was agreed with Ian Peill, the agent for the estate with whom, over the following years, I established a friendship. Our two moving men, Malcolm and Gordon, chuckling with disbelief because this was the seventh time they would move us in fifteen years, heaved all our stuff into their van once again and transported it all to the Chantry. We were in … and Saccie, too, soon realised how lovely it was to be there.

When I have been asked to define happiness, I have replied that happiness is something we remember. Which is to say that we rarely recognise that we are happy at the time. And yet, contrary to that definition, I don't doubt that Saccie and I were well aware of our happiness during the time we lived together at the Chantry. We each had our own interests and for Saccie it was to redevelop the greenhouse and the garden area which, although full of shrubs and trees, had become slightly neglected. In particular there was a most attractive old walled garden, which she transformed in time into a lovely flower garden. An unusual factor of living there was the availability of help from the team of four men under the leadership of John, the estate manager. This team, working full time for the estate, could put their expert skills as masons, carpenters, gardeners and even as plumbers and electricians to the building or repair of any property on the estate. If we wanted anything repaired, John would come with one of his men and do it for us. Thus, in this way, Saccie was able to have the old garden walls and the greenhouse repaired and some of the overgrown shrubbery removed.

On the top floor, there were two spare bedrooms and a kitchen so that we could from time to time invite friends to stay with us. The best part of the top floor was the big main room including a long, heavy oak dining table which may have been built by John *in situ* because it was so huge that there was no way I could see of getting it in or out of the house. The room and the table were ideal for me to set up my easel and paints because I was now painting again and so enthusiastically that I would have three or more canvases going all at the same time. The owner of a new and very grand art gallery in Ross asked to see my paintings at the Chantry and immediately, on seeing them, wanted to buy seven of them there and then. He offered a low price of £250 each for them unframed and, so chuffed was I at the thought of so much cash, that I accepted. Over the next few months, having framed the canvases very expensively, he sold the lot at an average £850 price. In all fairness, he spent a lot of money (as a good gallery should) in advertising the paintings in very posh art journals. But it was a lesson to me to raise my prices in future.

About this time too, I was engaged in 'teaching' my style of oil painting to others. But teaching is the wrong word because in my opinion painting cannot be taught; what one does is to suggest a method or means of achieving whatever the pupil (a word I hesitate to use) is trying to do, and maybe demonstrate a method. My best pupil, as such, was Ian Peill who, as well as his main obsession in life of shooting beautiful birds and animals, now wanted to paint them. I have a particular style and method of painting skies, which I regard as the key factor and the very essence of a marine, aviation or landscape painting, and Ian learnt my method so quickly and well that the wretched man (a good friend actually) started selling more successfully than me! He invited Saccie and me to his first exhibition at which all his many shooting friends turned up to buy his paintings of the beautiful birds they so enjoyed killing. Saccie was talking to some wives and Ian was busy selling his paintings, so I walked over to join a group of chaps, all dressed in tweed coats and knee-length bockers. They were animatedly discussing their various guns and, in due course, courteously turned to me and asked what gun did I use? I replied that my only experience of guns was that of using six ·05 Browning machine guns firing to converge at targets 240 yards distance which, I remarked, could be quite lethal. It was a silly reply, I know, but I likened my own experience of shooting to that of a pheasant caught in one of their organised shoots. In my analogy, the Admirals and Captains were the beaters who, back in 1945, had sent us off the Carriers to fly day after day to the airfields at Ishigaki and Miyako where batteries of Japanese gunners were waiting expectantly and patiently for our arrival, with their AA, cannon and machine-gun fire aimed in readiness at the inevitable direction of our attack, and with their fingers on the triggers just waiting for us. So I knew what it felt like to be a bird in the circumstances of a shoot and wished that I could convey the feeling of it to these younger chaps in their bockers. But, of course, it is not the sort of thing to mention, and I didn't.

Probably the greatest pleasure for Saccie and me was the shed which I caused to be built on the far edge of the back garden and overlooking the farming fields with a view all the way to the Welsh hills. It had windows and a little bogus balcony and we called it the 'sherry shed' because nearly every day, except in mid-winter, we drank our pre-lunch sherry there, not to forget our gin and tonics every evening. We spent a large part of our summer out there in and around the shed while reading, chatting or more likely just sitting in companionable silence, all of which is what real long-term lovers tend to do, inexplicable as it is to the young. In winter, we followed the same pattern using the warm and gracious living room in the house. We also held quite a number of parties for our friends as the arrangement of the two floors, with dining room and kitchen upstairs, and drinks in the living room downstairs, lent itself well to arranging a party. In the ground floor flat, I should have said, lived a nice middle-aged widow who proved to be a good and helpful neighbour as she had lived there for several years and knew the form. She kept herself cheerful and busy with buying and selling bits of old furniture and ornaments at local markets. I nominated her as Head Girl of the Chantry, which I think she rather liked.

The only snag to living at the Chantry was the hidden exit, from the long drive, onto the B-class main road. This was really quite dangerous because, looking to the right, there was a hill with the brow of it a mere two hundred yards away and drivers all seemed to accelerate as they came to the brow and could then see an apparently clear road ahead. But it wasn't clear, because I might be having to poke the nose of my car tentatively out, to see if I could safely come onto the road. There was a sign which warned of our exit but all drivers simply ignored it. This was just another little hazard to me, super driver that I was but, joking aside, I was very worried indeed at the thought of Saccie having to drive out of that exit. She didn't drive very much these days nor did she seem keen to do so. I was mightily relieved that, after giving it a lot of thought, she rejected the idea when I had reluctantly asked if she would like to have her own little car.

Came the time, however, when I developed another prune in a kidney. A stone really but I called them prunes because, in fact, they looked like miniature prune stones, all corrugated and prickly and about the size of the nail of the little finger. I was in pain and Saccie, who always responded so well to an emergency, drove me out of that horrible exit and through the city traffic again to the hospital in Hereford. It was too late for a zapping job, as the stone was out of my kidney apparently and in my urinary system somewhere, and there would have to be an urgent operation. Saccie left me in the ward there, intending to return in time to be with me immediately after the operation. It didn't happen quite as expected because, while preparing me for the operation and, just as I was being dressed in one of those pretty hospital frocks with a bare bottom showing, I desperately needed a painful pee. It was impossible to control and out shot the prune, like a bullet, onto the floor. Saccie returned to find me fully dressed and grinning like a Cheshire cat, ready to drive her home.

How weirdly variable is this business of age. I was about seventy-eight and, despite a propensity for prunes in the kidneys and recurring queer turns, I was enjoying a busy life. First of all I needed to paint up to thirty marine and aviation pictures for the Fleet Air Arm Museum at Yeovilton, where I had been invited to put on an exhibition in the summer of 1999. I was also playing eighteen holes of golf twice a week with my elderly chums but, whereas I was beginning to become physically very tired during and after a game, my three playmates, John Ovenell, an ex-Headmaster aged 81, Peter Farr, an Air Vice Marshall with a big left tit (as we describe gongs in the services) aged 83, and Bill a retired successful businessman and wartime air-gunner with a DFC, aged 87, were still bounding round their eighteen holes without any apparent difficulty. At times, to give myself a break, I might deliberately leave an iron club near the green of the previous hole whereupon John, sprightly as a young rabbit, would volunteer to run, yes run, back to get it while I had a breather. But I was still getting enormous fun from playing golf, largely because I realised that, having taken it up so late in life, I would never be any good at it and so was relaxed and did not mind a bit when I lost. On the other hand, playing squash at which I had fancied myself no end, I had been perpetually worried and stressed at the awful possibility of losing, which I hated. On finishing our round of golf, I was in a quandary because, much as I wanted to have drinks with my chums and gossip about the game, I also wanted to be back with Saccie for our customary happy hour before lunch, when we had our sherries together. The only solution was to have just the one drink with the boys and then drive back home fast to join Saccie for sherry. But it meant that I must make sure always to buy the first round, obviously.

For years I had bewailed having been forced to retire so early from Clifton College with heart trouble, but these last particular years at the Chantry made me realise how very pleasant life in retirement could be and how lucky I was to have sufficiently good health to enjoy it all. There was so much for Saccie and me to enjoy together living at the Chantry. Not just the garden and friends for Saccie and painting and golf for me, as I have written, but ordinary things too such as: watching the mass of swallows and martins that lived in summer in the nests all round the eaves of the house roof; going for strolls in the beautiful tree-lined paths and drives up to the manor house, watching the activities of the small farm next door and getting to know George and Verity who farmed it. Then there was the happy routine of the holidays in Tenby and the many trips to Wales in my latest car which was like a small Landrover, chosen for its capability of climbing over the kind of rough country which I liked to paint.

Moreover, we were looking forward to next year when Jeremy was planning to bring his elder daughter, Alice, for a visit to England. Despite all the difficulties in getting through to Kiribati on the telephone, we had been able to talk to Alice several times in recent years and admired how well she spoke fluent English, whereas Kate, the younger girl, was not quite so forward and still had some difficulty with the language. Jeremy wanted to talk about Alice's future education because she was evidently an unusually intelligent child and he didn't reckon schooling in Kiribati would do her justice. And, incidentally, it was apparent from photographs of her that she was also an astonishingly beautiful child having Jeremy's slim figure and the beauty of her mother's facial features. Anyway, he was thinking about sending her to New Zealand, or maybe to us in England for her further education, although he was doubtful of being able to afford either possibility.

Certainly, Saccie and I were willing to contribute whatever we could afford towards her education and we could discuss it when they came to England. In any case, it would be wonderful for Saccie and me to have them for a visit sometime over the next year and there was bags of room for the whole family, including Aza, on the top floor of the Chantry.

But before then there were also exciting developments for Aza, who after many years of having to run her own business, felt it could be a good time to leave it in someone else's hands and plan the trip of a lifetime to visit Jeremy and see his home in Kiribati. She was planning to go just after Christmas for several weeks and she and Jeremy spent months planning every aspect of it, including packing wine gums and marmite, which he missed so much!

In the meantime, following the success of my first exhibition at Yeovilton Museum in 1999, when twenty paintings had been sold and four commissions received, I had been asked to exhibit again in the summer of 2001. I would have to produce at least another twenty-eight paintings for it and I had already made a good start on the work, which was going well.

It was the year 2000, at the beginning of the twenty-first century. Our yo-yo lifestyle was at the peak of its climb, prior to its inevitable plunge down to the very end of its string. This had always been the up-and-down pattern of life for Saccie and me and, by now, we should have recognised it and been ready for a fall. But nothing could have prepared us for what was to come in the year 2001.

CHAPTER 20

A Private Family Matter

On the late afternoon of January 6th, 2001, the telephone rang and it was an unusual call from Mike Tinne, who travelled frequently to the Far East and the Pacific working for a Foreign Aid department of HM Government. Consequently he had met Jeremy in Kiribati and knew him well. He was telephoning from London to tell us that Jeremy had been killed in a car accident and with him was Alice, who had also been killed. Little Kate had been badly injured and had been flown to hospital in New Zealand, together with another little girl also in the car. But Kate too had died on reaching New Zealand. The other little girl survived. Early the next morning, Saccie and I drove to Aza's house in Bristol to tell her.

This was just six days before she was due to fly out to see him. With all the plans they had made and the excitement they had shared, it was a shattering blow for her. Although she could still have gone, and by going felt she had seen and been part of the life he had enjoyed so much there, thankfully for us she decided to remain at home, and immersed herself in work again.

We learned later that the accident had occurred as Jeremy was driving the three children back from a party. For the purpose apparently he had borrowed an old car, typical of the type of very elderly jalopy most people would use out there in that area of Kiribati. Jeremy was and always had been a bad driver. He was never a reckless or fast driver as are so many young men, but one who had always found handling the controls difficult. He had written off within days the small car I had bought him for his twenty-first birthday. He had subsequently suffered the appalling car accident which lacerated his face, blinded one eye and almost blinded the other. One would have thought, nevertheless, that he would have been safe enough on those small almost deserted roads in Kiribati.

Jeremy made many good, close and loyal friends during his lifetime but, as he had told me, his greatest friend was Derek, who was also his business partner in Kiribati. From Derek I learned that the most likely cause of the accident was that the car battery was failing and thus the engine needed to be kept at high revs. It seems probable that Jeremy changed into a wrong gear so that, with the engine still revving highly to keep the battery charging, the car would have been travelling very fast. He lost control on a bend and hit a tree.

That dear man, Derek, dealt with all the awful death procedures, which had to be undertaken quickly out there. He did everything that I, as the Father, should have done and it must have been absolutely terrible for him. I owe Derek a great debt. He arranged a funeral in the local style at which hundreds of people from the villages attended as well as Europeans. Communication with Derek was very difficult and there was information which I needed urgently to have, such as the death certificate, as I intended to obtain a pension for Atauea. The answer was to obtain a computer with email and learn to use it quickly, which I did.

Very shortly after our son and grandchildren were killed, Saccie, my very dear and so much loved wife and best friend of fifty-three years, was struck with pancreatic cancer. We were repeatedly told by her doctor that it was a gall stone and so we continued our life much as normal with this silly man painting his silly pictures ready for the exhibition at Yeovilton in August of that awful year 2001. Saccie, as I never realised until later, knew very well that the pain she was suffering and hiding from me was cancer, but she wanted me to do the exhibition and thus to keep my mind occupied and myself busy.

The exhibition was again a success. Among so many Fleet Air Arm friends on that day was that great fighter pilot and leader, Ronnie Hay, who had been my flying instructor in early 1941 and my Air Group Commander in the British Pacific Fleet in 1944-5. He too knew that he was soon to die of the same cancer as my Saccie, and no-one at that exhibition could have been aware of this from the manner and composure of these two courageous people. It was my practice, if and when I had a successful exhibition, to spend some of the proceeds on a dinner party for our friends afterwards at an expensive restaurant. Towards the end of that dinner, Saccie could cope no longer and collapsed with pain. At last this stupid wimp of a man, perhaps half aware of but afraid to contemplate such a possibility, had to face the fact of Saccie's terminal illness.

In September, Aza came with us for two weeks to the flat in Tenby, which was Saccie's favourite place to be. Afterwards, I took Saccie to the hospice near Hereford where the doctors and nurses treated us

A Private Family Matter

with understanding and kindness. After two weeks Saccie wanted to be in her bedroom at the Chantry where, from her bed, she could see the view and watch the swallows flying away, as they did every year, from under the eaves to the warmth of Africa. The district nurses and the nurses from Marie Curie cared for Saccie day and night with such kindness that I shall never forget them. And Saccie, with the help of the morphine pills and driver, carried herself throughout with quiet dignity and courage. She couldn't speak but would press my hand as if to give me courage too.

Aza and I were with Saccie and held her as she died. It was October 26th.

At Saccie's funeral, the village church at Linton was filled to capacity with her friends from Ross and Bristol. Aza had been superb in helping me through all the things that had to be done prior to the funeral and even more so afterwards and on her own, when I wimped out after the funeral.

I cannot write anything about the period of the seven months which followed Saccie's death, because my memory of that period of my life is, with the exception of one incident, an almost complete blank. That single incident started with a dull backache, which I recognised as of a kidney stone, which began to develop into intense pain. Instead of telephoning for an ambulance, I determined to stick it out by myself as a sort of guilty penance for my inability to either recognise or help Saccie during those months of her pain before my exhibition. I remember screaming aloud with the pain but it didn't matter as Head Girl had gone to Ireland and I was alone in that large house. The stone shot out of me in the morning but the pain had not assuaged my feeling of guilt.

I remember nothing else of that period. I didn't play any golf nor, as far as I can remember, did I paint. But I must have met people when shopping and that sort of thing and I believe that I behaved properly and was able to laugh and tell jokes whenever I did meet and talk to friends, since nobody has commented that I did otherwise.

I am so thankful that, apparently, I did not make a fool of myself because I cannot abide to see, for example, how immediately following a tragedy, the media march the associated family in front of the cameras and microphones to parade their grief in public. When a tragedy hits, I do believe it is important to contain grief and control it in front of all but very close friends and family. If not, at first your friends will give you their sympathy and do their best to help but, after a while if you continue, they will start to pity you, which is humiliating, and they may even get cross enough to boss you about; 'Why don't you sell that big old house and buy a bungalow?' they demand. Eventually, if you continue to grieve openly, they will come to despise you.

CHAPTER 21

The Residential Home

My first memory at the end of May 2002, and after some seven months of an almost complete memory blank, was arriving in Aza's van at Alma Vale Road in Bristol where, apparently, I was to meet some people who ran a number of Residential Care Homes in the city and had formed a company for the purpose. In their smart office, I met a lady who looked very businesslike indeed, I remember, in one of those masculine suits with trousers. She gave me to understand that she was a Director and the Secretary of the company and thereafter, in my mind, I always referred to her as La Petite Directrice. From there I was taken to a pleasant semi-detached family house in Clifton, quite near the College, where we were greeted by a large lady who showed me a basement room, with bathroom and loo attached. I would come to refer to this rather bossy lady, whose name was Jean, as the Gauleiter.

The room was of a size large enough to take a single bed with my desk and chair, table, armchair and small wardrobe. The rent for this room, including presumably the cost of food and care, was almost exactly the same as I had been paying for the lovely house and its ten rooms, gardens and garages at the Chantry and which evidently, as I now realised from my presence here in Bristol, I had left for good. I did notice, however, that the room had a door at the far end of it, which led directly up some steps to a garden. It seemed that I was required to make a decision on whether or not I would live there and so, when I realised this, I said I would do so if the little bathroom were to be fitted with an electric shower. The very businesslike Directrice and the large lady both exclaimed with horror at the cost but would agree to have the shower installed, provided I paid for it. It did occur to me that, having regard to the huge rent, this was somewhat mean but, so what? I reckoned that I still had a few thousand quid on deposit in a bank, so I asked them to get on with it, filled in a Form of Agreement and Aza made all the arrangements to have me moved into the room. It must have been a tremendous relief for Aza to do so, as she must have been worried out of her wits about me. She was working full-time at her own business in Bristol, and feeling responsible for her elderly Father, who appeared to be living mentally among the fairies, entirely unfocused on doing anything, fifty miles away on his own deep in the countryside. At the time and under those circumstances, a care home for Father must have seemed the only sensible answer. And anyway at the time, I didn't really care much where I lived although, truth to tell, I do remember feeling an unexpected sense of relief once the decision had been made for me to leave the Chantry.

However, before I had moved into the room, I realised belatedly that there was no space for me to put any tables and equipment for painting, and this lack would after all make the room unsuitable, since the urge was on me to start painting again. And here I have to write that the old Gauleiter came good with the suggestion of using half the laundry, located right opposite my proposed room, as a sort of studio. This seemed to be rather a daft idea at first because, as well as having a battery of washing machines and driers, the laundry was always festooned with garments, such as knickers, shirts, vests and pants, hanging to dry from wires stretched across the top of the room. In fact, however, this didn't really matter because, once I came to use the laundry as a studio, it was easy to duck under or through the hanging washing to reach the far end of the laundry, which had plenty of space and a window to give light. So I started to paint again there, and, as I did so, I was often watched by my fellow residents who would peer out at me through the hanging washing to see what I was painting.

I had not really given much thought to what sort of life I would have to lead in a care home for very elderly people. The first shock was to find myself sitting down at the big dining table with seven other residents and the housekeeper, all in our allotted places having trooped in at precisely 12.30 p.m. Without thinking, I had assumed that I would be having meals in my room or somewhere else, more or less in a normal manner. There were at the time seven other residents and I felt myself to be under intent but surreptitious scrutiny from them all.

Let me describe them because, after all, I was going to share my life with them. Around the table on my right was Mary aged 84 who appeared to be rather a grumpy old thing at first but I would find her to be an entirely kind old lady. Susan at 78 who had become more than a bit dotty with excessive doses, she told me later, of Terazapam sleeping pills. Nice old David aged 89, who had been nothing else than an accountant in a small town all his life and was now disabled enough to need a zimmer for walking. John at 83 who had been a carpet layer and, during the war, a searchlight operator in the army. He was a great fund of knowledge about the city of Bristol. Trixie, dear Trixie aged 90, who had been the manager of so many pubs in Bristol in her lifetime and was still full of fun and stories about pub life. Helen aged 80 who was rather genteel with stories which seemed of rather a grand background but she was nice enough with it. And finally on my left and at the head of this end of the table was Hazel who, at 83 appeared at first as a formidable lady with a sharp mind and certainly not one to tangle with particularly as, in wartime, she had been a Major in the WRACs in charge of three hundred girls at a barracks in Scotland. Later, when I came to know her, she would become my chum, a good companion and my Bridge partner.

Seated at the other end of the table, after she had served the meal to us, would be the housekeeper, Bobby, who was a good-looking young woman of probably about 35, born in Burma with an English father and, oh my goodness, what a super cook. She had a strong sense of her responsibility towards us and would go to endless trouble for those who became ill or needed her help. Bobby, as housekeeper, lived upstairs in a small attic flat where she could receive and respond to any emergency bells from the residents' rooms. She took one day off each week when a stand-in would have been arranged for the day by the management.

The management of the house was absurdly over-organised. In that pleasant family house with a maximum capacity of eight residents, there was a management committee of some nine ladies and one accounting clerk, chaired by the large lady, Jean, who had greeted me on my initial visit. These committee ladies were all volunteers so I must not be too unkind, but nearly all of them solemnly met regularly on an evening every two weeks to manage the household accounts and arrange for the cleaning, etc., of this simple, ordinary family house. Their main interest, as I would learn, was to hear the formal report from the housekeeper who, seated at the end of the table facing this battery of ladies, would have to account in detail for the cost of the meals she had provided and describe the menus she had prepared for the next two weeks. The only other function for each of the ladies on the committee was to 'do' a meal for the residents once every three months, when the housekeeper took her day off. This task consisted of putting a meal, already fully prepared by the housekeeper, into the oven and when it was cooked, dishing it up. Subsequently, all that had to be done was to put the used crocks and cutlery into the dishwasher, press the button to start it and then go home. Some long time later, I happened to overhear one of these ladies apologise to her friends that she would be unable to attend their coffee party next week because 'that will be one of the days when I do my charity work and cook meals for an old people's home.'

I spent the summer of that year 2002 sitting in the very nice garden while drinking my glasses of whisky. I did this every day for hours and hours at a time, under an umbrella if it rained, until well into the darkness of late evening, just vaguely thinking of this and that but mostly about Saccie and our life together. I watched the birds and noted their comings and goings amongst the surrounding trees and I had a favourite robin which would come and seemingly have a chat with me as I sat there. In the afternoons, I particularly enjoyed listening to the voices of the three children as they played in the garden next door. It was altogether a pleasant and soothing existence and did a lot of good to a ga-ga and still grieving old man.

I was always on my own, as my fellow old dears only came out occasionally in the midday sunshine, until one evening somebody came to sit in one of the garden chairs near me. It was Hazel and on that first evening she spoke very little and we just sat there in a surprisingly comfortable silence. She joined me on many afternoons and evenings after that until we began to enjoy quiet conversations together as well as the companionable silences, much as Saccie and I had always done. Hazel liked her whisky too and so we would share a bottle or two each week.

When winter came I retreated to my room where, instead of thinking about the past, I started to write about it on my lap-top computer and called it *A History of the Adlams*. I had never before written anything other than business reports and letters and became intrigued with this new form of writing and it started to occupy my mind. In the new year of 2003, after a Christmas made cheerful for us all by the efforts of Bobby, I received a telephone call from a lady quite unknown to me, who referred to the time when Saccie and I were living in Cornwall in a house reputed at the time to be haunted. She was in the process of writing a book about haunted houses, she said, and would I be kind enough to tell her about my experience at the house in Cornwall? I was about to agree to this when I suddenly had the thought: well, why don't I write the story myself? The lady was Mary James, already a successful author, who, instead of resenting my sudden decision that I myself would try to write the story, said she would help me to do it. And help me she certainly did and quite unstintingly. I sent my first attempt at the short story to her, which she read and in due course sent back to me with valuable corrections and comments carefully written all over it.

So I tried again, and again until eventually I had learned from Mary how to write a short story which might possibly be good enough for acceptance by a magazine. Mary warned me, however, that literally thousands of people offered their short stories to magazines every month for years and years and never had them accepted for publication. How fortunate I was to have Mary's guidance because, when I sent my ghost story to *The Lady*, one of the best-known weekly magazine on the market, the editor accepted it within a month although, as is normal practice, the story was not published until months later. This acceptance was a tremendous boost and so I set about writing more stories, but these were based on my flying experiences and I intended to send them to editors of aviation magazines.

I was coming awake from my coma or depression, whatever it was, and taking more interest at last in the people around me and the general state of affairs in this home where I found myself to be living. The institutional attitude of the people running it and the silly little rules they imposed, many no doubt prompted by those ghastly Health and Safety laws, now began to irritate me and so, for the first time, I took the trouble to find out how the management structure worked. There was a central Board of Directors for the seven care homes managed by the company which had been formed, so I understood, some five years earlier when there had been fifteen such homes. Since apparently eight homes had failed, it didn't say much for the competence of the Board. Each house apparently had a committee, such as ours, to run it. About half of us residents, and I resist using my usual name of inmates to describe us, paid the full rent whereas the others were assisted by Housing Benefits from the council. It was the job of the Directrice at the company office to negotiate these benefits for those residents who needed them, and there is no doubt that she did this well.

Hazel and I usually had a glass or two of sherry together, either in her room or mine, every morning before the holy hour of 12.30 for lunch. But I found when visiting Trixie, Mary or Helen in their rooms that they were also having their little sherry tipples, but on their own.

Opposite to me on the basement floor, however, was a bedroom kept empty in case an assistant housekeeper might need it. I proposed to Jean, our more or less permanent lady Gauleiter in the house, that this room be converted into a lounge and made available for the residents where they could congregate for their drinks and general chat each day. There was a whole lot of argument against this idea to begin with, mainly about the cost of furnishing the room, but I was able to quell that by offering to furnish it myself from the furniture which Aza had put in store for me. Once established, the room was immediately really popular, the only snag being the early lunch at 12.30. While we were still enjoying our gin or sherries, Jean the Gauleiter would trill from the top of the stairs, 'You may come through to the dining room now, Ladies and Gentlemen,' which of course was much more of a command than an invitation. She insisted that lunch be at that time because it enabled the housekeeper to have time off before preparing for tea. Which sounded reasonable but, when Bobby declared that she herself had asked previously to prepare lunch for a later time, there could be no more argument and lunch from then on was at 1 p.m.

Jean and her committee organised outings in a minibus from time to time, in conjunction with one or two of the other homes, but few residents in our house liked to go on these well-meant jaunts, feeling perhaps that they were over-organised. I decided to buy a second-hand Vauxhall estate car, large enough to take at least five of us on our own jaunts. Our first outing turned out to be quite different from that which I had imagined my fellow residents would want. I set out in the car, with Hazel, Trixie and Helen in the back and Mary in the front seat with me, to take them to the famous Westonbirt Arboretum about thirty miles away. The charge to enter was frightfully expensive but all the girls had plenty of cash there being little to spend it on normally. Hazel and I set off for a walk among the trees, having left the other three in the café. When we returned about an hour later, there was no sight or sign of our three girls and nobody had seen them since their arrival. I became extremely worried about them ... after all, their combined ages weren't far short of three hundred. Might one of them have fallen ill and all three been taken away in an ambulance? They couldn't possibly have been in the loo for the last hour and a half but, anyway, I asked Hazel to check. But they were indeed in the loo, and how relieved I was to see Hazel herding them out of it. Apparently, they had been frozen in the café and taken refuge all that time in the slightly warmer loo. I suggested that we

The Residential Home

now go for a warming lunch and a snifter at the nearby Hare and Hounds hotel, and their faces lit up with pleasure. This was more like it, they evidently thought. When they were all settled down in comfortable chairs, they all asked for a Horse's Neck (brandy and ginger ale), which was fairly soon followed by another. And then we had a good lunch before I drove us all back to the home for a kip. After that, we went on such jaunts regularly every month in the car but, since they were not interested in museums or famous old buildings and all that kind of thing, I would take them on a nice drive to a good pub or hotel for drinks and lunch.

Hazel and I started to play Bridge, first of all using my Bridge computer, and then playing as partners at the Clifton Lawn Tennis club, where previously I had been a member for many years. The club members had welcomed me back and were pleased also to meet Hazel, whom they liked very much. Hazel was an absolute ace at the game and I had a thing called flair which enabled me very occasionally to play a hand well and, of course, I always maintain that my bidding is faultless (who doesn't?). The tennis club held a tournament, which ran throughout the winter in which the members played in groups and, finally at the end of winter, the winning pairs from each group would play against each other for the prize. At half-time during the finals of our first year, I thanked our hosts who had laid on masses of wine and good food in their large house, and asked what had prompted them to provide such a generous party for the tournament finals. 'Oh, didn't you know,' they replied, 'the winners each year always host the finals on the following year.' I had a mental picture of Hazel and me, in my grotty basement room at the Old People's Home, hosting a large party for all these nice but really rather wealthy friends. But already at half-time Hazel and I were the leading point scorers and could well win the tournament so, without an opportunity for me to warn Hazel of the situation, we sat down at the card table for the second half session. I had an ordinary hand, yet I over-bid on it atrociously and deliberately so that, as I intended, we lost hundreds of points ... inevitably there was no possibility now of winning the tournament and therefore we were safe from having to host a party for next year's finals! Hazel never fully forgave me for my appallingly bad bid even after I had explained it and, as a result thereafter, I don't think she ever quite regained confidence in my bidding.

As we moved towards the summer of 2003, I suggested to my fellow old dears that we could abandon our 'residents' lounge' in the basement for our mid-day drinks and use the garden for which some garden chairs had been provided. The snag, as we found, was that the sun could be too strong for these elderly people and there was only one old and tatty garden umbrella to provide shade. I contacted both the Directrice at the office and our Gauleiter, Jean, but was informed that a new garden umbrella could not be provided because it would be too expensive. I gave some thought to our huge rents and, concluding that they were both talking rubbish, ordered a lovely new large and rather expensive garden umbrella to be delivered, and had the bill sent to the Directrice who, moaning as she did so, eventually paid it. The other silly difficulty was that access to the garden was through the kitchen and residents were never allowed in or through the kitchen without supervision. Thus all the old dears, except I who had my own access to the garden from my room, would have to line up outside the kitchen until Jean, our bossy Gauleiter, would trill, 'You may come through now, Ladies,' and usher them through the kitchen into the garden. And of course, the same trilling process in reverse would take place to marshal them back again after drinks for their lunch. I should add that old David would sometimes join the girls and me for drinks but John never did so, probably because it wasn't his custom to drink.

At the home, however, things were not going well nor had they been doing so for some weeks now. Quite unlike her normal self, Bobby had become sometimes impatient and a little irritable with us old dears, and she appeared to be upset by something. Eventually I learned that she was being given a hard time by our Gauleiter and her cronies on the house committee. At the meeting every two weeks Bobby had to sit at the end of the table facing alone this battery of committee hens all pecking hard at her about her bad relationship with the cleaning ladies. It transpired that she had one major fault, which was a tendency to bully the cleaning ladies, gardener or whoever came to work in the house under contract with the company. In her opinion the standard of their work was never satisfactory and, with her clarion cry of 'I am sorry but ...' she would criticise them and their work until they simply got fed up and would inevitably have to be replaced by the management.

The committee therefore had a point as Bobby seemed unable to modify her demand for perfection in the standard of cleanliness in the house, but their answer to this problem was to deprive Bobby of all responsibility for the supervision of the cleaning ladies and forbid her to have any dealings with them. But this bevy of ladies of the committee, these amateur managers lacking any management skill or experience, were unable to recognise that what Bobby needed so badly was more responsibility, not less of it. They should have given Bobby by herself the full responsibility for the appointment and supervision of the cleaning ladies and gardener, etc., while telling her clearly that, if she forced the employees into leaving, she would have to do their work until she herself had found and appointed suitable replacements.

That summer, Bobby, from looking ill, suddenly became very ill indeed and the first I knew of it was to realise just before mid-day that Bobby was not in the kitchen and that evidently no lunch was cooking or had been prepared. I couldn't get into her room but heard her trying to speak, so I phoned for the house doctor to come immediately, which he did. It was necessary, obviously, also to tell the Directrice at the office what had happened.

The next bit, other than the worry about Bobby, was really rather fun because all our eight residents had to be fed and I would have to produce a quick meal for them. It would not be difficult because there was a huge freezer containing a variety of frozen meats and vegetables. All this food was there for just such an emergency as this, because Bobby normally bought everything fresh from butchers and greengrocers. For that occasion, I gave them bangers and bacon all crisp and crunchy from the hot oven, with mashed potatoes.

Subsequently, I was reprimanded by the management for even entering the kitchen, let alone cooking the meal for the residents. In retrospect this was rather funny because, although we did not know it at the time, in the weeks to come I was going to have to spend quite a lot of time in the kitchen cooking meals in the absence of a housekeeper. However, I could understand their concern over Health and Safety regulations but they evidently needed a better back-up system for emergencies as they had been unable to call upon anybody quickly to do the cooking. None of the ladies on the house committee, who could have been of some value for such a purpose, were ever available except on an organised date in the future. To be fair, the Gauleiter would have come on call from her home like a shot, but she was abroad on holiday at the time. The management at the office had on their books a small number of professional cooks any one of whom could visit for the day and act as housekeeper, but they too needed at least a day's notice.

Bobby recovered after a couple of weeks and soldiered on for two more months, but the heart seemed to have gone out of her and she was unable to cope with the constant bickering and harassment from the house committee. Inevitably therefore, as the committee and the Gauleiter so obviously intended, Bobby resigned and left the care home where she had been so valuable and much loved by the residents.

The replacement for Bobby was a pleasant young Spanish girl who could speak and understand little more than a few everyday words of English. Her inadequacy for the job was brought to the surface when at lunchtime the elderly David was noticed to be missing. I asked the girl if she knew where he was but, unlike Bobby who used to knock on our doors each morning to check if we were all right, she had not seen David since the previous day and had no idea where he was. I left the table to go up to his room and found him on the floor, in the foetal position, unable to speak and wet with urine. Poor old boy, he was in a dreadful state after an apparent stroke and he had been there on the floor since getting out of his bed in the morning. I rang immediately for an ambulance and, while waiting for it, called down to the girl to help me put him on the bed where I dried him with a towel and put a warm dressing gown round him, ready for hospital. I followed the ambulance to the A&E department and waited until the consultant could examine him. His daughter arrived soon afterwards and I could leave.

David was transferred to another hospital where, when I visited him two weeks later, I was horrified to find him curled up in bed with his pyjamas and bedclothes soaking wet, and yet his bed was only a few yards from the table where the nurses congregated. I put on my pompous act and demanded that the ward matron be brought to see his condition, and stayed to see him transferred to a single room and a bed with an emergency bell close to his hand. It was unusual, in my experience, for the NHS to be so lacking in care.

We were obviously getting rather old and frail as a group because I had to make two more emergency calls for an ambulance during that year. The next was Mary. When she didn't turn up ready for one of our days out in the car, we her found in her room still sitting up in her chair not having gone to bed during the night. Again I stayed with her in the A&E department at the hospital until the consultant had diagnosed a heart problem. But Mary was a game old dear and came out smiling with relief at feeling better, five days later. The other was John who managed to pull the emergency bell in his bathroom after collapsing while having a shower. He was very seriously ill and I held him quietly, dried and covered him with towels while trying to comfort him, as the housekeeper, another new girl but this time one who spoke English, phoned for the ambulance. John died shortly after arriving at the hospital.

During the rest of that year, after Bobby had been hounded out, we had a succession of various housekeepers none of whom were suitable so that the management were relying more and more on the much more professional assistant housekeepers such as Anne who, by chance, previously had been one of my senior catering staff at the College before her retirement. It was a bonus day when Anne arrived as we could rely on her calm control and her provision of a good meal. Whenever we were without an established housekeeper and when none of the assistant housekeepers were available, as so frequently happened at the end of that year, the Directrice would make an emergency arrangement with an employment agency to send a cook every day for a week. Usually the agency girl would be a young student with a cheerful smile on her face at the prospect of a paid job for the week. Typically, the girl would have no knowledge of how to cook anything other than bacon and eggs in a frying pan. I would take her to the kitchen and tell her where everything she needed was to be found and show her the ingredients for the meal, which had been all set out by the assistant housekeeper, ready for preparation and cooking. If it became obvious that the girl had no knowledge of cooking even plain and simple meals, I would take her to the front door and bid her to be gone. My next step would be to inform the Directrice of the situation, before getting on to prepare and cook the lunch, in the expectation that a proper housekeeper would be found for the following days. At this stage, after a number of such inefficient temporary housekeepers had come and gone, the Directrice and the Gauleiter, although pretending not to be aware that I took responsibility for looking after the house and its people whenever there was no housekeeper on the premises, were all too obviously relieved that I did so and never again objected to my presence in the kitchen.

In December, the Directrice and the Gauleiter were well pleased with themselves to announce that, after interviewing three applicants, they had selected Kevin, a young bachelor and a professional cook, to be appointed as the new housekeeper. We all hoped that the management had at last found a suitable person because, truth to tell, we had not been at all a happy household since Bobby had left us. Our new young bachelor housekeeper appeared to be adequately competent to start with but, after a week or two, I noticed that more and more frozen fast-foods and vegetables were appearing in place of the fresh vegetables and meat from the butchers, which Bobby and the professional assistant housekeepers had always provided. It didn't really bother me personally as I like frozen foods, but I wondered how he could buy it within the strict budget normally given by the Directrice.

After a while too, our housekeeper's boyfriend started to visit him in his attic flat, although this situation did not particularly worry either me or the other residents, since there was no reason why the probability of his homosexuality need affect his job as our housekeeper. However, our tolerance began to be somewhat strained as we approached Christmas because the two men seemed to spend much of their time in the evenings having noisy quarrels or whatever up there in the attic. In response to complaints from the ladies with rooms below the attic flat, the Directrice came and rebuked her protégé housekeeper for the noise, but could not deny him the right to have a visitor who, incidentally, came and went via the outside fire escape. Of course, living in my basement room, I was the only one never to hear a sound from the attic.

As most of the residents would spend Christmas with their relatives, it was decided with the agreement of the Gauleiter that our Christmas mid-day dinner and party would take place on New Year's Day, and Kevin was briefed accordingly to prepare for it. Christmas for me was pleasantly quiet and spent with Aza at her little house on the far side of Bristol.

On the evening prior to the big day of the residents' party, there was no sign of Kevin who should have been there to prepare and serve the high tea which all the residents, except Hazel and me, would normally have in the dining room every evening at precisely five p.m. In his absence, I prepared scrambled eggs on toast with bread, butter and jam or cheese which was the sort of meal my old ladies liked to have at that hour. There was still no sign of our Kevin early the next morning and no answer at all when I banged on his attic door, which was firmly locked. I reckoned that he must have been out on a gay party with his boyfriends during all the previous day and night because, in the kitchen and larder, it was apparent that no preparations whatsoever had been made for the residents' big party. There was no turkey no Christmas pud, no nothing.

I telephoned the Directrice at her office, who said she would try to get one of the assistant housekeepers to come in, but it was obviously extremely unlikely that she would succeed and certainly not in time to produce the party dinner. So I raided the emergency cash store, which I knew was contained in a drawer in the dining room, having raided it on previous emergencies, and sashayed out to the shops in Whiteladies Road, rather looking forward to the challenge of producing a Christmas party dinner in quick time. There was only £84 in the cash box and I spent the whole lot plus some of my own money on a huge turkey, sausages, bacon, two puddings, cream, nuts, chocolates and two boxes of crackers from Woolworths and four bottles of wine. I dashed back to the home, set the gas oven at maximum and bunged the turkey into it, complete with prefabricated stuffing inside. All that remained to be done was to peel and parboil the potatoes prior to roasting, and make the bread sauce and gravy.

The main problem of providing a meal for the residents was always the dishing-up of it onto the table because the residents weren't happy unless it was properly done with each vegetable in separate dishes, sauces and gravy in sauce-boats and everything, including the plates, of course, very hot. There were two large ovens with grills and hot plates but, nevertheless, it was a manic time organising the various foods to be cooked *au point* while preparing all the hot dishes ready to serve the meal. On this occasion, I was getting ready for the dreaded ordeal when, hey presto, dear Anne turned up to apply her professional skill to completing the cooking and dishing it up. Thus I was able to greet my fellow residents calmly in our sherry lounge at mid-day as usual and announce that Anne had decided on this special occasion to serve the dinner at 2 p.m., and so to give us more sherry time. I have to write that the whole meal and the day went very well indeed, thanks to Anne turning up at such short notice. They didn't need any tea and so to bed.

The next morning there was still no sight of Kevin, but I thought I heard a slight sound from inside when I banged on his attic door. The Gauleiter was away on her hols but it was obviously time for the Directrice to give approval if the door was to be knocked down. She arrived quickly with a master key (which I did not know she had) and we found Kevin, dressed in shirt and trousers, lying on his back on the bed and looking extremely ill and in fact, at first sight, he looked to be a goner. I noticed that there were some white pills spilled onto the bedside table. Directrice rang for the ambulance immediately while, quite rightly, insisting that no-one must touch the pills in the meantime until the ambulance arrived. Kevin did recover in the hospital but remained there for two weeks, although the doctors would not disclose to anyone the illness from which he was suffering.

When he arrived back from hospital, he was unable to work but continued to occupy his attic flat while the full management team of the Chairman and Board of Directors were afraid under employment law to dismiss him and to repossess the flat. This ridiculous situation went on for another two months before dear Kevin was somehow (money?) persuaded to go. Had I been in charge, I would have given him a formal dismissal for his initial absence from work, gross irresponsibility and dangerous lack of care of the old people under his charge, given him a month's pay in lieu of notice, arranged for his possessions to be packed and put outside the house and a new lock put on the door of the attic flat. And that would have been that, because no court would have denied that his gross irresponsibility merited dismissal. I had been forced to take just such action twice, in very similar circumstances and for very similar reasons, when Bursar of Clifton College.

During the fiasco of Kevin's occupation of the attic flat, the residents had been without anyone to care for them in an emergency at night, but the Directrice had succeeded in finding and employing an excellent daily housekeeper. This situation was such a relief to everybody, after the shambles of the previous six months culminating in the management's adventure with Kevin, that it was decided evidently to let matters lie as they were, i.e. with having a housekeeper for the daytime only. It would be a lot cheaper anyway, no doubt.

This really was the crux of the whole problem in the management of this particular care home; they simply would not pay the proper going rate for a housekeeper capable of caring for elderly residents, day and night, feeding them and keeping house for them. I knew from Bobby that the salary for the job at the time was £7,500 p.a. with the free accommodation and meals and I compared this with the £11,500, also with free accommodation and meals, being paid at that time to a matron in a boarding house at Clifton College. Both jobs held roughly equivalent responsibilities, although a housekeeper in a care home had the more onerous task of providing and cooking all the meals.

I had been irritated at the start of my time in the care home by the constantly mean and pinch-penny attitude of the management, but my eventual fury at their niggling meanness was triggered off when, as was my custom, I asked the housekeeper for a piece of cheese to take to my room, because I never took the evening meal of high tea with my old ladies. It so happened, however, that the Gauleiter overheard me asking for the piece of cheese and immediately forbade the housekeeper to provide it because, she said, the home couldn't afford to operate, if residents asked for and were given more food than already provided for at meal times according to budget. I was angry enough to say, 'You ridiculous person, don't you realise that with these high rents this house must be making a huge profit?' Gauleiter huffed back to say that the accounts were none of her business, which was to ensure that the house was run within its budget. That did it. I remembered that in an earlier newsletter published by the management there had been a summary of the annual accounts for the previous year. In my uninterested frame of mind at that time, I hadn't bothered to study it, but now I went in search of the newsletter and its summary of accounts.

To cut the story short, I could establish from a study of the accounts that the annual administrative costs of this charitable company were over 21% of its income whereas a percentage of 6% up to a maximum of 11% is regarded as usual for charitable organisations. As regards our care home, I estimated from my precise knowledge of its salaries, wages and food costs, and assessment of other costs in comparison with similar and adjacent College properties, that there was an annual profit on the house in the region of £34,000 which thus, contrary to contract, was being used in support of other company properties. This profit was never refuted by management when I challenged them with it. Even more astounding was to find, from visiting other identically-sized and type of care homes in Somerset, Dorset and Wiltshire, that the individual rent paid by their residents was on average half of the rent we were paying. No amount of city weighting could justify such a difference. Little wonder then, from all these factors, that so many of the homes run by this company had closed in recent years.

During the following weeks, I kept up a correspondence with the Chairman of the company, a new man now and of considerable business and management experience, in the expectation that he would gradually effect the improvements which our particular care home so obviously needed. First and foremost was to provide adequate funds to pay a higher quality of housekeeper, able to take full responsibility for the operation of the house. Secondly, to get rid of the 'house committee' and replace it with a suitable and competent volunteer manager, such as a retired professional man, to be in overall charge and to act in support of the housekeeper. Thirdly, to reduce the rental for each room to a more reasonable level because, if not, the demand for this care home would inevitably fall until, as with the other properties of the company, it would have to be sold. More minor improvements for the comfort of the residents would be to install showers instead of baths, because very few old ladies or men can get in and out of a bath, and to install an electrically-operated seat chair for the stairs. And finally, of course, the separate office premises for the Directrice and her four clerical staff would have to be sold too. They were expensive and there was absolutely no need for them or for so many staff.

Except for the disbandment of the house committee and the reduction in rents, all the other improvements I had advocated were effected shortly after I had left the care home.

CHAPTER 22

The Last Lap

On a Saturday morning in June 2003, I received a letter from the Chairman of the Residential Home company which, although pleasantly worded, was yet another rather negative response to all the various points I had been making about improving our care home for the residents. I had been thinking for some time now that it was high time for me to bale out of the care home. After all, I had long since recovered from my ga-ga coma, as I called it, and I guess that I had been staying on simply in the habit of living there and, maybe, in the hope of effecting more improvements. Whatever the case, I felt strongly that it was time to go.

And so, later that morning, I walked to the top of Whiteladies Road, where estate agents abounded, and entered the very first one I came to and asked to see their list of flats for rent. At the top of the first list the agent showed me was a first floor flat overlooking the Bristol docks. The flat had two bedrooms, a kitchen-diner, bath-cum-shower room, a good-sized lounge with French windows and a balcony overlooking the dock waters. It also had a car-port at the back and a garden at the side shared with another flat. I hardly dared waste the man's time to ask the rental since such an apartment would obviously be far beyond my reach. In fact, as I calculated, the rent rates and service charges per month came to no more than £805, which was £15 less than the rent for my single room and food at the home!

By sheer chance it had so happened that on the previous Wednesday evening, I had been due to attend a meeting of ex-aircrew of the Fleet Air Arm at a pub located alongside the Bristol docks, most of which was now converted into a residential area. Because I was early, I had walked along the dockside and couldn't help thinking, as I looked at the attractive little houses and flats, what a lovely place for people to live, while never thinking of myself in that context at all at the time. And now suddenly and unexpectedly this agent was offering me an apparently lovely flat, which was located precisely in the area I had been admiring and coveting two evenings earlier, and at a rental I could afford. I took out my cheque book and said, 'I will have it, how much do you want as a deposit?' 'But you haven't even seen it or looked over it and, also, we have to check your credentials and there is a formal agreement to be considered and signed,' the man gasped. I asked him to stop looking like a stranded fish, to get his car and to drive me straightaway to the flat for me to view it. The furnished flat, except for the modern furniture, was every bit as lovely as I had expected and, to cut the story short, I had completed and signed by the following Wednesday an agreement with the very nice owner (an attractive young woman by the way) for a two-year lease. She was kind enough to dispose of her main furniture, which I didn't want, provided I increased the amount of the deposit. Aza, when I told her what I had done and so quickly, despaired of me and my impetuosity, but could not fault my decision once she had seen the flat. As always when I needed her help, she beavered around getting my furniture out of expensive store and moving me into the gorgeous little flat, which had plenty of space for all my remaining bits and pieces as well as my furniture. So began five years of a contentment very close to happiness, such as I had never expected to enjoy ever again after that tragic year for me of 2001. But I cannot lose that sense of being always alone, that feeling I have without Saccie with me to share the gift of life in the environment of this lovely flat. I am not lonely because I am fortunate to have many friends still, but I am 'alone' which is different.

I don't know whether my painting or writing was the major factor in this new life, because both of these two activities blossomed like mad soon after I moved into the flat. To take the writing first:

I had already enjoyed the thrill of having the four short stories I had written, accepted and published in magazines and these had been written while I was still at the care home. But now I would try to write a book. It would have to be an autobiography because, although I had some ideas for a novel, I had little idea of how to plan a story and make it suitable for a book. At least with a biography, the story was already there and I could write it as it was. Moreover, having made a point of reading a couple of autobiographies to test the water, I was struck by how dull some of their stories were. Surely, I thought, I can drum up more interest than is in either of these from my absurdly varied life?

The Last Lap

I started my story, for some reason, from the age of ten as a schoolboy although, come to think of it, perhaps I particularly wanted to analyse the odd and unhappy relationship with my Father and writing about it would be a way of doing so. The writing went happily along and I was getting a lot of pleasure from it, until I came to my age of eighteen, when I joined the Royal Navy in 1940. I seemed to come to a grinding halt just there and I didn't really feel that I wanted to continue, which would mean writing about the war. I had an undistinguished war although a very dangerous one, which had given me the frights over a period of nearly five long years flying from Aircraft Carriers. I had never talked about it ever to anyone, even Saccie, except very rarely when I might have met an old wartime flying colleague. When I did eventually make a start on writing about the war, all the stories and happenings just came flooding out of my memory, each one with extraordinary clarity. In particular I remembered all the many friends and squadron comrades with whom I had flown and decided that my book would be as much about them as about me. Most war books deal not unnaturally with those men who are innately fearless leaders, whereas my book was going to be about ordinary chaps, such as myself, and how difficult it sometimes was for us to cope with wartime flying.

Nevertheless, shortly after beginning to write the book, I had all sorts of doubts about it and its potential interest to anybody other than Aza, my only family. Thus, in the early days, I gave the typescript to Nigel, a very good friend, to be the first person to read what I had written, and to cast his analytical solicitor's mind over it and give his opinion. He did more than that, he gave me the boost of his support and he encouraged me to get on with writing the book. Another good friend, David, who had been a teacher of English at Clifton, not only kept an eye on my grammar, but he too gave me continuous encouragement as well as suggesting a good title for the book. Aza surprised me with yet another of her abilities, of which I had been unaware, by doing an excellent job of editing all I had written so far.

I finished writing the book in December 2006 and now came the problem of how to get the thing published. I had made a list of possible publishers to whom I intended to offer my book when I had a stroke of help from a naval chum who, although not in the book business, happened to meet someone in a firm of publishers to whom he mentioned my name and my book. So, at least I now had the name of somebody in the publishing business. I wrote to this chap with a synopsis of my book and attached a typed copy of one of the chapters and, while I was sitting back and waiting hopefully for a reply, I had the biggest bit of luck of all.

This was to meet Victoria again, who had known Jeremy and Aza years ago in Abbots Leigh when they were all teenagers. Vicky was a former Managing Director of a printing and publishing business and, if there could be anything about publishing books which she didn't know, then it wouldn't be worth the knowing. Moreover, she had a sharp and bright brain like a razor blade. But, better than all that, she was a kind and sympathetic friend.

Vicky came back into my life just on time because, unbelievably to those who have experience of book publishers, I received a brief letter from the aviation editor of Pen and Sword Books Ltd asking to come and meet me at my flat to discuss a contract for the publication of my book. Thank heavens that Vicky was there to take me in hand because, so pleased was I with this letter from the editor of a well-known publishing company, that I might have lost all business sense and possibly might have given away all my author's rights. Vicky and Aza joined me at the meeting three days later at my flat with the editor when, so anxious did he seem to be for a contract, that he even conceded advance royalties for me.

There followed a period of hard and hectic work and, without Vicky to help me through every step of the publishing procedure, I would have been at a complete loss. My first problem was that the editor, with all his experience, wanted to present me as a dashing Errol Flynn-type of heroic figure, whereas the whole point of my book was to show the reality of life for the ordinary guys such as myself in a wartime fighter squadron. I even wanted the title to be *Ordinary Naval Airman*, but the editor, wisely I have to admit, refused point blank to use such a title. We settled in the end for the excellent title suggested by David of *On and Off the Flight Deck; Reflections of a naval fighter pilot in World War II.*

I was to learn that the main means by which publishers advertise their books is the descriptive writing, the 'blurb', on the book jackets and on the fliers which they send out in large quantities to distributors. Once again however, in his blurb, the editor endeavoured to portray me in an heroic light and I managed to insist on rewriting the book jacket. Unfortunately, we failed to agree entirely on the vitally important description of the book in the fliers, which went out to thousands of people.

The Last Lap

The book jacket was designed as the result of telephone discussions and emails between Jonathan, who was the jacket designer for the publishers, Vicky and me. Jonathan decided to use two of my paintings as a major part of his design and I reckoned that his eventual jacket cover was excellent and I was delighted with it. I found I was expecting too much to receive a fee for this, however, as I had done for other book jackets in the past. Nor did we receive any payment for the typesetting of the book, which was done by Vicky because she wanted to be quite sure that it would be to a good standard. And so, although the book had been written, there was much to be done all through the year 2007 before the publishers launched it in October. This included my making contact with all the various Associations of which I was a member, to ask that they distribute the descriptive fliers about the book, which they very graciously did.

Despite all these difficulties for an author prior to launching a book, of which most people will be as unaware as I was, it all seems to have gone well in the end since a year later in December of 2008 nearly all copies of the hardback book had been sold, and the publishers apparently intend to print a paperback edition. The main thing for me is that it has been an exciting episode in my life and, in the hope of repeating it, I am writing the final chapter of this my second book.

The other activity of painting also bloomed once I had moved into the flat. Maybe I was inspired by the open skies which I could see all day from my balcony window, and by watching the beautiful old sailing schooners and boats of every sort which passed in front of my lovely flat overlooking the dock waters. I also had the benefit once again of a suitable place to do my daubin', as I had converted one of the two bedrooms into a studio. It started with a commission from the Bath and County Club whose committee wanted a large painting with a subject relating to Nelson's fleet at Trafalgar. This was a bit scary because completion of the commission depended on the committee viewing my painting at the half-way stage and approving it. I had never agreed to such a thing before and disliked it so much that I put a hefty but realistically professional price on a finished painting under these terms. When they crowded into my little studio, they liked the painting, bless 'em, even unfinished as it was, and moreover, they didn't baulk at my price when it was completed. In due course, I was invited to the Trafalgar dinner and the formal hanging of the painting at the Club, where I much enjoyed the company of the many members who attended it. Another piece of good salesmanship was accepting an invitation to exhibit two paintings at Christie's in London. One was purchased by a famous London club and is hung in the main public room where, on the occasion of the Club's formal centenary celebration, my painting in particular was admired by Maggie Thatcher. Rather proud of that, so forgive me for mentioning it.

A number of people from Bristol presumably viewed the painting at the Bath club, and maybe at the London club too, because I began to receive more commissions at much the same prices. The commissions were nearly all for marine paintings and I established a practice of discussing the type of ship together with the weather and sea conditions, so that I could be fairly sure of painting what the customer wanted. I insisted on taking my own reasonable time over each painting because I was having to fit painting in with time needed for writing the book. It was all rather fun and I was a very lucky old man.

The money earned from painting was coming in at the right time too, because Aza was struggling to start a new business after an intensive course on ceramic restoration, which she had just completed at West Dene College and where, incidentally, she had received a special award for her work. Thus she needed some capital to make a start and to obtain all sorts of equipment to cover that and her other subjects too of miniature painting and stained glass. I never quite know what to do with money when I have some, except spend it, and at this time there was something worthwhile on which to spend it, in the form of helping Aza to get started. This was much more useful than shoving the stuff into a deposit account and made me feel less guilty for charging the higher prices. It so happened too that, at this later stage in her life, Aza was proving herself to be a natural teacher of art and was becoming in demand for teaching at art centres in the south and west counties. How strange that both my children, Aza now as well as Jeremy, should have a natural bent for teaching. It was a profession which I too would have wanted.

A lucky and fortunate old man indeed I have been since moving into the flat although, in more recent years, that damned old yo-yo has started a bit of a wobble downwards again. I didn't worry much about being rather deaf because, after all, the NHS has supplied me free with an expensive and super gadget to stuff into my ear 'ole, which is quite effective. But I had already gone 90% blind in my right eye from dry macular degeneration when, quite suddenly, everything I looked at with my remaining left eye became distorted. This apparently is another, wet, macular degeneration and would have made me almost entirely blind by now but for the new miraculous Lucentis drug which, despite the infamous NICE committee, I am receiving free from the Eye Hospital. So far, the drug has arrested the degeneration. A slight fault seems to have developed in the communication system between legs and brain so that I have a tendency to fall about and cannot walk far but, yet again, this problem has been overcome by the purchase of an electric sit-upon scooter.

All these disadvantages are just par for the course at this age and I remind myself that there are hundreds of thousands of other elderly players with much higher handicaps than mine.

But that's old age for you and the secret of living it out is to know your limitations and enjoy whatever is left to you. The best thing for overcoming the inevitable depression of old age is to enjoy the number of friends remaining to you in your life. Those friends remaining with you as you become old will be fewer, but they may well be the very best of them. Sadly, in addition to those comrades killed but remembered from the wartime days, a whole lot of good friends also will have fallen off their perch in recent years. It has to be faced too that, when you are very old and grotty, some of a younger age group, whom you regard as your friends, will fall away. This is normal and inevitable because, in the different circumstance of your old age, you may no longer be able to share the same interests with them. And so you must go out and about as best you can and make new friends in the pubs, in the shops or wherever. The main thing when you are old is to talk to people. When the girl behind the bar at the pub finally comes to serve you and asks, 'Well dearie, what can I get you then?' then you chat her up and make her realise that your mind is every bit as young as hers and rather sharper, in fact. On the pavement, in the shops, on the bus, wherever; be that garrulous old man who starts a conversation with people. It is amazing how interesting people are and how many additional friends can be made. But it isn't only to seek friendship that you talk to strangers, it is because you must refuse to be ignored, as old people so very often are by the British people, some of whom seem to fear contact with the very elderly and act as though they are not really there at all.

Perhaps the best part of my good fortune has been the particular friends I have made during the period of this flat. First and foremost is Aza, the daughter I love who, in recent years, has become a good and close friend, my best chum. About Vicky, I need say no more than that I could not be writing this book without her friendship. Then there is David Hoey, whom I met in a pub and to whom initially I chatted about art, since he is a keen artist. He is a kind and gentle man who laughs with me at my disabilities, goes shopping with me to carry the parcels and is there to pick me up when I fall over. Dear Tony Thomas, the most modest of men I have ever known, who has been a sailor in small boats sailing across the world and also, as a one time electronic engineer, comes to mend my various electric gadgets when they so frequently fail. Nigel Sommerville, who has never failed in these years to cheer me up almost every month with a chatty and cheerful lunch together. Not to forget John Rogers who still props me up, no longer with accounting figures, but just with his friendship. And there is David Reed, my mentor of English grammar, who continues to encourage me.

'Luck'; it cannot be just luck that has been such an enormous and continuous influence on my life over the past eight years. More likely to be an all-powerful love. Love from Saccie and Jeremy up above who have found some magic wand up there which they have been waving about over me. It is as if they knew that I needed the time in that care home where I would have to learn to look after and care for other and older people, before they 'arranged' so craftily and smoothly for me to move into this lovely flat. It wasn't just luck that made me write short stories and a book and get them published, it was more likely a hefty push from them two above, and from Aza down here. And I bet that the committee from the Bath and County Club, who commissioned my first big painting, didn't find their way to my flat by chance; they were given a damn good shove towards it from above!

Any reader who has been interested enough to stay the course of this autobiography, will have realised that it is as much about Saccie, who was my other half all through, as about me.

I realise that the many mistakes I made in my life were the cause of the up-and-down, yo-yo lifestyle I have led and these mistakes were, in turn, the result of my impetuous character. I have sometimes looked wistfully across the divide of my age and experience towards my younger friends, now in their late sixties and seventies, whose post-war schooling and time at university or training had made a level lifestyle possible for them. But in retrospect I am in a way glad of those rash decisions I made, mainly because they led me to my wife Saccie, but also because I worked with people of all types whom I would never otherwise have met and to environments, which I would otherwise never have known.

END

Index

Abbots Leigh, 152, 284
Abbott, Mrs Betty, 50, 94
Accra, 130
Adlam, George, founder of George Adlam & Sons, 23, 52, 87
Adlam, William, grandfather, 87
Admiralty, 9, 15, 37, 38, 39, 40, 43, 47, 101
Aircraft Carriers, 7, 8, 42, 49, 84, 90, 91, 129, 146, 182, 251, 283
Airspeed Oxford, aircraft, 7, 8
Aldwell, Buzz, 115
Alice Adlam, granddaughter, 230, 243, 259, 261
Alice Leaman, mother-in-law, 21, 22, 24, 26-28, 32, 100, 138-140
Alvis, car, 97
Andrews, Stuart, headmaster of Cliftion College, 200, 201, 214, 218
Annie, kennel maid, 53, 56, 73, 88
Apprenticeship, 85
Argyle, Mr, headmaster of St Columba's College, 141, 142
Atauea Adlam, Jeremy's second wife, 230, 239, 243, 245, 262
Attlee government, 18
Auster, aircraft, 103
Austin, taxi, 45, 69, 72, 78
Aza, daughter, 36, 45, 99, 107, 108, 116, 117, 119, 133, 135, 136, 140, 144, 145, 151, 152, 155, 156, 160, 164, 165, 186, 211, 215, 229, 230, 231, 233, 235, 238, 240, 245, 252, 253, 255, 260-265, 270, 276, 282-288

BAE, British Aerospace, 148, 149, 150, 151, 165
Bailey, Ace, 42
Baker, Mick, 156
Baker, Mr, solicitor, 50, 51, 93
Ballet Russe de Monte Carlo, 83
Ballyholme, 113, 115, 139, 144, 146
Bangor, 101, 113, 114, 117, 133, 135, 138, 141
Barnes, 51, 52, 55, 56, 60, 62
Baron, aircraft, 127, 128, 129, 130, 131
Barracuda, aircraft, 115
Bath and County Club, 285, 288
Beechcraft Corporation, 121-129, 131, 134
Beggars Bush, 216, 217, 226
Belfast, 46, 96-100, 102, 105, 106, 107, 112-114, 116, 123, 124, 125, 139-142, 145, 211, 243
Blair, Tony, Prime Minister, 223
Blue Train, 74, 80
Bobby, housekeeper, 267, 268, 270, 272-276, 278
Boycalls, 65
Brazil, 163, 164
Brighton, 56, 62, 70, 73, 79
Bristol, 14, 23, 24, 26, 54, 77, 85, 86, 87, 89, 148-155, 159, 160, 163-165, 167, 170, 185, 186, 188, 203,

206, 207, 209, 216, 229, 231, 232, 238, 240, 245, 253, 261, 263, 265, 267, 276, 281, 286
Bristol-Siddeley, company, 160, 163
Britton, Jack, 170, 175, 190, 198, 203, 204, 216
Brooke-Smith, Tom, Chief Test Pilot, 101, 126
Brown, Ken and Irene, 249
Buick, car, 74, 75, 81, 84, 85
Bull Terriers, 6, 52, 55, 56, 73, 77, 79
Bull, Mr, maths teacher, 61
Burgage, The, house, 249-251, 254, 255
Bush, Admiral Sir John, 204, 206, 208, 210, 216
Butler, Mrs Roma, secretary, 177

C.C.S. Company Ltd, 226
Cairo, 223
Calloway, Roy and Betty, 156, 160
Camilla, niece, 146
Canberra, aircraft, 101
Cannes, 80, 84
care (residential) home, 265, 266, 274, 278-282, 288
Castle Rock, 47, 50, 96
Cavendish Hotel, London, 11
Central Flying School, 8, 42, 102
Chamberlain, Neville, Prime Minister, 85
Chantry, The, house, 254, 255, 256, 257, 259, 260, 263, 265, 266
Chippendale chairs, 95
Christian Missionary Alliance, 111
Christie's, 286
Citizens' Advice Bureau, 243
City Art Gallery, Bristol, 204
Clifton Club, 194, 217

Clifton College, 166, 167, 177, 180, 184, 185, 189, 198, 203-205, 208, 210, 215, 218, 222, 225, 226, 253, 259, 278
Clifton High School, 151, 212
Clifton Lawn Tennis Club, 271
Cloverhill Park, Belfast, 99, 113, 115
Cobbie, dachshund, 236
Coffinswell, Devon, 88, 89
Cole, Peter, catering manager, 173, 196
Colet Court, preparatory school, 53
Collar, Roderick, 191
Collins, John, architect, 127, 218, 219
Columba, St Columba's College, 141-145
Commemoration Day, 205, 208
Composition Fee Fund, 193, 194, 213, 218
Conway, Hugh, 122-127, 159, 160
Cooper, Charles, 191, 209
Copycat, copying machine, 25, 26
Corsair, aircraft, 38
Cosker, Ellie, 242
Côte d'Azur, 74, 85
Cottesmore, preparatory school, 54-66, 69, 77, 82, 134
Coulson Centre, Clifton College, 214, 215
Coventry, 28, 29, 30, 32, 33, 35, 38, 113, 160, 161, 164, 165, 231
Coverack, Cornwall, 1, 3, 4, 9, 13, 15, 16, 18, 19, 27
Craigavad Golf Club, 114
Crawfordsburn Country Club, 114
Crufts, dog show, 55
Culdrose, Royal Naval Air Station, 1, 2, 7, 33

INDEX

Davies Jones, Martin, 238, 250
Development Fund, 201, 214
Discount Scheme, 213, 218
Dominie, aircraft, 101, 102, 106
Druries, Harrow House, 65, 68
Dwerryhouse, Jim, 109

Eastleigh, 229, 230, 239, 240
Eglinton, Royal Naval Air Station, 43, 44, 47, 49, 93, 97, 98
Ellis, Herbert, 15
Eve, Tony, 119, 209, 210, 219, 228
Eye Hospital, Bristol, 186, 287

FAA, Fleet Air Arm, 6, 8, 9, 39, 42, 44, 84, 90, 91, 94, 110, 146, 165, 258, 262, 281
Fancourt, Captain St John, 96
Farquhar, Mr, draughtsman, 23
Father, 11, 23, 50-54, 60-62, 67, 69-71, 74-89, 93-95, 119, 147, 187, 230, 283
Fern Lea, house, 240, 242, 243, 245, 246, 253
Fireflies, aircraft, 39, 101
Ford, Royal Naval Air Station, 94
Forster, Mr, headmaster, Cottesmore, 58, 61
Frenchay Hospital, 186

Gardner, Nigel and Margery, 8, 15
Gastrell, Mrs Estelle, 75, 80, 85, 88, 89
Gedge, George, 148
George, ghost, 3, 9, 18, 19, 20
Ghana, 130, 131
Gibson, David, 173
Gieves, outfitters, 63, 72
Glenlola, girls' school, 117, 133, 144, 145
Gosport, 90
Gover, Tom, 209, 216, 226

Groomsport Road, house, 133, 138, 139
Gulson Road, house, 33, 34, 35, 36, 38, 249

Hambrook, Bill, 109, 112
Handoll, Mrs, nanny, 54, 77, 78
Harper, Malcolm and Gordon, 232, 235, 236, 255
Harrow, 2, 61-69, 72, 73, 75, 78, 79, 82-87, 119, 187, 192, 212, 215
Harvard, aircraft, 4, 8, 41
Harvey, Bob, 123, 126
Hay, Ronnie, 262
Hayley, Robert, demonstration pilot, 125
Hazel, care home resident, 267-271, 276
Headfort, Jeremy's second preparatory school, 134-136, 141, 142, 144
Health Insurance scheme, 194
Heather, *see* Saccie
Hellcat, aircraft, 115
Hereford, 229, 237, 244, 245, 251, 258, 262
Hicks, Sir Denys, solicitor, 176
Hill, Peter, assistant bursar, 177
Hill Samuel, 191
Hilliard Society, 231
Hillman cars, 28, 47
HMS *Illustrious*, 94, 146
HMS *St Vincent*, 90, 91
HMS *Unicorn*, 96
Hoey, David, 287
Hollander, Brigadier Vivian, 71, 72
Holywood, 106
Hong Kong, 230, 231, 253
Hornby, Jim, headmaster of Clifton College Pre, 166-168, 173, 178, 179, 180, 195, 196, 214

Houghton, Professor, 210
Howard, Mark, 110
Howe, Ben, 223
Humber cars, 28, 32, 47
Humphreys, Pat, Phoebe's fiancé, 94, 146
Hurricane, aircraft, 29, 90
Hyde, Eric, 148

Innes, Mike, 226
Inverdale, John, 197
Irvine, Ron and Liz, 115, 120
Isaac, Gwyl, choirmaster, 222
Ivy Hotel, Richmond, 155

Jackson, Mr, consultant, 117, 118
James, Mary, 269
Janine, 81, 82, 84, 90
Jeremy, son, 11, 14, 15, 16, 18, 19, 20, 23, 24, 32, 35, 36, 46, 99, 107, 116, 117, 133-145, 151, 155-157, 164, 165, 185, 186, 215, 229, 230, 233, 234, 239, 240, 243-245, 253, 254, 259, 260, 261, 284, 286, 288
JOAC, Junior Officers' Air Course, 41, 42

Kano, Nigeria, 127, 128
Kate Adlam, Jeremy's adopted daughter, 259, 261
Keith-Lucas, David, 126
Kevin, housekeeper, 275, 276, 277, 278
Kiribati, 230, 239, 240, 243-245, 259-262
Knight, Peter, 214
Korean War, 37- 39, 96, 97

Lagos, Nigeria, 127-131
Lane, Tubby, 103, 105
Lang, Duncan, 9

Lee-on-Solent, 8
Leslie Adlam, half-brother, 50
Lewis, Reverend Mark, 111, 112
Lewis, Sir Ian, judge, 204, 216, 226, 228
Linton, 263
Liz Adlam, Jeremy's first wife, 229
Lossiemouth, Royal Naval Air Station, 102, 106
Lowder, Johnnie, Phoebe's second husband, 94, 95, 146, 147
Lucentis, 287
Lucille, Renault car, 13, 14, 15, 18, 19, 20, 21

Macaleese, Mr, 136, 137, 138
Maddie, Mother's companion, 4, 5, 13, 40, 52, 56, 57, 70, 71, 83, 85, 88, 91
McDermott, Bobby and Gill, 47, 50, 96
McWatters, Stephen, headmaster of Clifton College, 169, 172, 173, 175, 178, 190, 199
Methody, Methodist College, school, 145, 146, 211
MG, car, 5, 9, 12, 13
MGB, car, 160
Michael Adlam, brother, 54, 77, 78, 88, 93, 95
Milward, Robert, 237
Monaco, 74, 75, 80, 81, 83
Monmouth, 249, 252, 253
Montauban, Mr, second master at Cottesmore, 58, 60, 62
Monte Carlo, 75, 83, 84, 93, 95
Morley Road, house, 160, 164
Mother, 4, 5, 7, 9, 13, 23, 24, 32, 40, 50-57, 60, 62, 63, 69-79, 82, 83, 85, 86, 88-91, 134, 157
Musketeer, aircraft, 122, 125

INDEX

Navy, Royal, 1, 2, 6, 7, 8, 12, 15, 17-23, 33, 38, 39, 40, 44, 47, 49, 50, 84, 90, 91, 96-99, 110, 116, 146, 147, 149, 151, 283
Nesbit, Hubert and Dorrie, 115
New Zealand, 94, 230, 239, 259, 261
Newman, Roger, 191
Newtownards, Flying Club, 97, 99, 102, 132
No. 7 New Street, house, 236, 237, 240

Old Cliftonians, Old Cliftonian Society, 175, 190, 201, 208, 218, 228
Orford, O.O., 160, 164, 165

Palmer, George, 176, 185, 194
Paris, passenger ship, 3
Parrott, Brian, 176, 192
Patey, Antony, 143
Pearson, Chris, 143
Peill, Ian, 255, 256
Pen and Sword, publishers, 284
Perkins, Major, 3, 5
Peters, Mike, 158
Philippa and Howard, 91
Phoebe, sister, 54, 62, 70, 71, 74, 76, 78-84, 93-96, 146-148
Piggy Cottage, house, 48-50, 97
Piper, aircraft, 104, 105
Piper, Raymond, 120
Plessey, 153-156, 158, 161, 165
Polack, Ernest, 175
Potts-Harpers, 47
Price, Harry, writer, 20
Pushings, 99, 100

Queenair, aircraft, 122, 124, 126
RAF, Royal Air Force, 7, 29, 42, 87, 90, 101-105, 110, 122, 167, 237
Reserve Fund, 200, 209, 214, 218

Richmond, 155-157, 160, 164
Ringo, Jackie, 3
RNVR, Royal Naval Volunteer Reserve, 2
Rockport, Jeremy's first preparatory school, 116, 117, 135
Rogers, John, 174, 188, 192, 288
Rolls-Royce, 159-167, 200
Ronald, at Plessey, 158
Roope, Michael, domestic bursar, 213
Rootes Group, 28, 47, 152
Rose Cottage, house, 246-250
Ross-on-Wye, 234-236, 242, 247, 254
Rouse, Michael, Phoebe's third husband, 147
Rowe, Archie, 3, 4
Royal Ulster Academy, 121
Ruth, secretary, 124
Royal Ulster Yacht Club, 115

Saccie, Heather Adlam, 1-30, 32-41, 44, 45, 47, 48, 49, 96, 97, 99, 100, 102, 106, 107, 112-120, 132-157, 160, 163-169, 172, 181, 185-189, 195, 196, 199, 200, 203, 204, 206, 208, 215, 219, 222, 228-263, 268, 282, 283, 288
Sainsbury, Teddy and Toni, 232, 233
Salisbury, 9, 20, 21, 24, 25, 27, 29, 30, 32, 35, 36, 51, 96, 113, 139
Samaritans, The, 106, 107, 243
SC1, aircraft, 101
Scoffham, Doug, 122, 124, 125
Sea Furies, aircraft, 38, 39, 101
Seafires, aircraft, 39, 101
Sealand, aircraft, 101, 110- 112, 121
Short Bros. & Harland, 96, 97, 99, 101, 103, 104, 106, 109-112, 116,

120-129, 132, 133, 148-151, 159, 165
Singer, car, 70, 72, 78
Skyvan, aircraft, 121-131
Slattery, Sir Matthew, 97, 99, 109, 121, 123
Solent, flying boat, 38, 39, 40, 110
Sommerville, Nigel, 283, 288
Spastics Society, 152
SS *Uganda*, 222
Strangford Lough, 116
Stuart Leaman, father-in-law, 21-24, 26-28, 32, 35, 36, 133, 138-140, 148
Suspension Bridge, Clifton, 216
Swanage, 133, 138, 139, 144

Taplow, 4, 13, 79, 83, 85, 88, 89
Tenby, 252, 259, 262
Thatcher, Margaret, Prime Minister, 219, 223, 286
Thomas, Tony, 288
Tiger Moth, aircraft, 103, 105
Tinne, Mike, 261
Torrens-Spence, Commander Air, 49
Travis, Norman, 171, 198, 199, 204, 205, 210
Trinity College Dublin, 142, 157
Trixie, care home resident, 267, 269, 270

Ulster, 46, 78, 97, 100, 115, 120, 131, 133, 138, 140, 148, 149

Varah, Chad, 107
Vian, Rear-Admiral, 165
Villa La Quieta, Roquebrune, 75, 76, 83, 84, 93, 94, 95, 96
Viper engine, 161, 163, 164

Waley-Cohen, Bernard, 191, 210
Ward-Thompson, Lt, Phoebe's first husband, 13, 79, 84, 94, 146, 147, 148
Watch House, first home, 1-3, 5, 7, 9, 15, 18, 20
Waverley Drive, house, 113, 114, 117, 132, 133
Well House, The Old, 88
West Dene College, 286
Westonbirt Arboretum, 270
Weybridge, 74, 76, 150
Whatley, Terry, 187, 196, 215, 225, 226
Whybrow, Charlie, 171
Wilkinson, Jonathan, cover designer, 285
Wilson government, 200, 208
Winterbottom, Derek, 227
Woolmer, Bill, Shorts Company Secretary, 114, 133
World War II, 110, 284
Worthington, Brian, 215
Wrens, Women's Royal Naval Service, 242

Yeovilton, 1, 2, 8, 9, 33, 98
Yeovilton, Fleet Air Arm Museum, 258, 260, 262